M000107403

Bless and Release

A Mother's Journey Through Mental Illness

By Karen Elaine Greenwell

© 2019 Karen Elaine Greenwell. All rights reserved.

No part of this document may be reproduced or transmitted in any form or by any means, electronic, mechanical, photocopying, recording, or otherwise, without prior written permission of the author. Failure to comply with these terms may expose you to legal action and damages for copyright infringement.

ISBN 978-0-578-45691-1

Even Balance Publishing

Photo credit: Rachel Badali

PREFACE

Statistics say one in four people will suffer from a mental illness sometime in their life. That is a lot of people. It includes your friends, coworkers, neighbors, family and maybe even you. The effects of mental illness can be brief or lifelong but will always leave an indelible mark on a life.

Such is the case for me and my family. My husband Dale and I have three children and of the five of us, three have bipolar disorder; me, Sarah and Taylor. When we married we never anticipated our life together would include things such as mental health treatment, medications, suicide, therapy and crisis planning. We, like most individuals facing chronic illnesses, have to quickly learn to identify our needs, decide a plan of action, and follow through in ever changing situations. We have not always done a great job, but we have always intended to do our best.

This book is about our journey. But like any real-life story, the journey may look different from one person to another. This is my story and is written according to the world of Karen; my perception of our life. Perception is a way of regarding, understanding, or interpreting something. Perception is not necessarily good or bad, it is just different. I have tried to be accurate, fair, and sensitive in sharing some pretty difficult things. The conversations, of course, are remembered to my best ability. While Dale and our children have read this book and have given their approval, they would all agree that in some things our perception is different. Perhaps they will also want to write their story someday, but this is my story.

The book is organized into four parts and an afterwards. Each part is written with an overall focus which also includes a mixture of pieces of our life story sprinkled in. Part one shares experiences from my teen years, our marriage and life as a growing family. Part two focuses on Sarah's story from diagnosis to young adult. Taylor's story is part three. In part four and the afterward, the threads of our story's tapestry are brought together to discover some of the lessons from our journey.

Except for the names of our family, all the names of individuals in the book have been changed. There are many wonderful people who have impacted our family. I sincerely hope you see yourself in these pages and know of my deepest appreciation.

Every person will experience hard challenges in life. That's just how it is. For me, for Dale, for each of my children, the task for us was how to meet these monumental challenges as individuals and as a family. This story is about having the will, the faith and the courage to face our challenges head on. And we won.

TABLE OF CONTENTS

INTRODUCTION

The room was packed with people, the air thick and stuffy. After nearly two hours, Dale's name was finally called, and he stepped forward to a table that was bare except for a single microphone. He faced a diverse group of legislators armed with the task of deciding how best to spend millions of dollars set aside for services for programs through the Health and Human Services Committee. Represented were the aged, the autistic, released inmates, the homeless, and various others. Dale stood as the only voice for children with mental illness. He had only three minutes in which to tell our story—not even time enough to be nervous.

Placing an eight-by-ten photograph of our family on the table so the committee could see a smiling mother, handsome father, three beautiful children, he began.

"This family of five, as you look at them, appears to be healthy, happy, and a contributing part of society," he said. "You might think, as you look at this family and other families like them, *I can remove $2.5 million from public mental health services and allocate it elsewhere because this family and others like them don't need it.*"

Dale paused to look each legislator in the eye. "I challenge you, for just a moment, to listen with your heart as I talk about the true needs of this seemingly typical family of five."

"Three of the five—60 percent—of my family suffers from mental illness. Two have contemplated suicide, feeling the world would be better off without them. One is struggling to maintain their health while changing medications and fighting various side effects for a third time. A year ago, one experienced daily fits of rage and uncontrollable mood swings and was unable to function in the classroom or establish healthy relationships with peers. However, with the aid of mental health services, this person is now able to function in the classroom, no longer has these fits of rage, and testifies, 'I am making good choices, and I enjoy school.'

"One of the three had the opportunity to attend a summer camp sponsored by the local mental health center, where this child developed social skills they lacked due to mental illness. The child now is forming appropriate relationships with peers and feels a sense of pride.

"This is my family. We struggle with mental illness, but we are not mental illness. We are not broken. We are a family with individual interests, needs, challenges, and dreams. We are a family of strength and commitment. We are your constituents, and we need your help to continue to access the services we need."

At the end of the session, Dale found himself surrounded by media from radio and television. It was surprising he received any attention at all. Ours was just one of many stories. Maybe he received the attention because he was so well spoken and because no one had put such a face on mental illness before. But the truth then, and the truth now, is that from the outside we look like anyone else. We are your siblings, your neighbors, your teachers, your friends. We are your employees, physicians, and those you meet at the grocery store. You wouldn't know we struggle with mental illness unless we told you. It's a hidden disability, but it impacts everything we think, feel, and do. Sometimes you need to look beyond what you see. And always you assume that the road for someone with mental illness has been long and hard. You realize how brave someone must be to continually fight this battle.

HELP WANTED

You had to have a black belt in parenting to be the parent of a child with mental illness. You had to develop a commando style of disciplined mental agility. The ability to conduct an interrogation without your child realizing what was going on. You had to know how to hand out consequences in the most sophisticated manner, without tipping your hand that you were not really after hardcore consequences but a little cooperation. When Dale and I compared notes, we found that the most effective parenting tools were in our facial expressions, eyes, and voices. It almost didn't matter what message we were delivering; all that mattered was how it was delivered.

It started with nonthreatening body language, a softening of the shoulders and knees. And a healthy respect for personal space. Sneaking in a deep breath now and then was helpful, but too much of a show of deep breathing gave off the message that we were preparing ourselves for a fight. We learned early on that yelling didn't help. The message didn't get across any faster, and it only challenged our children to amp their volume to meet ours. I learned one of the games I could play to keep myself in check during these times was to change the volume of my voice to a lower decibel. For example, I once brought Sarah to a gentle landing from a tantrum by whispering to her so quietly she had to lower her voice and intently listen to hear what I said. It was exhausting but effective. Interestingly, our kids didn't seem to notice what we were doing. We just brought the breathing rate down with calm voices and enough space in between comments to slow everything down to a more manageable place.

Having a neutral face was hard, but necessary. There was so much going on in my mind while trying to defuse a crisis. I could hardly keep up with my thoughts, let alone try to compartmentalize them to make sure I kept a situation under control. First, I went to assess whether anything had to be done immediately to protect or preserve safety. Next, I considered the environment I was in. Sarah was known to pick the most inconvenient, public, or uncomfortable situations in which to pull a punch. But she knew there were things we would not discuss in public and she would not be confronted with the issue until we got home. I was sure she hoped by the time we got home the misdeed would be forgotten and she wouldn't have to deal with us. That might have been true in some cases. Unfortunately for her, we had a pretty good memory.

The next key factor was timing. Not only whether this was the place to have a parent-child tête-à-tête, but was there even time to deal with it? Usually time would be made immediately, but we also learned the art of delaying the discussion to allow our kids a chance to think about how they wanted to respond to the situation. Taylor and Sarah hated the delaying part because it prolonged the time they had to carry their angst before we had a resolution. We sometimes asked them to think of what they might consider a fair consequence for a behavior. Then we assured them we would talk about it later. By the time we got around to talking to them at the end of the day, both had often come up with a consequence far worse than we would have picked. I loved that part of having them parent themselves.

By not reacting to their reacting I believe we avoided many potential crises. When Taylor couldn't seem to calm himself, it was best to have him see me across the room being an example of open body, soft voice, gentle hands and face, and easy breathing. He probably was not conscious of what I was doing, but it was important.

Our parenting style had to change as the kids got older. I sometimes thought it would have been easier to simply wrap our arms around them and hold them tightly until the overwhelming feelings went away or at least weren't so potent. Teaching and modeling skills in communication, problem solving, arguing fairly, ignoring, and downright outlasting someone's meltdown was exhausting.

Most days I would debrief Dale when he came home from work and tell him what happened and how I had responded. He was generally positive and supportive of my efforts, and when we needed to rethink a situation, we were mindful of each other's strengths and weaknesses. He usually had to run interference with Sarah because Sarah and I could be like oil and water. I had to run interference with Taylor because Dale and Taylor could be explosive together. We were fortunate to have each other. We were both committed to help and love all our children in whatever way we needed to. But, boy, sometimes I perceived it to be a bigger-than-me and an impossibly hard job.

On those days when it seemed I had been totally ineffectual, I shut down and put myself on autopilot. There were days I felt too overwhelmed and was not exactly emotionally there for the kids. I did the job of detached mother and stoically made sure we all had what we needed. I went to bed at night, prayed for help, regrouped, and hoped to wake with my mommy hat on the next day. Sometimes it took the total combined effort of the two of us to rise above our limitations as parents to do what needed to be done. We took it day by day.

Otherwise we felt so overwhelmed it would have been hard to have any perspective of what the future should be and to hope that tomorrow would be better.

PART I

CRAZY

From the outside, my family growing up looked like a normal family. My dad was a hardworking computer programmer; my mom stayed home to take care of us. We lived in a nice, safe, middle-class neighborhood in the same house for more than twenty years and had good neighbors. We played outdoors, went to church on Sundays, and lived a generally typical suburban life.

My four brothers—two older and two younger—were involved in things I didn't care much about, like sports, which left me a lot of time to spend doing what most interested me. I loved books, books, and more books. I also liked to color, sing, and write. I happily shared my treasured pictures and stories with my parents. They dutifully praised me and bragged about me to family. My brothers teased me, but I didn't care. We teased each other, a lot. Everyone was an equal opportunity target. I didn't really have close neighborhood friends, but I found I could often be happy by myself.

My mom had her hands full with five active kids. She also babysat, and so we usually had a miscellaneous two or three additional children at our house. She kept busy with activities she chose for herself. She enjoyed her soap operas, reading to and playing with the younger kids, and always had a well-worn biography nearby to read. She hummed or sang as she went about her activities. She was generally busy or distracted, and I was frequently on my own to find something to do.

In public and to everyone else, my dad was a "jolly" man who took an interest in people. He had a big laugh and enjoyed telling a good story. People were drawn to my dad, and he was always one to do a kind turn for another. My parents were supportive and involved in Little League and many church activities in which we participated. Occasionally I would hear his big bass voice join with my mom's soprano, the two belting out church hymns and other songs. That made me happy and I felt more connected to my parents.

I was always aware my dad was different with us at home than he was with others, but I never questioned why. My dad liked his job and worked long hours. He often felt under pressure to perform and put all his energy into doing a good job. He wore himself out each day, but didn't let it show until he came home. At the end of the work day, he immediately went to his bedroom, dragging his feet as he climbed the stairs. Once he went into his room, I wouldn't see him until the next day. At home his room became his sanctuary. He was never unkind and he didn't ignore us as he went on by. I always knew he loved me, but I also knew he was going to his room to be alone just like always.

I don't remember hearing my parents talk to each other about my dad's isolation. My mom would make dinner for us kids, and then go get fast food for my dad's dinner which he would eat by himself in his bedroom. That was the almost daily routine, and nobody said anything to indicate that level of separation was a problem. I might see my dad if he called me into his room to change the television channel and to ask me how school went, but that didn't happen every day. Sometimes days would pass and the seven of us would almost orbit in our own remoteness, not really connecting on an intimate level. Who knew the cycles of isolation, binge eating, irritability, and seemingly never-ending sadness my dad only showed within the family were symptoms of a deep depression? Not me. As a child I didn't understand the complexity of living with depression in a time when it was not socially okay for my dad to admit he was struggling. I didn't recognize the impact of my dad's chronic depression in his life, and in our lives, because I didn't know anything different.

My mental illness came to light in my early teenage years, though I wouldn't be able to define it until decades later. Around age thirteen I became more secretive about my feelings, because I didn't know how to explain what was going on inside me. I grew confused as I found myself distracted with sad and depressed feelings that wouldn't go away. I couldn't shake them, no matter how much I tried to be happy. My thoughts became increasingly intense and I was stuck in horrible cycles of thoughts of death and dying. I became increasingly withdrawn, spending all my free time alone in my room. There, I wrote dark stories about death and drama, and read books about loss and heartache. The gradual change in my mood and increase in irritability stemmed from more than the beginning of puberty and adolescence; this was my first remembered depression. I felt lost. Panic threatened me when I found myself unable to stop crying in my room. I hated to cry and went to great lengths to not cry, but now it seemed all I ever did was cry by myself. I had questions about things I couldn't find the words to describe, but I didn't believe I had anyone I could talk to who might have answers.

I pretended to be all right with my family. We were not a close family; we cared about each other, but we just didn't connect well. Each person focused on doing what they wanted to do as we passed each other in the halls of our home. Mom and dad had their lives. My older brothers were oblivious to what was going on with me, and my younger brothers were too young for me to consider them allies. It wasn't difficult to hide my sadness because we didn't spend time together. No one seemed to notice me anyway.

Because I had no one to confide in, it seemed crucial that I find someone to help occupy my time and to show they needed me. I suddenly had an intense desire to be best friends with a particular girl at school. Though irrational, this need was something I could not let go of. I wanted to hang out with her every day after school and talk on the phone every night. If she spent time with other friends, I became jealous without really knowing why. My demanding behavior probably scared her; at any rate, she didn't stay my friend for long. Her abandonment left me crying silently in my room, inconsolable and lonely. I didn't understand my feelings, but I recognized I had embarrassed myself. To spare myself further heartache, I withdrew more from other people at school.

For what felt like a long time, I lived in this sadness. I chronically did not want to interact, only wanting to sleep and do the minimum for weeks on end. I didn't know what to do. In my memory, I have little recollection of my parents attending to my sadness or need for connection except as a younger child. I didn't know of any adult or even a peer who would understand the odd thoughts and feelings in my mind. I was stuck. To me, my withdrawal to my room and lack of any interaction screamed out loud that something was wrong. My efforts to hint at my sadness went unheeded. I had never learned the skill of asking for help, it just wasn't part of our family culture. So, the only thing that made sense to me was to expend my limited energy

17

to make everything look normal to the people around me. I knew if my brothers saw me cry I would be teased, or worse, discounted. My parents didn't seem to see what was going on behind my lethargic, sad countenance. I wanted them to care enough to ask me without me having to come clean with how I was feeling. I couldn't imagine anyone in my family understanding how I felt, and I wasn't brave enough to find out if they would.

After a while, the funk in my head seemed to lift. My view began to change, and it seemed I could face each day a little better. Ironically, I became alienated, even angry, with everyone because it seemed like no one had taken note of my deep sadness. Only I had seen the difference in my world. It made me sad; it seemed I didn't have anyone or anywhere to turn.

Sometime after the depression lifted, I attempted to talk with my mom about that confusing and lonely time. It appeared hard for her to even recall any changes in my mood or activities. My efforts to describe and share my experience seemed to fall short as she responded back to me, "Well, you have always been a moody child." In just a few words she made my depression a non-event. I felt offended and demeaned that she would describe something that had been traumatic for me—something I had gone through alone— with such a patronizing comment. She had not been there for me and if she noticed my moodiness, she made no efforts to see if something was wrong. There had been no gentle moments of sympathy and concern from anyone in my family. My sadness had been real, profound, and heart-wrenching. I felt misunderstood.

Many years later, as a parent, I would understand the tendency to see my child's intense emotions as just a phase. It was easier to ignore or explain my child's unusual behavior as a temporary issue rather than a deeper need. Parents generally just don't consider a child could be depressed. I guess nobody knew any better.

Grudgingly, I came to accept that my family would not be a reliable safe place for me to land, but inside I hoped they would see the cracks in my life. Far worse than having my depression ignored would be to have it mocked. Out of experience and necessity, I realized I would have to fight my depression and get up, go to school and do what looked normal for many days on my own. My reality of just having to be what I wanted people to see protected the vulnerability I held inside. That first experience with depression and subsequent experiences defied the simple explanation of moodiness.

Perhaps with my first depression I formed the idea that any emotional suffering should be done in silence, that depression was a personal thing and should be held close. Isolating myself in my misery but acting like everything was okay has been the hallmark of my bipolar depressions—a legacy I unintendedly learned from my father. I learned to have multiple faces—one real, one sad, and the one everyone else saw. Coping was best when it looked detached and inconspicuous. It wasn't hard when people tended to overlook obvious signs of distress or accounted them to something trivial. Crying and tears didn't seem to be useful in my efforts to hide my sadness from the outside world. It was easy to hide my bipolar disorder in plain sight if I tried hard enough.

My ups and downs of adolescence were not fantastically vivid or long lasting. I performed well in my classes, excelling in journalism and as a Sterling Scholar in English. I sometimes acted invincible and a little cocky about my confidence to manage my responsibilities. But at the edge of all this busyness, feelings of sadness and at times hopelessness lay hidden just beneath the surface. I refused to share my real feelings with anyone. Some friends knew I could be in a funk, but they had no idea how depressed I really was.

Sometimes my dad would see me struggling and would reach out to spend time with me. His favorite way of cheering me up involved taking me out to eat, always just the two of us. We wouldn't necessarily talk about the real emotion of what was making me feel down; that was not a part of our relationship. Instead he wanted to know how I was doing in school, and what I was planning in the future. We looked at the big picture part of things rather than the here and now that was making either of us sad. He wrapped up our time together with a bit of advice and a bit of encouragement and we were on our way. After the calorie splurge, we would both be happier. It became our way of dealing with the sadness together, something we shared my whole life.

I graduated from high school and knew I wanted to attend college away from home. I wanted to live outside the little world that had been built around me. I received a scholarship to Southern Utah State College and majored in English. I lived in a lovely, large, old-fashioned pioneer home on a quiet street with three roommates—a grandma who owned the house, a thirty-year-old newly transplanted high school music teacher, and a forty-year-old woman who'd grown up in a town of less than one hundred and fifty and struggled to cross a busy street because she got confused by the stoplights. Then there was eighteen-year-old me. We were a strange combination. We came and went, and I found I could pull back into my own world once again. A lonely place to be.

I made few friends and returned to the comfort of isolation as I studied and worked hard to get good grades. My freshman year consisted of me being kind to myself and not pushing myself to socialize if I didn't feel like it. I often didn't. While not horrible, college life didn't live up to my expectations. Withdrawing from anything outside of school was a way to manage my funks and to focus on my education. I realized I liked my independence and didn't want to live with my parents once school ended. I determined to live on my own or with a roommate once I finished my freshman year. I happily transitioned to life as a young adult living on my own with a roommate. I juggled classes at the University of Utah and worked my first grown-up job. I rejoiced in the freedom of making my own decisions and making new friends.

Overall, the next few years of single life gave me a sense of happiness and satisfaction. There were dark periods of insecurity and angst that slammed into me at regular intervals, especially during the winter. My childhood friend and roommate, Elise, learned to help me roll with the mood swings. She was a sounding board when I was down and someone to do things with when I felt well. She learned to see what nobody else saw and was my friend regardless of my ups and downs. She wasn't scared of my extreme moods and we enjoyed being young, single and untethered to heavy responsibilities. Elise was a safe place for me. I knew I could trust her with the craziness that filled my mind more and more often.

I had become accustomed to the ups and downs of my life. I knew to expect a surge of energy during finals week or when under a deadline or some outside pressure. I would sense the revving deep within me and knew the energy would soon follow. I liked that feeling. I felt like I had electricity filling my body and coming out of my fingertips. I could get so much done. Once, I had to present a large, detailed research project in class. As I was finishing my final draft, the energy surge inside of me bubbled over, and I started moving around my apartment in agitation. My dog Abby got excited and started to follow me, barking and jumping on my legs. That ramped up the energy; it was like the air was pulsing. I started running through the house with Abby racing around with me, both of us going as fast as we could. Then I spotted the multicolored wrappers of a large bowl of miniature Reese's Peanut Butter Cups on the table. I had only one thought, "I like them and I want them."

I quickly grabbed a few as I ran past. I ate them as fast as I could, enjoying the chocolatey peanut-butter flavor as I continued my circuit. Elise came into the room and stood watching me and the dog. She said nothing, watching us go back and forth, looking concerned. For at least ten minutes I ran, frantically unwrapping the chocolates and shoving them in my mouth, hooting to Abby until the candy ran out. I had eaten the whole bowlful and hadn't even noticed. Stopping to catch my breath, I experienced the whoosh of my brain trying to catch up with the rest of me. Then I ran to the bathroom and threw up. Purging my body helped me calm down and refocus.

I knew vomiting was not healthy, but it didn't matter. It made everything stop for a time. It became my go-to in any stressful situation. It gave me a sense of being in control of something—a way to control my "out-of-control". I would have phases of bulimia on occasion throughout my adult life, lasting one to two months at a time, where I threw up consistently almost every day. I never tried to fool myself into thinking my bouts of bulimia were helpful or healthy for me. I knew bulimia served as an awful and punishing distraction from stress. It wasn't about food. It was all about not being able to cope. For a short time, bulimia would give me something intense in which to focus and micromanage. I would focus my energy on the eating and purging instead of whatever was making me feel so overwhelmed.

The ultimate deterrent from bulimia was the threat of having someone find out I was purging. For Elise or later Dale or my children to hear or to be made aware of my active purging would have been devastating for me. I guarded my secret at all costs. Other than that risk, I was compelled to do something to release the pressure building in my mind. So, in an effort to control something tangible, I chose what and how much to eat, and when and how much to purge. Crazy on top of crazy.

But after a time, I would experience a sadness inside—a kind of nondescript angst. I'd cocoon in my apartment, sleeping and staring at the television. I wouldn't answer the phone and called in sick to work. I would still go to school but do only the minimum. I would ignore the signs of isolation and my tendency to be impatient with the world and other people, thinking they were unnecessary. I was too tired and disinterested to engage.

Usually this depression would last a month or so and then lift. I would return to what seemed like my normal. Strangely enough, I didn't notice the pattern. It had become a part of my personality. I didn't think other people noticed. I didn't like all of it, but I thought I could manage the roller coaster ride. Except for the times I couldn't.

The downward spiral started typically enough—I'd trudge through the days, sleeping as much as possible so I wouldn't have to engage in anything. But it got harder to hold on to my regular routine. I called in sick or went home early. I didn't eat much. I smelled or looked at food and felt sick. I was a little alarmed when I found myself feeling dizzy when I stood up because I hadn't eaten, so I forced myself eat a minimum amount. I cried easily—very unusual for me. Crying gave me the sense of being on the verge of losing control. I did all I could not to cry, but I couldn't stop. I spoke in monosyllables to my roommate and stared at the wall. I remember staring at the wall in my bedroom where I had hung a sampler that said, "I am a child of God." I could see it, but it didn't resonate within me. I kept staring at it for a long time. It was difficult to think God could love me if I was so messed up. I existed like this for about two weeks, showering only when I needed to and eating only because I knew I should.

One night, deeply sad, I laid alone in the dark on the couch, staring blankly. I began to scratch at a spot on my arm; it must have itched. Then I scratched the same spot over and over and harder and harder. The rhythmic and soothing sensation brought the realization that I was capable of feeling when everything seemed so dead and hopeless inside. The area began to tingle, then burn, so I kept scratching and scratching. I just focused on that one place for a moment; my mind blissfully blank. I became distracted when I realized my fingers were wet. I stopped and looked at my arm. Three distinct three-inch gouge marks stared back at me. Deep, thick, angry scratches that bled freely. Disconnected from any pain, I closed my eyes and cried. I didn't mean to hurt myself. It seemed as if all conscious thought had fled and left behind was something to remember the experience by. I vaguely remember getting up off the couch and washing off the blood and going to bed.

In the morning my arm looked like it had been dragged on asphalt. For the first time, I realized how easily I could hurt myself. That frightened me. I knew I was in a deeper depression than ever before. Conflicting thoughts in my head considered the benefit of taking the well-worn path of hiding my pain and depression and not letting anyone know I hurt myself, or I could actually reach out for help. I worked as a psychology research assistant at the University of Utah and enjoyed a pretty open relationship with the professor with whom I worked. With a lot of apprehension, I told my professor what had happened and showed him my wounds. Always kind, he helped me know things could change, but he said I needed to accept help from others. He would support me, but I needed to get into therapy to help myself. He was the first person to recognize my symptoms as something definable, such as depression. Nobody had mentioned those words before, but it made me think this seesaw I lived on might have a solution. I walked away from our conversation forever grateful he pushed me to get the kind of professional help I would need over and over in my life.

I was seeing my therapist, David, twice a week but my depression was worse than ever. I didn't know how I would get through the day from the time my feet hit the floor until I lay my head down at night. I could plan nothing, and I could commit to no one.

Even though I just sat there, I went to work every day because David, my boss Rosa, and I agreed I would be safer and less likely to harm myself if I went to work rather than sit in my apartment alone. Rosa, once aware of my risk of self-harm, compassionately agreed to allow me to come to work and sit in my cubicle doing the easiest of tasks. She respectfully kept an eye on me, letting me know I could come to her as a safe person if I needed one. Everyone basically went about their business, checking in to make sure I knew they were there for me. I was numb and just waiting until the hours passed so I could go back to bed. Too depressed to even be embarrassed, I let my coworkers float in and out of my day as they kindly let me know they were available should I need them. This went on for about three weeks, when I had the oddest sensations and series of thoughts, which literally changed my life.

While at work one day, my body suddenly felt as if it was glowing from the inside out. My whole body shook as if I had two-hundred volts of energy surging within me. My thoughts became crystal clear. My hearing became acute; I heard the sound of the coffee percolating in the breakroom across the hall, I could hear the tap, tap of coworkers' fingers on their keyboards as they labored at their desks. I felt the heat from the sun coming through the glass that surrounded our workspace. It was so bright. Everything felt so crisp and accessible.

I knew—no, I was convinced—I needed to run a marathon, twenty-six miles, starting right there and right then. It didn't matter that I, in no stretch of the imagination, was not capable of running more than half a mile or that I didn't even possess the right shoes. I knew what I needed to do, and I needed to do it right then. I decided I would start by running through the thick plate-glass floor to ceiling windows that circled the area. I never considered I couldn't do it or that I would get hurt. The absoluteness and clarity of the moment was immediate and profound. The depression had totally disappeared, evaporated into thin air, and I floated on a lofty high of well-being and direction.

I found Rosa. "I need to leave." I said forcefully.

She started explaining I needed to stay until the end of the day like we had arranged. She then looked more closely at me and could see that something had changed.

"You don't understand," I said. "I know what I have to do. I *must* leave right now. I've got to run from here to downtown and back before it gets too late."

Upon hearing what I planned to do, she quickly convinced me I should call David to discuss the idea. I talked so loudly and animatedly that she took me to an outside area to share my grand plan. Thankfully, she remained calm and told me I would have to talk to David before she could let me go for the day.

I was impatient with any delay, but I agreed to call David. I called and told him of my epiphany. I had energy and focus that I hadn't known in months. While I had experienced parts of this energy before, it didn't compare to the intensity of my mania at that moment. I was positively buzzing. Excited about my new thinking, I waited anxiously to hear his approval. Instead I heard him take a huge deep breath and begin to apologize for what he had done. I didn't understand; what had he done that was so terrible?

He told me he was sorry for not recognizing the true signs of what was now obviously wrong with me. He said I had manic depression (later called bipolar disorder), and we needed to work to get me well. He said we would have to work differently than we had been, because manic depression was a more serious illness that could be unpredictable, and we needed to establish better safety limits. He spoke calmly and with great compassion. I couldn't think of what would be so bad about having manic depression if it created feelings which were so amazing. Still feeling good, I got off the phone not understanding why he expressed sympathy for me. I didn't really understand what David was telling me about this new diagnosis, but I did understand I would not be able to run a marathon that day. I was confused and feeling agitated about what to do with all my energy. I was left with the task of keeping myself on track and safe until this new part of me could be figured out.

It took a few days and some time for me to research manic depression before I would begin to see how the pieces of my depressions and times of mania fit together. I understood why David felt such a sense of urgency to resolve my manic episode. He believed a sudden end of my mania could put me at risk of a severe depression, even increasing my risk of suicide. He explained it as "the higher you go, the harder you fall."

As I transitioned out of the mania, I began to have a sense of peace because now I knew what was wrong with me. I didn't have to live with the ups and downs and wonder why I lived so out of control, why as a person I was so messed up. With a name to the illness, it didn't have so much power, and I could learn about it. There were people who specialized in knowing what to do.

Hallelujah. I finally had an answer.

The next few months of therapy were intense but focused and, thankfully, short-lived. I followed David's every suggestion and direction. It seemed once I had the right diagnosis, I could develop the skills to manage my mood swings. I put healthy tools in my emotional toolbox. I learned about cognitive behavioral therapy—how my depression or mania drove the thoughts that started a vicious cycle of hopelessness or craziness. These then ultimately affected the way I thought about my world, usually in an unhealthy and emotional way. The circle continued until I had a total breakdown or blips of mania. This became my lifelong pattern. I would have to manage my thoughts and behaviors and live with the new diagnosis. Finally, a sense of empowerment meant that I could actually do something about it and not ride the roller coaster of my past. At twenty-one years old I believed knowing was power, and I liked power.

Over the next few years I continued to cycle between highs and lows, but they weren't as extreme or long lasting. I knew how to better identify things and situations that triggered my moods. If I found myself on a downward slope, I would hunker down with people who were my support system until I could ride it out. The highs meant a few days of incredible well-being. I didn't get crazy manic, wanting to run through windows or race through the city. I felt a pleasant buzz and energy that allowed me to be a little "more" for a day or two. I didn't see it hurting anybody, including myself, so I enjoyed the moment.

I hated having to take my emotional temperature every day; I focused too much on what was wrong with me. But when I performed my daily checkup, I became more confident in my ability to predict things that might set me off. If I made sure I got enough sleep, ate regularly, and enjoyed some regular leisure time, I could manage my illness.

Bipolar disorder didn't knock me flat anymore. Over time it wasn't even on my radar.

I DO, I DON'T

From the beginning, Seattle felt like coming home. The Pacific Northwest was a balm to me. Totally and deeply in love with my new home, I reveled in everything about it—the green, the water, the rain, the culture, the attitudes, the people. Even just breathing the Seattle air made me feel embraced and welcomed. For Elise and me, moving to Washington was the beginning of an exciting adventure.

Living in the University District was exciting. There were students in their Birkenstocks walking along the Gilman Trail, and students with their noses in their textbooks. There were students playing Hacky Sack in the park or strolling down the eclectic University Avenue with its tiny ethnic restaurants, shops, and markets. The sights, smells, and sounds were foreign but familiar at the same time. I loved the "I can be here because I want to be here" attitude. I loved it because it was new, and it wasn't like Utah. Believing I had truly found a place I belonged, I began to make new friends and embarked on a time of exploration. I wandered the walking trails, Green Lake, Pikes Market, and enjoyed looking out over the water knowing everything was a fresh start.

I attended a local community college to finish my Associate Degree and remembered how much I loved learning. My classes were dynamic, and I took advantage of every opportunity I could. I looked forward to whatever exciting things would happen around the corner. No longer plagued with significant depression or sadness, I enjoyed a sense of happiness. I knew good things were going to happen.

31

I remember the first time I saw Dale. We were at a singles activity with our church and he was playing Twister with some friends. Being new to the group, I was able to sit on the fringe and watch him. I instantly fell in love with his infectious laugh. He laughed easily and often. It seemed everyone enjoyed being around Dale. He was competitive, yet he was genuinely engaged with all the other players. He was confident without being cocky, and as his winning streak affirmed, he was very good at Twister. He was the kind of guy everybody wanted as a friend.

A few weeks later, Dale invited me and Elise to his house for Sunday potluck. It sounded like fun, and we were ready for an adventure. I rarely had been part of a spontaneous group activity, and it was exciting to be with so many people. Aware of being self-conscious, I wondered if it was obvious I didn't know how to mingle. I decided to give it a try anyway. I don't remember much outside of watching Dale as he played host and appreciating his kindness and sense of humor.

Later, everyone divided up into pairs to play Pictionary, and Dale and I ended up as the only two without partners. When the realization hit me, I felt an awkward pause that seemed to go on forever. Dale hadn't done anything to make me feel unwanted, it was just my insecurity rearing its ugly head. While I was embarrassed, he soon convinced me that being partners with me was exactly what he wanted.

We were both horrible artists, but it made for hilarious drawings. He would take his time methodically drawing an intricate picture, then proudly present it to me, repeatedly tapping the pencil point on the notepad to try to get me to divine what he had drawn. Usually I didn't see it, but his intensity and sincere desire to win made me laugh until I couldn't breathe. We both had tears running down our cheeks before long. I don't remember who won, but it didn't matter, because I had a great time and I wanted to get to know him better.

A few days later he called me. I guess he wanted to know me better too. On our first date we went cross-country skiing in the Cascade Mountains. When he called to ask me out, I had a split-second vision we would one day be married. Where this came from, I don't know. I had never thought of someone this way. I figured it was best if I set the thought aside as a passing moment of strangeness.

We had a clear and a brilliant blue sky that day, and the space around us seemed hushed except for our voices. Dale showed great patience in teaching me how to ski. Unfortunately, I didn't show much promise as a student. I was awkward and stiff but decided to give it my all and allow myself to have a good time. Our ski date ended up being much more than just the skiing; we talked about ourselves, our families, and our history as we spent the day on the snow.

As Dale talked about growing up in Utah, I realized our experiences of being raised there were very different. Our parents and families differed, and we had been exposed to distinctive opportunities. It was intriguing. Talking to him was like picking up a book I wanted to devour.

Near the end of the day as we trekked back to his truck, my exhausted, wobbly legs gave out and I fell. I kind of laid there like a lump of clay, not wanting to get up but knowing I needed to. I glanced up at Dale and saw him unsuccessfully trying not to laugh. I told him he could laugh, in fact, we both had a good, long laugh before he helped me get upright again. He was so easy to be with, and I let go of my insecurities. I was comfortable just being myself, clumsiness and all. We got back to his truck and settled in for our ride home. Although sad the day had come to an end, I had a sense of well-being and peace. I hoped I would see him again.

By the time I got home I was very stiff but tried not to look it. Elise helped me peel my layers of clothes off, and I was startled when I saw my right leg. My knee resembled a purplish-blue cantaloupe. That was a problem. After a three-hour visit to the emergency room, I left with a full leg brace, crutches, a bottle full of pain pills, and a prescription for six weeks of physical therapy. What an ending to the perfect day!

When I saw Dale at church the next day, he gasped.

"I broke you!" he exclaimed.

I had to reassure him over and over that no blame existed. Believing himself to be responsible, he anxiously asked what he could do to help. I assured him that between him helping me keep my leg elevated and my taking the pain killers, I was fine. He settled down, but he glanced down at my leg a few times throughout the meeting. As we spoke about our skiing adventure, I was pleased when he admitted he'd had a good time too.

Elise and I became a part of a group that included Dale and a few other couples from our congregation. Dale and I spent time together at church, during group activities, and on dates. On my twenty-third birthday, my friends from our singles group gathered at the park across the street from my apartment to celebrate—on my behalf! Growing up, I'd never belonged to any group. It was one of my most memorable birthdays. How could it not be with all my friends and Dale being so attentive as we celebrated? Dale and I quickly grew close, each interaction seeming magical.

I was the first to say, "I love you." One night as he held me close, I experienced such a sense of connection and without even thinking about it, the words tumbled out. Dale looked a little shocked and told me that, while he deeply cared for me, he didn't feel he could say it yet. He told me when he knew he also felt that way, I would be the first to know. He said he didn't intend on saying it just for the sake of saying it.

"Okay, that was awkward," I thought. My face turned red and I felt embarrassed for blurting out my feelings.

He explained that to him, it spoke of a declaration, a kind of bond not to be taken lightly. I was disappointed, but what could I do? I appreciated his honesty and found him to be a man of integrity. So, I had to wonder and wait. A few weeks later while saying good night he told me he loved me too. A smile spread across my face, and I pulled away from his embrace and looked at his face. I could see and feel the truth of his words in his eyes. It was a wonderful feeling.

We spent late nights talking in his truck in front of my apartment. It seemed like we had so much to say and not enough time to say it. I loved to listen to the timbre of his bass voice. His eyes would twinkle when he found something funny, and he often thought I seemed to be most amusing. He wasn't overly physical, but when he reached across to hold my hand, or when he touched my leg to emphasize a point he intended to make, I would feel the heat and be reassured I wanted to be with him exclusively. He said he liked to watch me talk and found me entertaining. He liked my quirkiness and the way I saw the world. Pretty early on we knew we were compatible; our goals were matched, our determination to live according to our faith was the same, our perspective of the world around us similar. We had an awesome, strong friendship that ran beneath all aspects of our relationship.

Dale's unofficial proposal came as he lay on my couch in my apartment with me on the floor next to him, talking about nothing and everything. He so casually said, "What do you think about getting married?" I gave him a hard look to make sure he was serious, and then grinned. I tried not to squeal as I told him I thought it would be a good idea. He smiled and giggled, and we began to talk about a life together. What an exciting but scary time. Although I had known I wanted to be with him from almost the moment I met him, we had only been dating five months. I tried to not think negatively and decided to have faith in our timing being exactly as it should be. I didn't want to wait another six months. That would be forever when I didn't want to be away from him for even a day.

I considered the Salt Lake Temple in Utah "my" temple and the only place I ever wanted to marry. The Salt Lake Temple was part of my growing up. Every time I went to downtown Salt Lake City, I would look for the majestic spires of the temple. I loved the feeling of peace I felt as I walked along the temple grounds. It was a way to orient myself both physically and spiritually. Since Dale also grew up in the Salt Lake City area, he shared similar feelings, and we agreed our marriage could only take place in the temple surrounded by both our families.

There was so much to do! We headed to Utah to make all the arrangements—renting a reception center, purchasing a ring, and meeting each other's families. The days were chock-full of preparations, and we found ourselves exhausted and stretched to the limit.

The day before we left to return to Seattle, Dale and I broke away from everyone else and he drove me to Ensign Peak. It was a hot, dry July day, and we were a little tired and punchy from all the many things we had to do to get ready for the wedding. We were anxious to have some uninterrupted time away from everyone else and the pressures around us. I didn't care what we did; I only wanted to be with him. From Ensign Peak we could look out over the Salt Lake Valley almost as far as the eye could see. Most beautiful from this point was the view of the Salt Lake Temple. That spectacular building stood as a symbol of our shared beliefs, values, and our faith in the future.

Dale parked his truck, so I could sit in the truck bed and see the valley. Then he suddenly got all nervous and began fussing around. He told me I had to sit in the truck bed and not look at him. I found that odd, but I could sense his excitement and anticipation, so I did as he asked. After a few minutes he came and sat next to me, taking a deep breath, and with a shaky voice handed me a yellow rose.

He said, "I want to marry you in the temple because you are my friend, and this yellow rose represents friendship."

He then added to the yellow rose a white rose and said, "I want to marry you in the temple because you are pure, and white represents purity."

He then added a red rose and said, "I want to marry you in the temple because I love you and red represents love."

Dale then added the greenery typical of a bouquet and said, "I want to marry you in the temple because it will be forever, and green represents forever."

He reached around him and brought out an exact duplicate bunch of flowers. He put them all together and read the Bible scripture that states that a man is not to be without a woman or a woman without a man. He then pledged to be unified in our marriage and offered an official proposal.

It took my breath away and rendered me speechless. Dale showed himself to be a thoughtful, loving man to work so hard, and consider a message which would touch my heart forever. I loved him to the moon and back at that moment. As we drove down from Ensign Peak on that beautiful July afternoon with our windows down, I shouted, "I am getting married! I am getting married!"

Early morning on September 8, 1989 found us in the Salt Lake Temple. We were actually getting married. I floated through the day, giddy, boisterous and so happy. Celebrating the joy of being in love, we shared an amazing day with friends and family. The reception that evening was perfect. The guests waiting to go through the reception line stretched out the door and through the parking lot. I loved standing near Dale and calling him my husband.

Then we were off to Hawaii. I enjoyed being spoiled to have such an extravagant and exotic location in which to spend time with my new husband. Dale took me snorkeling, kayaking, touring, and we learned to hula. I saw things I had only read about.

However, as the week went on, my emotional seams began to unravel, and I knew I was headed for a funk. I worked hard to not show my feelings to Dale. I didn't want to ruin Hawaii for him, but I wanted quiet time to myself and with Dale. The excitement and stress of the previous two months was catching up with me, and I was aware of being extremely tired inside.

At the end of our last day in Hawaii, we spent a relaxing evening in the hot tub under a beautiful star-filled sky and surrounded by the scent and colors of the flowers. We found ourselves sharing things we hadn't had time to talk about when dating. During our conversation, I told him about my battle with bipolar disorder in previous years. He asked how I finally got diagnosed, and we talked about how I had come to cope. He mentioned he had family who had bipolar disorder but said he didn't know much about it.

That was that. We didn't discuss how bipolar disorder, or our family history might affect our future. I marvel now at our naïve understanding of such a devastating illness. Truly, if we knew then what we know now, our lives may have been very different. Bipolar disorder just didn't have a big place in our life nor did we think it ever would.

As we settled into marriage, everything seemed different but also comfortingly the same. I loved that I could more freely spend time with Dale. Seeing life from both our perspectives was interesting.

I was invigorated to leave behind the limits of single life in favor of sharing experiences with someone I loved. Along the line we deepened our sense of companionship. I remember feeling so complete whenever we were together.

Now, as a couple, we had to learn how to give each other space, when to push, and when to pull. We were both going to school but on different schedules, and I worked in the evenings part-time. My life became busy, and when we connected, we enjoyed our time together. Dale had less to do as he took only a few classes at school and worked sporadically for his grandfather. But at the end of the day, we were grateful for the many blessings in our life. Our relationship as a married couple grew, as did our relationship as friends.

I enjoyed playing the role of wife and homemaker with Dale as provider. We rented a nice condo and worked together to make it feel like our home. It was deeply satisfying to sit together on the couch and look around and realize we were exactly where we wanted to be, and with the person we most wanted to be with.

Dale and I both had distinct visions of our marital roles. Dale and I had strong beliefs of what we considered the right and wrong ways of doing things. While we shared similar values, sometimes our strong convictions would put us at odds with each other. At times our priorities and timing clashed, but usually we tried to accommodate each other and put our personal feelings aside.

As a business major Dale handled the finances with an iron fist. He could account for everything and was extremely organized and frugal. I was responsible and practical about money but enjoyed buying what I wanted from time to time. He insisted I learn his money management system, but I couldn't grasp it, it was so detailed and precise. After explaining it over and over, he would become frustrated with me and speak with what I called his "Mr. Rogers" voice. It made me feel stupid and incompetent. This quickly became a point of contention between us, so I decided to leave the finances up to him. It didn't have to be a problem, but rather than find a place of financial compromise or agreement, we just had Dale do the money. It was our first all or nothing stance, and while we didn't think it was too big a deal, it impacted our unity.

I liked to plan how I wanted to spend my day and would think about what needed to be done and the best way to go about it. Sometimes I would expect Dale to comply, but he wouldn't be able to or had other plans. He would suggest other ways to accomplish my goals and accommodate both our schedules. Not being inherently flexible in my thinking, I resented trying to change five things just to make one thing happen. Generally, things were black or white for me, and when Dale introduced a dizzying myriad of alternatives to what I thought unnecessary, I thought he was sabotaging me. I became stubborn and stopped communicating. My bipolar way of thinking seemed to be creeping into our relationship.

Whenever we were likeminded, life was good. We were good together. The laughter we shared when we finished each other's sentences with ease and regularity warmed our relationship. We loved engineering days away from school to wander through downtown Seattle and people watch. Frequent trips to Green Lake were never mundane. Dale held my hand and listened to me chatter all around the three-mile walking path of the Lake. It was our time.

But there were days we were at odds. Neither of us liked to argue or fight. We seemed to have a preset limit for conflict and once we reached that limit, we would stuff our feelings away and partly shut down. This didn't help with our disagreements as we weren't able to reconcile the problems we'd buried and tried to ignore. Frustrations weren't out of sight or out of mind.

Although we had briefly discussed my bipolar disorder on our honeymoon, we didn't give it much thought until I began to cycle soon after we were married. I became obsessed with losing weight. I wanted to lose weight and lose it right away. Dale, never having had weight issues, tried to understand my thinking and my intense need to do something about it *now*. When he told me I looked beautiful, it frustrated me because I fixated on how much better I would look if I lost twenty-five pounds.

Though finances were tight I insisted Dale find the money, so I could join Nutrisystem. I'd learned that if I met my goal within six months, I would get a $100 rebate. The rebate would be like a bonus I could give to Dale to show him I had been worth the financial sacrifice. So began a downhill slide as Dale handed me the money to start the program.

All I thought about was losing weight. I sometimes even skipped a few of the required meals so I could lose weight faster. I walked six miles at Green Lake each night, seven days a week and choked down more salad than I could physically handle. I reignited my bulimia. Throwing up after eating diet food didn't seem like a big deal to me, but I would have been mortified if Dale ever found out.

As the weeks went on, I continued to be weighed and measured at each weekly appointment, and I lost weight. We were stunned to see how many inches came off. After a few more weeks, the weight loss slowed down a little, so I exercised even harder and saw more progress. In four weeks, I'd lost twenty pounds and many inches. Over the next two weeks I only lost half a pound. It made me crazy when I realized my goal continued to elude me, and the inches I'd lost didn't count toward the rebate. I didn't know what else I could do.

Then suddenly I was done. Nutrisystem didn't matter anymore. I refused to eat any more salad or rehydrated dinners. I became as disinterested in weight-loss as I had been focused on making it happen. It was as if a switch had shut off, and I would not even discuss the situation. My mania about weight loss ended as suddenly as it had begun. Baffled, Dale stood back and shook his head.

In retrospect, neither of us tried to understand what really happened with the Nutrisystem experience. With a mania brewing, I could latch on to a ready-made opportunity to not only lose weight but show my new husband my ability to earn $100 in the process. I wanted him to be proud of me. I just had to put my mind to it and I knew I could. Dale for his part, had never seen me be so committed to something, and felt to just stay out of my way. What he didn't understand was that for me, it was all or nothing. This was Dale's first experience with my mania.

As time went on, we experienced deepening miscommunication. Our pattern of shoving our real thoughts and feelings under the rug continued, and along with it, a growing sense of resentment. It became apparent we didn't know how to effectively communicate with each other. We spent our time avoiding conflict and rarely took the time to be honest about how we were adjusting. We didn't make ourselves have those deep, searching conversations about the not-so-good things, and it started to take a toll.

When Dale did talk to me, at times it felt reminiscent of my father lecturing me. He didn't know this was a trigger for me, because I didn't know it was one either. Yet, it had a direct impact on my emotions. I didn't want anyone controlling me or speaking to me like a child. Although I knew I needed to partner with him for a successful marriage, I didn't know how to tell him what was bothering me. We hadn't shared our more honest, darker thoughts before and I was afraid of rejection. I was convinced if Dale looked hard enough at me he would decide I wasn't worth the trouble. I was fearful of having my husband find out I was a bad person. But I wasn't, and he never thought of me that way. I spent a lot of time consumed with the belief that I was not good enough for him.

I yearned to make changes to get relief from some of the stress. Dale seemed okay with how things were going. Although he could see and feel the contention between us, he thought it was something I was needing to work out. He thought I'd figure the problem out better if he stayed out of the way. I kept telling myself to focus on being grateful for what I had.

The longer this impassivity went on, the more I receded into the black-and-white thinking typical of bipolar disorder. I had been experiencing mild depression for months, blaming myself for not knowing why I was unhappy. I was angry with Dale for not grasping the problem, which was unreasonable since he couldn't guess at or help me when he didn't understand what was going on. We couldn't continue to live that way.

Wanting things to be different, I finally started sharing my true feelings with him. I tried not to worry so much if it hurt his feelings. He didn't seem to want to hear what I had to say and told me I needed to figure things out for myself. I expressed if either of us is struggling it is always an "us" problem and we need to be invested together, always. He just didn't see any responsibility for the conflict at that time. I told him I couldn't do it alone and perceived he was abandoning me when he wouldn't come around. I was scared and overwhelmed. How would we ever break through the now ingrained pattern keeping us apart?

The love and friendship we'd developed while courting allowed us to stumble along for a while, but eventually it became fight or flight for me, and Dale didn't know how to hold me to the earth. My agitation became even more pronounced when I got pregnant and had to suffer through all the emotions that came with a combination of changing hormones and bipolar disorder. We had to fix ourselves before I had the baby. But how?

Nothing seemed to be changing, and I began to give up. Then, finally, amazingly, Dale seemed to grasp the gravity and immediacy of the problems in our marriage and resolved to do something. But for me, it was too late. His version of a fix was far different from mine. We were just not on the same page, and I was too tired to keep trying. The time had already passed for Dale to recognize how dire our situation was, and I, with sorrow and remorse, threw in the towel. I took my pregnant self and moved out. We had only been married a year and a half.

Getting a divorce was an uncomfortable thing to think about as it was in direct conflict with our faith and how we viewed marriage—that it should last forever. Yet there we were. We loved each other, but I couldn't conceive of a way for us to stay together. We tried to talk it out, but ultimately, he left the decision up to me. How would we ever be able to have a breathing, viable, meaningful marriage based on what we then had? Convinced we couldn't bring a child into a marriage that suffered from lack of communication and was disconnected on the most intimate level, I realized my efforts to fix it had failed. Once Dale understood he had lost me, the decision was made.

It hurt like crazy.

UNEXPECTED MIRACLES

In the meantime, a child was growing within me. How would we share our baby through her childhood? We had many awkward conversations, hurt feelings, and fears as the pregnancy progressed. Emotionally, I wasn't open to Dale, and I was protective of the space I had created between us. Being just friends became our safe place because we could still claim a connection, but the ultimate commitment didn't exist. Why open myself up to possible heartache and risk my sense of being? My decision, and therefore, Dale's, had been made. I mourned for what we'd lost, but in my head, it could only be done this way.

Sarah came on her due date. Dale came to the hospital, but I was unable to have him in the birthing room; I felt too vulnerable. Having a baby was an incredibly intimate experience, and I didn't believe I could do what I needed to do if Dale was there. Protecting myself was a priority so I could take care of Sarah. I was sad to hurt him. Later I watched him as he held her, cooing and marveling at her perfection. He was a good man, and I knew he would be an exceptional father. We would figure out a way to share her.

And yet, as much as I wanted to share our baby, I was insecure. The day after Sarah was born, Dale threatened me he would one day be married, have a new family and take Sarah away from me. I knew he was saying that out of anger, but it frightened me more than anything else he could have said. That threat remained at the back of my mind. I worried about making him mad or having him perceive I was alienating him from his relationship with Sarah. Could we make single parenting work? We both had different ideas about how things should be, but with a little time, we were able to find a compromise. Neither one of us wanted to hurt the other. We certainly didn't want to hurt Sarah and knew a strong relationship between her parents would bless her life.

The first few years of co-parenting flew by. Sarah became a happy, charismatic child. She loved both her mom and dad and thrived on the attention she received from us. We decided we were doing a decent job. We had established a routine, and Sarah did well between life with me and life with Dale.

As we moved on with our lives, I finished my bachelor's degree and teacher certification. Teaching school would allow me to share as much time with Sarah as possible as she grew up. My first teaching job allowed Sarah to be on-site in childcare. I made new friends and was able to cope when my moods cycled and I needed to manage my stress. Dale moved on to better things at his job, things he enjoyed. He started dating steadily, and I watched to see how it would all turn out. I was not jealous but perhaps uneasy with his dating. I didn't know how to prepare for the time he found another woman to be his wife, and stepmother to our daughter. That unknown was unnerving, but I dealt with it.

Eighteen months after we divorced, I became increasingly aware that my feelings about Dale were changing. I looked forward to seeing him when he came to get Sarah. I enjoyed when we took the time to talk and listening to him laugh about something cute Sarah had done. I was interested in his well-being. Being drawn to him, I found myself pleasantly surprised to admit I wanted to spend time with him.

Typical for me, I decided to rush in and approach Dale about the possibility of getting back together. Our friendship had miraculously remained strong. I now thought about why we had gotten divorced. I better understood the factors that led to the separation, and recognized the divorce came because neither of us had done anything to stop it. I believed our maturity and my efforts to understand and have empathy for him would be sufficient to at least discuss reconciling. But when I brought it up, no dice. In fact, Dale became so upset he wouldn't even discuss it, and he asked me to leave his apartment.

Dale later shared that, at that point of time, he had finally figured out how to reconcile what our relationship was to be. When we separated and divorced, he had to learn how not to love me, as his wife. He felt like he had put his life back together and was finally in a good place. He said he had to let our marriage relationship go and enjoy how we worked together as Sarah's parents. For me to come along and shake things up seemed inconceivable. Threatened that getting together again would drastically disrupt the life he had rebuilt, he refused to discuss the possibility and asked me to leave. That was okay; I decided to settle into being friends for the sake of Sarah. I could move on with life knowing I had at least broached the subject. I would watch from the outside, always having a connection to Dale. It seemed to work. Sarah never saw us upset with each other and never questioned why we were not together like other mommies and daddies. She never knew anything different.

Then Dale got serious with one of his girlfriends, and I had a hard time thinking someone else would be taking my place as Sarah's mother. When Dale took the woman down to Utah to meet his family, I knew it was serious. Dale had told me early on in our divorce he wanted to have another family and would be actively looking for a partner. It seemed he'd found her.

So, in my new confrontational fashion, I asked him for permission to have lunch with his girlfriend. That freaked him out. Only after I explained that I wanted to have a chance to get to know a potential stepmother for Sarah, he said he'd think about it. He never did give me the chance to meet with her. Shortly thereafter, he decided he did not want to be with her and broke off the relationship. I was relieved.

That spring Dale and I spent some time together with Sarah. I surprised Dale by showing up at a surprise birthday party for him given by a mutual friend. I didn't find it odd, but I guess having your ex-wife at your party was a little unusual. I didn't intend it to be anything more than me celebrating his birthday with friends, but I later found out it made him uncomfortable.

On Sarah's third birthday, we decided to take her together to Chuck E. Cheese. We had decided to share her birthday each year. This ended up being the first year that it was just the three of us. It seemed like an out-of-body experience to me. From the moment we walked into the restaurant, things were noticeably different. As we ordered the pizza, it seemed as if we were a married couple out with our daughter for a celebration. It was like I had imagined it would be so long ago. Dale accidentally bumped into me, and I was aware of an electric but natural feeling at the same time. I was unexpectantly attracted to him, which made me pause. Then I realized I was totally okay being with him, not as Sarah's dad out for her birthday party, but being with him. I liked it. The air felt charged between us as we got our drinks and pizza and we began to eat. Later, while we watched Sarah play, we sat across from each other and freely talked about things that were important to us. It was as if we were swept back to our courting days. Sarah would cry out, "Mommy, look at me." Or "Daddy, look what I can do." I perceived it as a magical yet scary moment, but neither of us said anything to each other. We were afraid to find out what the other was thinking yet hoped it was the same.

About a month later, Dale called me on a Sunday evening, totally unexpected, and asked if he could come over to talk. He never called unless he needed to arrange something regarding Sarah. He specifically asked to have Sarah at someone else's house, so she wouldn't see him come over. I was so nervous. I called our mutual friend to see if she knew if I had done something to offend him. This was it. I was afraid he wanted full custody. What had I done to warrant this surprise visit?

When Dale came, he was noticeably nervous and didn't want small talk. We sat down across the room from each other, and he got right to the point. He asked why we had gotten divorced. Taken aback, I answered him as honestly as I could. I remembered it from my perspective. More than three years had passed, and I had played the situation over and over in my mind. I knew he had too.

He listened and then said, "If we can figure out what went wrong, maybe there is a chance for us to figure out how to fix us and get back together again."

I was shocked.

And I was surprised to find the connection and my affection for Dale reemerging. That was why I had gone to him almost two years before. He had not been open to me when I had approached him but was definitely open now. When I asked him why he wanted to reconcile, he said he still had feelings for me and couldn't move on without trying one more time to see if we could be together. He said he didn't want to live with the regret of not having tried.

Well, here's to not having regrets. It certainly felt fortuitous to me.

Maybe I'd healed faster, because for me everything had fallen apart faster. Or maybe my bipolar brain jumped ahead and understood it would work out in the end. Even if I couldn't see what the end would look like. I had recognized by this point how much my bipolar mood swings, skewed thinking, and my impulsivity had contributed to the divorce, even though I knew it took two people to bring us to that point. But as our conversation continued and Dale relaxed his guard more and more, we got excited about the possibility of getting back together again. He wanted to point out this was not an official formal reconciliation but an effort to start dating to see what came of it. If that was how he made sense of it, that was fine, but my head and heart had already leapt ahead of him.

Dating my ex was weird, plain and simple. We had so much history—and a child. When we went out together it seemed sneaky and we hoped we wouldn't see anyone we knew. We thought we were something unique, but to everyone else we were only another couple. After a time, we acted like any other couple. We talked a lot about what had happened and began to open up to the hurt the breakup had caused. But we mostly enjoyed spending time together; and soon we knew we wanted to be married again.

One of my requirements for us getting back together was to attend couples therapy. I wanted us to resolve the issues we'd had during our marriage and during our time apart. I was so grateful Dale understood how important that was to me.

A history of therapy had taught me that much good could come from us going to sort out our difficult issues with a third party. We methodically picked apart the mess we had made when we first married, recognizing our need to learn and use effective communication skills. We recognized it was okay to be frustrated and mad with each other, but we understood the importance of being responsible for what we did with our emotions. There never was conversations of blame or fault; we didn't have time or a place for that. We were committed to being forward thinking, to acknowledge mistakes of the past, but chose to learn from them in the future.

We became more understanding of the different worlds we grew up in, and ways we wanted to mold our marriage and family to fit our values. We finally talked about the reality of my bipolar disorder and how it colored the way I saw things. We devised ways for me, and for us, to cope when I had my ups and downs.

We went for more than a year, building a foundation based on the things we'd learned, from our days in the beginning, to our breakup, to our single lives, and back again. We had come full circle.

What had we learned? So much. Even things we refer to now, more than twenty years later. We learned, foremost, about forgiveness. The depths of our individual and collective sorrows ran deep and powerful, and we had to claim them. To move through the stages of recognition and acceptance of things we had done to each other and ourselves proved difficult. But we learned to let go so we could move forward. We also learned to communicate more effectively, having the courage to talk through our problems instead of around them. We've used these skills throughout our married life. We learned to laugh at ourselves and the things around us. We learned patience and loyalty. We learned compassion and empathy. We learned how to be peaceful and calm in life's struggles and in the face of unexpected events. We learned about ultimate commitment, about never walking away. We learned how to be soft with each other, and when to rejoice together. In our counseling sessions, we planted seeds of hope, but it was through the actual living together that we grew and cultivated them to where they've become a part of who we are.

Since then, I can say that despite the ups and downs, marriage to Dale has been wonderful. He is my strength and my best friend. The road has been long. It is a miracle we were both single when we talked about finding our way back to each other again. It is a miracle God helped prepare us for the moment when we could reconnect. It is a miracle we have been able to stand strong throughout life's difficult circumstances. It is a miracle we deserved.

DEPTHS OF DARKNESS

We quietly remarried exactly five years to the day of our first marriage, with only a few people attending the ceremony. To us the real marriage happened five years before, the remarriage just a legal formality. Dale and I decided to keep our story mostly private because we felt protective about the road we had just traveled. Life for the Greenwell family was good.

Within two months, I was pregnant. We wanted to have another child right way so the age difference between Sarah and her sibling would be as small as possible. I started the new school year teaching first grade and PE at a private school in our area, and Sarah came with me every day for prekindergarten classes. Sarah loved having her daddy living at home with us, never questioning why things had changed. Life fell into an easy pattern. Dale had a demanding job as an area representative for a commercial carpet company where he was on the road three of the four weeks in a month. He always appreciated coming home to our enthusiastic welcome. We missed Dale and looked forward to the fun weekends we shared with him. Although it seemed as if we picked up where we'd left off, we were much wiser and devoted this time around.

On July 14, 1995 our son Taylor came into the world. It was also my dad's birthday; and as it ended up, his last birthday before dying of cancer. To have Taylor born on that day made my heart tender. Having Dale at Taylor's birth was so gratifying. I could finally give Dale something to make up for not allowing him to be at Sarah's birth. Dale wept as he saw and then held Taylor, and my heart soared with the satisfaction of being bonded to my family. Sarah couldn't wait to show love to Taylor and take care of him.

However, from the beginning, affection seemed to agitate Taylor. We had waited such a long time to have him; but he became distressed whenever he was held, and he refused to be cuddled. He even refused to breastfeed because he didn't like being held close. After having an amazingly positive experience with Sarah, Taylor's absolute refusal to let me feed him left me sad and rejected. He would cry and push against us as hard as his baby arms could push; and once we put him down, he would calm down. At times we had to swaddle him tightly in a blanket and rhythmically pat his back to soothe him. Many nights found him in his car seat on top of the running dryer as this helped him calm down. Bonding with him was difficult because I didn't want to agitate him. I tried to find other ways to interact— talking to him, playing toys with him, and reading books with him. But Taylor was in his own bubble and remained most content when left to his own world. To make things worse, he developed colic. He was miserable. Many times I cried, feeling unwanted as his mother, and I didn't know what to do to connect with him.

That fall, Dale's uncle, who lived in Fairbanks, Alaska, approached Dale to see if we would be interested in relocating to Fairbanks so Dale could run the family carpet store. We were intrigued to think of a new start in an area not associated with the memories of our past. We also liked the idea that Dale would be home every night, not having to travel. Dale had lived in Fairbanks for a time as a young adult and warmed up to the idea of returning. I didn't know anything about Fairbanks, but I figured I could be adventurous and decided to give it a try. I trusted Dale's judgment. Since Sarah and Taylor were both young, their adjustment would be minimal. While we did have friends in our area, we weren't attached to anyone besides my brother who lived in Seattle. So, we decided to sell our condominium and see what happened.

In the meantime, my dad grew sicker. Not being with him in Utah for his last days broke my heart. However, a week before he died, we said our good-byes, and we both knew how much we loved each other. He was only fifty-five years old. I couldn't help but be wistful about all the things he would miss as we raised our children. My dad and I had a unique relationship. With him I was always special, and we shared a history of mutual depression. When he died the end of October, we gathered with the rest of the family to bury a man who'd had a profound influence in my life. His coworkers and friends, coming through the reception line, told me how my dad loved to talk about me and how proud he was of me. I held it as a tender message of love from him to me.

While I stayed behind in Utah with the kids for a few extra days after the funeral, Dale returned to Washington. Not long after he arrived, he called me and said we had an offer on the condominium. We discussed if we were really wanting to make such a big move. The offer came in at full asking price, and we couldn't see any reason not to go. Soon we were packing up and buying cold weather clothes. We thought we knew what we were doing, but we had no idea how this Alaskan adventure would turn out.

The Alaska I first experienced felt harsh. We arrived in Fairbanks two days before Thanksgiving and experienced the cold sting of winter as soon as the airplane door opened. We were told the twenty-degree weather was mild. Maybe for Fairbanks, but compared to our sixty-degree weather in Seattle, we all shivered in the frigid air. Then there was the darkness—at 3:00 p.m. it looked like night. Driving to our lodging, everything was in shadow and blowing snow.

The staff at the carpet store was anxious for Dale to arrive and welcomed him immediately. I anticipated caring for Sarah and Taylor and being the homemaker I'd always wanted to be. Cooking, playing with the kids, doing art and science projects, and decorating—all these activities beckoned to me as I'd contemplated what coming to Alaska meant. To me Alaska meant freedom and a fresh start for us. We could define what we wanted to be. But in the end, the cost of freedom turned out to be very high.

Dale's aunt and uncle who owned the business arranged for us to stay in a small two-bedroom apartment on the outskirts of the neighborhood in which they lived. They were generous to let us live there for free, and it had all the basic amenities we needed to make us comfortable. Everything we owned was packed up to be shipped in a big freight container to Alaska. We literally only had the clothes on our backs and what we were able to fit in a couple suitcases. It certainly started out like an adventure, and I went to bed that night thinking if I could only keep that perspective, I would be able to roll with the punches that were sure to come.

And come they did. We didn't have a crib for Taylor, and he refused to sleep between us on the bed. I did have his sheepskin blanket with him, so we folded some additional blankets and made a nest in the bedroom closet with the sheepskin on top. If we made sure he remained safe and left him alone, he seemed to be content. Sarah was a little scared to be in a new place but was excited to spend time with her cousin Emma. It was wonderful to have someone to help her make the transition. With Sarah's contagious enthusiasm, we all went to bed the first night, excited for the next day to begin.

As it was his nature to jump in 100 percent, Dale began work the very next day. He kept busy with his daily responsibilities and would come home for lunch excited to share about the enhancements and how his vision would come together. He met new people and made contacts with customers every day. This was great for him, but it left the kids and me alone in the apartment with little to do and no way to get around. Every day I would look out the windows of the apartment only to see blowing snow, four-feet-high piles of the stuff, and perpetual darkness. I became frustrated and lonely and wished for activities we could do, but most things required us braving the cold and snow and I didn't have a car.

One day I tried to go for a walk with the kids. We had been tutored in the type of winter gear we would need for Fairbanks. With the extreme cold, venturing out was not for the faint of heart. We bought the gear to specifications, so the kids would be ready to play safely and stay warm. The thing I didn't expect was how long it took to get us all ready.

Armored in her new magenta snowsuit, Sarah sat on the couch to watch me dress, or rather fight, Taylor to get him ready to go outside. Taylor wouldn't sit still; he cried every time I tried to get his flailing limbs into the snowsuit. He hated being zipped and buckled up. I persevered because I really wanted to get out of the apartment.

By the time I got Taylor dressed and wrapped in a blanket, poor Sarah had become overheated and red-faced. She still wanted to give it a try, so out we went into the blowing snow and negative twenty-five-degree weather in the 11:00 a.m. semidarkness.

At twenty-five below, your nose hairs freeze, and the snow sticks to your eyelashes. It was hard to breathe without a scarf or other barrier in front of your nose and mouth. Trying to move about in our new Alaska snow boots looked comical and was tiring. Dale had warned me I would need the chunky Sorrel boots, but I'd balked at getting them because they were ugly. When we had trudged about halfway across the parking lot on our anticipated trek to Kmart, I looked at my children. They looked miserable and overwhelmed. I realized it would be best if we went back to the apartment and ended our escapade with a cup of hot chocolate and their sheepskins. We didn't go out much after that except with Dale in the van. I'd learned my lesson, but it made for a lonely time.

Once Dale's brother got to Fairbanks with some of our belongings, our spirits lifted. Familiarity was supposed to bring comfort, but every time I looked outside, I was reminded Alaska did not feel like a familiar place. I spent part of my days on our computer emailing family and friends. I wrote we were having a good time, we were well, and that Fairbanks was an interesting place. I lied with every email I sent, but I wanted to believe everything would be all right, so I pretended. I had lost my adventurous spirit.

Then we had a breakthrough. The house across the street from the apartment, which we could literally see through the front window, came up for sale. It seemed a gift from heaven. We put in an offer, and the owners accepted. Finally, something to look forward to. I looked out the windows now and stared at the house, wishing the days away until we could move in.

Christmas in Fairbanks was unique. We had to have enough money for the down payment on the new house, so we knew Christmas would be lean. Luckily the kids were young and easily pleased, so they didn't have expectations of a big Christmas. Dale and I decided more winter snow gear was the way to go. For our Christmas tree we were a little stumped. Fresh trees had to be flown in from Washington and Oregon, and they were expensive. The Fairbanks trees looked like Dr. Seuss trees, all misshapen. The artificial trees from the store were also expensive, so I got creative. I purchased shiny green Christmas wrapping paper and carefully cut a large piece in the shape of a Christmas tree, then taped the tree on the wall. Dale and I acted so excited about our new cool tree, Sarah decided she liked it too. Thank goodness for children's acceptance of things they cannot always understand. Christmas for the Greenwells had come to Fairbanks, Alaska. Though our leanest Christmas, it became the most memorable and cherished.

As the weeks went on, I steadily sunk into a depression, but I had reasons. Taylor continued to be a difficult baby, my dad had recently died, financially we were limited in our resources, and we'd moved from a familiar place to a foreign land. I spent a lot of time isolated in our apartment, and there was little or no light to be had. I carried a lot of sadness in my heart, but I believed most of it was circumstantial. I thought I would be able to outlast the depression. But I couldn't. Dale and I went to see a doctor who gave me a prescription for an antidepressant and sent me on my way. It was the fastest appointment I had ever had. I'd never taken prescription medication for my depression. Before, I had always managed my moods with coping strategies, but I didn't have it in me this time. I tried to figure out why the doctor seemed to be so cavalier about my depression when I came to the realization that depression was likely a common problem in Fairbanks. It was the illness du jour.

When we moved in the house, the first thing I did was lie in the middle of the front room on the soft carpet like a snow angel, close my eyes, and smile. It was so spacious and light. The perfect house for us. There were big windows in the front room, which promised to offer lots of light in the spring and summer. Sarah and I enjoyed unpacking and rediscovering our things. For us it became like Christmas all over again.

Getting settled with the kids gave me a sense of purpose and something to do. I got a calling at our church to work with some of the young women in the congregation. I started to make a few friends. Sarah had a few friends, Taylor's colic finally lifted, and Dale excelled at work. Things were getting better. By the end of March, I began to feel more like myself and stopped taking the antidepressant. Then came "Green Day." The snow in Fairbanks suddenly melted, leaving deep puddles and shrinking snowdrifts. One night we went to bed with everything still looking like winter. When we woke up, the buds were like a beautiful green blanket of leaves covering the trees, promising the coming of spring. I loved that day. Each day we added six to seven more minutes of daylight, and my spirits soared. I enjoyed this Fairbanks much more than the winter one. I wished it could stay this way forever, with months of light and sun and warmth and no need for snow tires.

As our family happily moved into April, it looked like we would finally claim Fairbanks as home. But things were not as they seemed. At first, I didn't notice the changes inside me or, more specifically, inside my head. Now always cheerful, I sometimes acted even giddy. I loved spending time with the kids, and we often went to meet with friends at parks or visit a friend's house. We enjoyed an exceptionally clean home. I would sing as I worked and got Sarah to sing Disney songs with me. Taylor would squeak and kick his heels as Sarah and I put on our own concert. I was a fun mom and a good wife, serving Dale a hot dinner and offering a listening ear each time he walked into the house. I thrived in being good and doing good to the people around me, but it didn't seem to be enough. It was so subtle and so unexpected, but even in Fairbanks the mania found me.

During this time, I met a friend named Kim who introduced me to scrapbooking and Creative Memories. Creating photo books for memories and journaling about things which were important struck a chord in me, so I decided to start my own Creative Memories business. I had never had my own business before and didn't know where to start, but it didn't matter. I embraced the opportunity and would make it work. My theme was "It speaks of who we are and how we want to be remembered." I committed all my time and energy to it in addition to taking care of the mommy things. I wanted to go big, so I decided with Dale's approval that we needed to make the financial investment to stock up on inventory. I inherently knew I could sell anything and make money. I couldn't fail. Dale trusted me, and I spent thousands of dollars over the next couple months amassing inventory and working the business. I held two to three events a week in our home, teaching others how to scrapbook and helping them accomplish their scrapbooking goals. Soon I had people approaching me to see how they could become Creative Memories consultants. I had never wanted to do any recruiting, but if people were coming to me, what could I do but sign them up? I signed thirteen consultants in my first quarter, becoming the highest recruiter in the company. Creative Memories even invited me to speak at the upcoming national convention.

People were drawn to me and my success, and I enjoyed having a social outlet that also brought in some income. Kim watched from the sidelines, pleased to see my business and influence growing exponentially. But I sensed a little apprehension from her about how fast everything seemed to be happening and how much of my time I dedicated to the business. Somehow, I managed everything and made it look easy. Invigorated and excited I moved forward at breakneck speed.

My life moved fast every day, full of activities and people. I buzzed with energy and found myself motivated to try new things and reach out to new people. I started making good money and spending time thinking of new ways to sell Creative Memories. My to-do list grew daily, but as I moved through the items on it, I started to stay up all night to accomplish everything I needed or wanted to do, pulling all-nighters two to three days a week.

Dale didn't seem to mind, or if he did it wasn't apparent to me. I figured if I took care of what I needed to do at home, he would be okay with my lack of sleep. He rarely mentioned it, and I didn't bring it up. I even started skipping meals because I didn't have time to eat with all the activities I had going. I dreamed up and organized activities for my Church calling that were so grandiose the husband of one of the leaders I worked with said his wife would come home from our activities and cry because she believed she could never live up to the standard I set. She thought I could do anything. In truth, I thought I was great, and I thought everything I touched would be great.

I was unaware of how obnoxious I had become. Nowhere down this road did it occur to me that my crazy midnight oil burning, skipping meals and alienating people life was mania in full swing. It all felt so good, so how could it be bad? I had moments when I recognized that I was feeling weary with the activities I was juggling, but then I would chide myself and say not to be such a baby.

By mid-July I occasionally stayed up two to three nights straight. I would get everyone down to bed, then quietly go downstairs to my scrapbooking area and either organize, create handouts, or do my own scrapbooks. Periodically, sensing my brain slowing down a bit, I remained compelled to keep going. One night I started scrapbooking my wedding album around 9:00 p.m., worked through the night, and finished at 7:00 a.m. the next morning in time to get breakfast for Dale. I believe it was one of the best scrapbooks I have ever made. It was crazy, and I started to feel crazy.

After being up for that many days, I would sometimes pause in the wee hours of the morning; and if I happened to be standing, I would get a rush of vertigo and become woozy. I was nauseated from not having eaten much the previous day. My eyes burned from lack of sleep. This scared me a little, and I especially worried Dale would find out and make me stop my whirlwind of activity. I knew something wasn't right. I began to sense how out of control my life had become, but part of me didn't want it to end. However, the end came whether I liked it or not.

I felt as if I had been running on a treadmill inside my head for months. I started to get shaky and wished I could slow down or stop. I didn't know how to ask if I seemed to be acting strange because I didn't have words to describe what was going on inside me. Although compelled to try to keep up with everything, I began to drop things I was responsible for. Life outside of myself marched on, but my brain became foggy, and I would suddenly forget what I had to do. I didn't think anyone else could see me falling apart, but I received "Are you all right?" comments from several people as the next few weeks went by. I still had a whirlwind of thoughts in my head, but it seemed I could no longer access or execute them as well as before. I became scared.

After driving a bunch of youth home from a church activity, I was shocked to realize I didn't remember driving most of the one-hundred miles home to Fairbanks. This new land didn't offer fun, creative or invigorating times anymore, and I didn't like it, but I didn't know what to do. I sat perched on the edge of a precipice, and the only way to go was down.

Late on an August night, Dale and I were sitting on the couch facing each other, talking about nothing and everything at the same time. I suddenly had an incredibly breathtaking physical and mental experience that came out of nowhere, knocking me to my knees. As Dale talked, my perception changed, and he seemed to be sucked away from my vision like into a vacuum. I could still hear his voice, but I couldn't understand him. He remained totally inaccessible to me. I then envisioned myself standing before a huge, beautiful, intricate stained-glass window. I was looking up and admiring it when I saw out of the corner of my eye a small piece of glass dislodge itself and fall ever so slowly to the ground. I heard the distinct tinkle of the shard as it hit the ground. Then silence. Looking up, I saw another piece falling, then another, and another. To my dismay I saw all the pieces of this beautiful window crash to the ground with a mighty force, the sound of which deeply frightened me. I wanted it to stop, but I didn't know how to get away. The noise and sensations swallowed me, seemingly to never end. Then it became silent. Deathly silent.

When that vision ended, I knew something essential about who I inherently was had forever changed. I was left acutely frightened and in despair. Dale must have seen something change because he started asking me if I was all right. I could only say no, and then I started to sob, deep heart-wrenching sobs, because it was all I could do. I couldn't be touched, and I couldn't be comforted. I couldn't explain the emptiness inside me. It was like having an immense weight pressing down on me. Profoundly sad, I never knew what hit me. I cried for hours into the early morning. I tried to sleep but couldn't let go of the fear. I couldn't explain or understand why I was so afraid. My mind, my soul, all of me shut down and shut out the world because I could not process anything more than to keep breathing. It hurt to even just be.

I only remember snippets of the next few days. Dale stood constantly nearby, taking care of me, managing the kids and the house, trying to figure out what needed to be done. He tried to keep the kids distracted so they wouldn't be exposed to my sadness. I don't know what he told Sarah, but she kept checking on me. I couldn't care for myself, let alone the kids. Dale wanted to understand what I was thinking and feeling, but I didn't know how to explain it. He would lie next to me on the bed and hold my hand, trying to comfort me. He called my mom and arranged for her to come to Fairbanks for a couple of weeks to take care of the kids. This, at least, allowed him to go back to work, and Sarah and Taylor had a gentle grandma to watch over them. With the nearest psychiatric hospital in Anchorage, Dale decided to keep me home and do his best to keep me and everyone else taken care of as best as he could. Dale's aunt helped by taking Sarah to play with her cousin to keep her away from my withdrawn behavior and endless crying.

I cried a lot, and I slept a lot. All I wanted to do was sleep, because then I didn't feel so hopeless, helpless, and dead inside. I slept up to eighteen hours a day, more if I could manage it. I stopped eating because nothing interested me. I didn't have the energy to eat, and nothing tasted good anymore. I stared out the window or at the wall. I know I didn't communicate well, and I hated that Taylor and Sarah had to see their mom in such a state. We all did our best to get through the day. I did my best just to exist.

I remember realizing that I didn't want to live in this condition, with these circumstances, early on in my depression. It became exponentially bigger than I was, and I wanted to get away from the sadness and inner pain. Without calling it suicide, I starting to envision how I could make everything go away by making me go away. In the beginning I was so debilitated I wouldn't have been able to commit suicide. I floated from minute to minute, waiting until I could sleep again and forget. But as the immediate crisis ebbed and my mom left, I realized I needed to pull myself together enough to at least provide the kids a safe environment while Dale worked. My job consisted of making sure Taylor didn't fall down the stairs or encounter other physical dangers. My goal was to keep both children fed and in front of the TV or with a toy until Dale got home from work. My life was pathetic. Even the simplest mothering had become impossible. I camped us all in the front room with all the things I thought they might need and laid down on the couch and slept the day away. Both Sarah, age five, and Taylor, age one, were curious why I cried so much, but since I couldn't explain it, I withdrew into myself and tried to hide my pain. I resented that I had to care for my kids and they couldn't just manage themselves. This was our pitiful existence until Dale would get home from work. I would then move into our bedroom and check out of life, removing myself from conscious thought for the rest of the day and night. It was horrible.

After three weeks of living in these conditions with the depression not lifting, Dale set up a three-step plan I had to follow every day. First, I had to get dressed. Second, I had to eat something at least once a day. By this time, I had lost more than fifteen pounds. I lived on one English muffin per day. Third, I had to get out of the house, even if only for five minutes. This could be a walk around the block or a walk through the nearby Kmart parking lot, so long as I got outside. That was it, the totality of my self-care. Luckily Sarah went to kindergarten, so she stayed at school part of the day, and Dale's aunt made sure Sarah got to and from school for me. It worked as well as could be expected.

Around the fourth and fifth week of this ordeal, I began to formulate a plan to die, because dying meant being released from the oppressive and strangling depression, for both me and my family. It made so much sense at the time. Many people think suicide is a selfish act, but for me, I saw it as unselfish. I saw, as much as I had the capacity to perceive, how much pain I'd caused my family, especially Dale. I no longer existed as the wife and mother I had been, nor did I really believe I could ever be that person again. Deeply sorry, so sorry, I couldn't see any way the situation would get better.

As the source of the pain, I believed I had the ability to remove myself from the situation and thus release them from the burden of caring for me. I would be doing them the ultimate favor. It was an effort to cease to be, and in intense psychic pain, all I wanted to do was no longer be. I didn't know where God fit into this picture, but I believed He knew how bad I felt, and He wouldn't want me to live like this.

I had to consider how to do such a thing. Dale had already removed all the knives from the kitchen to keep me safe. I decided to walk in front of a semitruck on the road as I ventured out for my mandatory walk each day. I could hear the noisy truck coming from behind me and would begin to cross over the white line as it approached. I would count down: five, four, three, and at the last second would veer back onto the shoulder of the road--back to safety. The truck would blare its horn at me, shocking me into reality. I decided after a few attempts that it would be a horrible way for my family to see me die.

I could easily starve myself to death. Six weeks after the onset of my depression, I had lost more than thirty pounds and still I had no desire to eat. But I knew that form of self-destruction would take far too long, and soon Dale would step in to intercede. I was in too much pain to stretch out my demise.

Then I thought of what to me was an ingenious plan. In the weeks since the beginning of my depression, time had marched on, and with it came an early winter. How I hated the snow, but now it would provide me a way out. I realized that a thick blanket of snow and exposure could mean my death. I decided I would lie down in the deep snow on our deck late at night and lie there until I froze to death. It wouldn't be an ugly death. I would just go to sleep and never wake up again. It seemed perfect.

I chose the day I wanted to kill myself—just an average day in our now not-so-average life. I spent some time with Sarah and Taylor and told them how much I loved them and that they were extraordinary children. I straightened the house and tried to formulate a plan to take care of their immediate needs after I died. I was the most self-directed and focused I had been in over eight weeks. I planned the details of how and when in the night I would get out to the deck without Dale noticing and stopping me. After dinner, I sat Dale down and asked him crucial questions relating to my death. I never revealed my plan to him, but he wasn't blind.

I asked what he would do if I died, like where he would bury me. I was adamant I did not want to be buried in Alaska. He told me they could put me in a temporary coffin and fly me to wherever I wanted to be. We discussed the benefits of being buried in Seattle, which I loved, or in Utah, where our families were. We kind of left it up to him. I told him how I wanted my funeral to be, which music to be sung and whom I wanted to speak. I asked him to place our special bouquet of red, white, and yellow roses on my casket and to explain to people what it meant to us. This conversation was painful, but it had purpose. I can only imagine what Dale thought. He was patient, not overreacting, and mirrored the methodical thinking of my questions.

After we talked, we put the kids to bed. Since I had become depressed I would go to sleep very early, and Dale would stay up to clean up the house and get ready for the next day. But this night we both got ready for bed at the same time, and he laid down to sleep with me. He wrapped me in his arms and held me until I fell asleep. I experienced one of the most peaceful nights I'd had in more than eight weeks. Waking up in the middle of the night to retire myself to the frigid deck had been my plan, but to my surprise I woke up to a new day, still in Dale's embrace. He had protected me from myself and my destructive plan. I took it as a sign I didn't need to die but to get better. He had literally saved my life.

I was honest with Dale after that about the suicidal thoughts and about my deep-seated fears and the pain of my depression. He tracked down a neurologist who prescribed a strong antidepressant, but it never really helped. Over the next many weeks, I became more proactive, and some of the suicidal depression started to lift. I grew more capable of taking care of my responsibilities at home. I finally found some fight left. But it was still slow going, and there were more days I was down than up. My Creative Memories business was on hold for a few more months, but eventually I even returned to a limited schedule of workshops and classes.

Somehow, I got through another winter. I dreaded each day and trudged through the days in fear that my severe depression would return, and my life would again be upside down. Still sad, but not to the extent of the previous months, we tried to keep life as normal as possible for the sake of the kids.

One way to do that was to periodically volunteer in Sarah's kindergarten class. She was clingy, especially in the evenings, wanting us all together as much as possible. If she saw me being sad, she would offer a hug and tell me she loved me. She made me special pictures of "happy people" for me to hang up. One morning I got a phone call from the manager at K-Mart. He asked if I was Karen Greenwell and if I had a daughter named Sarah. When I replied in the affirmative, he told me he had Sarah with him and that she was fine, but he wanted to tell me about something my amazing five-year-old had done. Sarah evidently had dressed and sneaked out of the house before I awoke and had gone to K-Mart with her total savings of thirteen cents. The store wasn't open yet, but she banged on the window, and the manager came and opened the door for her. She told him she wanted to buy a present for her mom because her mom was sad. She showed the money she brought and asked if she could look at the earrings. She carefully picked out two pairs and asked how much they cost. The manager told her they cost exactly thirteen cents. She was thrilled.

Taylor grew quickly from the twelve-month-old he had been when I got sick to an energetic and loud toddler. As long as he had his bucket of toys and books, some Barney to watch on TV, and his sheepskin he seemed content. Sometimes he would become so intense trying to get my attention when I laid down after a hard day. He would use a broad range of noises to growl, squeak, and yell to tell me what he wanted. There were many days it was hard to connect with the kids or play with them at all. But we could always fall back on reading book after book while we snuggled on the couch.

Dale kept us all together; he had to. He would fill in with the grocery shopping when I couldn't manage to get dressed for the day. He was a practical person and very task oriented, so when he walked into the house after a day at work, he would assess what needed to be done and then get started. He was always so kind to check with me to see how I was, and he took time for me to ramble on about my many fears and angst of the depression. At a time when I was feeling so isolated and worthless, he let me know he loved me no matter what and he would never go away. He was a rock, always trying to find the positive, even if the highlights of my day were making the bed and emptying the dishwasher. Because of him we had come through a very scary time together. It must have been overwhelming trying to care for me when I couldn't even care for myself. I don't know if he had anyone he talked to when I was so sick; probably not. But our children were loved and nurtured during this difficult time because he understood the importance of being a daddy and gave them the affection and attention they needed. I was saved by God's grace and by Dale's love.

As we neared the spring and more sunlight, I started to experience more energy, but it was far from normal. Almost everything was a drudgery, and my thought processes still reflected the ups and downs of my disorder. In May, Dale and I finally had a conversation where we asked honestly if this depression would ever get better. I had been functionally depressed for eight months. By scheduling positive activities, I became more productive, but it didn't seem to be enough. The medication didn't have much of an effect, and we were fearful of what another winter would bring. Dale made the courageous decision to move our family out of Alaska as soon as possible in an effort to save me from myself. He was convinced I wouldn't survive another Alaskan winter. He knew his decision would put our family on another unfamiliar path, but something had to change. We were united in our decision to leave, and with faith and a vision for our future we moved forward.

The house went up for sale by owner, and we immediately found a buyer. We had a massive yard sale and sold all we needed to sell for the money we were asking. We would be leaving Fairbanks with only what we could fit in a U-Haul truck. We were grateful the whole process went so smoothly.

Dale left the carpet store on good terms, Sarah was out of school and would be able to start anew, and Taylor was content to go along with any plan. Overcome with a sense of freedom, Taylor and I boarded an airplane for Utah. I could breathe again. It seemed as if I was being released from all the ramifications of bipolar disorder and a land inhospitable to people like me. I turned away from Alaska and have never looked back.

SETTLING IN

Coming back to Utah was overwhelming. Nothing in our lives had any structure, and we didn't know what path to take. Welcomed in the arms of our family, we had a soft place to land. Worrying about where to live, employment, school, and doctors could wait for a few days until we allowed ourselves to relax with our families. But after those precious few days, reality smacked us in the face.

We lived with Dale's parents while we searched for a place to live. Although we greatly appreciated their generosity, after eight weeks we were anxious to have a place of our own. We had a sense of homelessness we couldn't shake no matter how helpful our families wanted to be. Even with a sense of being displaced, weary, and sick inside, I tried to run interference for Sarah and Taylor who didn't understand why our lives were so undone. They seemed hesitant and overwhelmed by family they did not know. We had no real income yet, so we couldn't be too choosy, but we found an average three-bedroom duplex in a nice neighborhood. We moved in with the money we had left over from our move from Alaska and with what few possessions we brought with us. We borrowed a table and folding chairs so we had a place to eat, and my brother gave us a couch. The kids still had most of their toys, and we had a few miscellaneous items, but for the most part we didn't have much. Feeling discombobulated and a little lost we hardly knew where to begin.

It was sobering to realize how much we had walked away from to get out of Alaska. We knew we'd made the right decision, but we spent many hours contemplating where we were going to go from there. Besides our parents, none of our extended family had seen or could really understand the devastation we'd experienced. We were lonely even as we were among those who loved us. It was hard to explain what a black hole Alaska had been for us; and when we tried, many shared their opinions about what they thought we should have done, which often did not help. We also realized this was the first time either of our families had spent time with us since we were first married, and they essentially were still being introduced to who we were.

Dale and I had been living in Washington and Alaska; and we now found that, because of our divorce and remarriage, there were old feelings of sadness and misunderstanding within our families which had never been sorted out. Sometimes things seemed awkward with our families and we realized there had been many things that should have been said after we remarried that had been left unsaid. We didn't have a lot of experience with them as a family, and vice versa. Dale and I had a lot of water under the bridge, and we were both rather protective about our past. Ultimately this led us to somewhat isolate ourselves, which caused heartache and confusion as many times our families didn't know how to help us.

Our number-one priority was finding me a psychiatrist. Dr. Matthew O'Reilly was referred to me by a friend who knew of my history of depression in Alaska. Dr. O'Reilly worked through the university and specialized in mood disorders. While initially frightened to go see him, I had become motivated to do whatever it took if it meant I could become better and reestablish my role as a wife and mother.

Right away Dr. O'Reilly struck me as a man of compassion and practicality. He patiently listened to us as we struggled to tell our story. I could tell he understood us, as nothing we said seemed to surprise him. He had heard it before, and now I knew he would help me too.

He clearly and carefully explained how my brain had experienced physiological changes due to my long and severe depression in Alaska. Dr. O'Reilly believed the only way to stabilize my current depression and to have lifelong health was to use medication to stabilize the chemicals in my brain. He talked of the risks and of expectations we should have, but I was undaunted. I committed right then to do something proactive to take back my life. I may have had second thoughts about taking medications when first diagnosed years before, but after what we had been through, I knew I owed it to all of us to try medication.

In Dr. O'Reilly's opinion, my depression could never really be resolved without a mood-stabilizer. He stated I was probably at a greater risk for more depression or a manic episode only being on an antidepressant. He continually stressed that no medication would "cure" my symptoms, just manage them. This was heavy stuff for me to process. I'd never embraced the idea of being sick or crazy. I had always pushed my way through my mental health issues in the past. I wished I could do it again, but it was bigger than me now. I'd initially seen myself overcoming bipolar disorder, eventually never having to deal with it again. Now, with the reality of what had happened in Alaska, I doubted that would be true. Before I could accept what Dr. O'Reilly wanted to do to help me, and before I could hope to improve, I had to surrender to a new way of seeing my illness.

Dr. O'Reilly started me on both Depakote and Wellbutrin. I was enthusiastic—until we went to the pharmacy and had to pay for the medication. We didn't have health insurance and therefore had to pay in full—almost $400 a month. I almost backed out, but Dale was adamant we would find the money. I remember thinking he probably shared my desperation for me to get better, so I trusted his word and tried not to worry. The medication knocked me out, sometimes for more than fifteen hours a day, for almost three weeks. I was groggy even when awake and became disoriented and disinterested in things. Daily nausea made it difficult to interact with the kids. They probably wondered who had switched their mother and given them this zombie. Once again Dale and I focused on getting through each day, keeping the kids safe, and having faith that we could ride it out. It was a hard transition, but within five weeks I had less side effects, and I began to feel better. I was tentatively hopeful the medication would provide the balance I needed to manage my illness. As the weeks went by, I found I could do some of the things I used to do. I could become the wife and mother my family needed, and the person I wanted to be.

Still, secretly in the back of my mind I feared never really being able to be better. The medications gave me a sense of being different, like another person in my own skin. I wondered if every sad moment was the beginning of the end, when it generally ended up being only me having a normal reaction to something that was sad. It seemed I spent my time always taking my emotional temperature, being too focused on my feelings and not enough on who I was. I questioned my future and how I could stand as a partner with Dale. I didn't want a marriage where he would have to take care of me. I wondered if I could be fully there for Sarah and Taylor because I would be unable to emotionally nurture them. Worse, I didn't know how to make sense of the thoughts tumbling through my mind enough that I could share them with Dale. So, I sat, quietly afraid of my future.

Life developed into a sort of routine, but Dale was still unemployed. The pressure was staggering. He worked odd jobs— laying carpet, apartment maintenance, sprinkler installation, telemarketing, and bookkeeping—whatever he could do to take care of us. He kept our heads above water, and each week as we counted what we needed and what we had, it was mighty close indeed. We had to put my staggering monthly medication costs on our credit card, hoping that we'd have some form of income soon. Dale worked with an employment agency that helped him better target the types of jobs at which he would excel, but after eight months we still didn't have anything. He continued to take piecemeal jobs, working wherever he could. He was relentless in his search and maintained hope that something would come along. I know he was overwhelmed and defeated at times and probably a little panicky, but he never let it show. We tried to keep our hopes high that something would happen and spent many occasions giving each other pep talks about the value that comes with struggle.

Mid-February, eight months after arriving in Utah, I received a strange call for Dale regarding a job for an organization I had never heard of before. We had a bad phone connection, but it sounded like she said something about a veterinary company in California. The woman on the phone wanted to talk to Dale and said she had Dale's résumé in front of her and would he please call her back. I tried to get in touch with Dale, but I couldn't reach him. I wondered what this was about. As I tried to go back to my task, a sudden warmth washed over me. This was the job we had been waiting for, the answer to our prayers.

National Veterinary Association, based out of California, owned and managed veterinary hospitals throughout the United States. Dale was being considered for the job of Hospital Administrator for a group of veterinary clinics and hospitals in the Salt Lake valley. He would manage about eighty-five employees at seven sites and would be responsible for the day-to-day operations with an emphasis on customer service. This job fit his qualifications and his desires for a career exactly. After a series of interviews and training at other veterinary sites in the country, he settled into his new job, and we settled into the security of a steady income and health insurance. We were thrilled at the prospect of having my medication paid for, but these benefits were denied as the insurance deemed my disorder a preexisting condition. I would have to wait eighteen additional months to be covered for any mental health costs associated with bipolar disorder. The benefits for our medical plan were vastly better than the benefits for our mental health plan, and we were told it was simply policy. This unfair difference between medical and mental health coverage would continue for a long time, impacting our financial well-being again and again.

Nevertheless, we felt liberated as Dale started his new employment. Gone were the days of just making due, and back were the days of productivity and pride in his work. Dale absolutely blossomed at his new job, exceeding expectations from the beginning. He was sparked by opportunity and the chance to finally use his skills and considerable customer-service talents in ways that helped customers and employees. He enjoyed the load of responsibility and the chance to think deeply about issues and problems at work. It thrilled me to see him with an outlet for all the pent-up frustrations he had been carrying for months. He enjoyed being provider, and I loved his commitment and the energy he brought home with him.

Sarah and Taylor were the highlights of our lives, although raising them was not without its challenges. Being four years apart in their age, they weren't really playmates, though they would occasionally play together. They would get along at times, but Taylor could bother Sarah to tears. Taylor, on the other hand, was one tough kid and could bulldoze his way through any situation. He rarely cried when he got hurt and seemed to tolerate a fair amount of physical pain as he played his rough-and-tumble games. Sarah couldn't keep up with that kind of self-abuse. Taylor would sometimes corner Sarah and have her crying because she was scared to try to get away from him because he might hit her. He would also upset Sarah by talking to her when she didn't want to talk to anyone. In a maddening cycle, she would freak out, which of course fed Taylor, and he would continue to harass her. He had almost a joyful but mean look on his face when he saw his sister cry. Sometimes I marveled at how Taylor, at only three years old, could so influence Sarah's moods, but I tried to stop him before he got her too worked up.

As Sarah grew, she showed an increasingly sensitive and emotional side. She could be easily cajoled out of a bad mood with a kiss or a hug or if we spent some special time with her. However, she would cry at the drop of a hat and would be inconsolable for an hour. Dale and I discussed how having a sibling like Taylor could be Sarah's undoing or it could toughen her up. The jury was still out.

Dale and I recognized that in buying a house we would have to make sure it came with a large yard, and perhaps a special room for Taylor to get his energy out. Everything he did was at a hundred miles an hour, and at one hundred decibels. We had to restrict his extreme physical play to either his bedroom or outside, or our whole apartment would be in shambles.

One weekend some of our family visited us and saw Taylor at his worst. It started with Taylor being so loud and intrusive we asked him to go outside. He refused and went to play in his room instead. Sensing disapproval from our family when we let Taylor just bang around in his room, we still knew better than to try to amp him down before he was ready. Our goal was to keep his energy to a manageable level. I thought it would be unkind to limit our little boy's play, much like breaking the spirit of one of the horses he loved. Nonetheless, I cringed at what he might be like when he got older and bigger. While we termed his personality quirky, I knew others might not see it that way.

It was also during this time that Sarah and I would come to loggerheads over things which to me seemed trivial but to her were huge. When we were out of sync, it was difficult for us both. On reflection, I realize we often had the same goals in mind; we just had different ways of accomplishing them, and neither of us wanted to back down. We both innately sought for control in our environments and were upset when unexpected things happened. I later realized I needed to be the adult and an example to my seven-year-old. But it seemed so hard to know how to manage Sarah. She was emotional; I was not. She would get upset, I would withdraw. When we had a particularly difficult day, I would retreat to my room and go inside myself, protective of my mental health. Sometimes dealing with her and Taylor could chip away at my wellness if I didn't find ways to insulate myself.

A little more than a year after we returned to Utah, Dale and I decided to stir our now calm and predictable life with thoughts of having another child. For about six months I had been feeling we should have another baby, but I fought it. We had wanted to have at least four children when we first got married, but that was before life happened to us. I finally found the courage to approach Dale about it, and he surprisingly agreed. He also desired to have another child, but was apprehensive about broaching the subject. As he considered my history of morning sickness with both Sarah and Taylor, and especially because of my bipolar disorder, he felt he couldn't ask me to have more children because it might be more than I could bear. We didn't know then about the possibility of bipolar disorder being genetic. I'm not sure we would have changed our minds if we did know. We talked it over and prayed a lot. In the end decided it was the right thing to have another baby.

I talked to Dr. O'Reilly before getting pregnant, so I could come off my medications. Science didn't know what was safe for babies and what was not, and I didn't want to take any chances. Although Dr. O'Reilly was supportive, he expressed a lot of concern and insisted that I monitor any bipolar symptoms and do what I could by making healthy lifestyle choices. There was no guarantee I would respond to the medications the same way after the pregnancy. That possibility made me hesitate, but he acknowledged that sometimes there were other considerations in deciding to have a child than just medical science. If Dale and I hadn't been so in sync over the decision to have a baby, I might have changed my mind. In what seemed like a moment, I became pregnant. Thus, began a very long nine months.

We were all excited to have a new baby come to our home. However, I experienced extreme morning sickness the first six months and then continued to feel sick throughout the remaining pregnancy. Again, I had to set aside my role as wife and mother as I lay in bed day after day wishing I could stop throwing up. Dale and the kids tried to cheer me up, and the kids tried to be helpful as Dale managed the household again. Our family and church members chipped in with meals and some babysitting. But as the weeks went by, everyone left me to myself to try to find ways to be less miserable than I was.

Dale and I were counting the days until the baby came, but soon became more concerned about my bipolar disorder as around the seventh month the depression started to creep in. We tried to manage it with stress relievers, such as a variety of structured daily activities, exercise, funny movies, and long conversations. I tried to stay as busy as the morning sickness allowed with the kids' gymnastics and church activities. But as the days went on, my depression grew. Every day I would will myself to be happy and healthy for myself and my baby, but I continued to march down the road to sadness and then moments of despondency. I didn't know how to turn it around. My obstetrician and psychiatrist were working together, and we all decided we should induce labor, so I could restart my medications as soon as possible. But what if the baby was not mature enough? I worried. On the other hand, if I waited too long and ended up with a severe and long-lasting depression, would I be able to take care of the baby? We did tests to check on the baby's well-being and found that everything pointed toward a healthy birth.

Our son, Alex Emerson was born three weeks early on a beautiful day in May. He had to spend a few days in the NICU before he came home, but we were anxious for our family of four to grow to five. Before Alex's birth, Dale and I had to make some serious decisions. We both wanted another child after Alex, but we had to think of the ramifications of another pregnancy and another child to care for. Because I got pregnant with Alex I had to go off all my medications, which had been working well, to avoid any medication passing through to him. Going without medications put me at extreme risk; I could have either depression or mania, which would impact not only me but the whole family. We knew with this pregnancy I hadn't been able to keep depression at bay no matter how many happy thoughts I put in my head. I knew I would be willing to go through another pregnancy knowing the risks but being willing and having it be good for our family could be two different things. The part which most concerned us was what would happen afterward.

Would it be like Dr. O'Reilly said? Could I have other physiological changes in my brain that affected me not only medically but affected my very sense of self? Would my medications cease to be effective after going on and off them again? Would I increase my chance of having depressions that would keep me from taking care of the children? What would the effect of chronic episodes have on the kids and how they functioned? Could I even parent another child when Sarah and Taylor were already a handful? Could we be happy as a married couple if Dale continually had to care for me, along with the kids? It was sobering to consider all the what-ifs, and I hated we even had to. But it was the responsible thing to do. After much discussion and prayer, Dale and I decided we would not have any more children, and I had a tubal ligation after Alex's birth. We were okay about the decision and recognized we were fortunate to have three beautiful children we would love and care for as best we could.

Alex was a calm baby; happy, and so easy to care for. He brought joy to our home and a sense of belonging to all of us. We were looking forward to some peace and routine in our lives. Funny what you wish for.

BLINDSIDED

Sarah started third grade and worked hard to fit in, but she didn't seem to know the secret to making friends. She showed verbal maturity and loved to talk to the other girls, but she didn't always know what was appropriate to say. She talked easily about her thoughts and feelings in a rather adult way and seemed to either intimidate or make the other girls uncomfortable. It was like talking to a twenty-year-old woman in an eight-year-old body. Her teacher worked with her, encouraging her to read others' body language and listen to the conversation to see what the other girls were talking about before starting to talk herself. Sarah tried, but she merely had a lot to say and she needed to share. When she sensed any rejection, she would try to control the situation by being bossy; and when that didn't work, she would shut down and isolate herself. She cried easily and would lament about her life being a catastrophe. We saw her anxiety increase as we tried to help her by giving suggestions or role-playing. We only seemed to make it worse, which further affected her self-esteem, and she would temporarily pull away from us. Then within a few months, everything changed.

When Sarah was a few weeks shy of her ninth birthday, she was diagnosed with bipolar disorder. Looking back, we recognized the many signs she showed since she was very young. Dale and I had been concerned with her overcharged emotions. It seemed that everything Sarah experienced was overwhelmingly intense. She would cry so hard she would hiccup, unable to find the words to tell us what was wrong. She would cry for thirty minutes, sometimes for an hour, rocking back and forth, vacillating between whimpering and a sobbing. We would either hold her, or she would go to her bed and try to calm down. Sometimes we had to lie down with her to keep her from hitting her head on the wall. After she had worn herself out, she would fall into a heavy sleep, and after a time would wake up perfectly fine, rather unaware of her meltdown.

Then, on the flip side, she would be ecstatically happy, singing at the top of her voice as if on a Broadway stage. She was unbelievably creative, drawing beautiful pictures which she generously gave to us. She would be silly and make up jokes, being the one who laughed hardest at the punch line. She was enthusiastic, loud, and gregarious, and lovable, but her sad times were disturbing. We had always tried to keep tabs on Sarah and her peaks and valleys, because if we could catch her before the fall, she would recover quickly. We were aware of her moods, but we didn't think to look deeper to see if there were some underlying problem.

She could be a little bit of everything—happy, sad, frustrated, mad. We saw it as her unique personality, and though troublesome at times, it could be managed. What had become normal and acceptable for us ended up not being normal at all.

We were at a family barbecue at our house early on a Saturday afternoon in May, and all of Dale's family was there. It was the first big party at our new house. I had been talking to someone when Dale sidled up to me and whispered that we needed to take care of Sarah. I could tell by the look on his face that I needed to ask questions later. The only thing he said was she was in the kitchen, so we headed into the house to find her there. As we walked to find her, I was totally unprepared for the story Dale shared.

His niece had told her mom, Sarah had a big butcher knife, and Sarah had told her young girl cousins she wanted to hurt herself. I looked to Sarah for a denial of the story, but she looked back at me unflinchingly.

"I took the big knife from the kitchen when everyone was outside and hid it by the hedge," she said matter-of-factly. "I was feeling sad. I thought that if I killed myself it would be better."

"Why would you want to kill yourself?" I said. "And why would you want to do that in front of your cousins?"

Sarah said, "I didn't want to kill myself in front of them. I wanted to say goodbye."

"Sarah, that's not okay," Dale said. "You scared them. They don't understand why you said you want to hurt yourself."

"I didn't say I was going to hurt them. I said I wanted to die."

I leaned in close to her and asked, "Do you still want to die?'

With a serious look on her face she looked from me to her dad and nodded her head yes.

Why would a nine-year-old want to commit suicide? What could be so wrong in her world she would want to leave it? We wondered if she was seeking attention or if she was serious. Unfortunately, we couldn't tell the difference, and we were alarmed that our usually gregarious redhead thought such sinister thoughts.

She obviously didn't understand dead meant dead forever, but for her to even entertain the thought shocked us. Dale and I had to fall back on what made the most sense to protect Sarah from herself until we could get professional help. We were running blind but doing the best we could. We told Sarah we were going to help her and that she could trust us to make good decisions to keep her safe. Strangely, through the whole situation she didn't shed one tear. She seemed numb.

Suicide watch was critical when there was a crisis, but it became hard not to hover, overanalyze, or create more drama. The first thing we did was take all the knives and lock them in our bedroom. Momentarily embarrassed for hiding our knives, I wondered, what if someone came in the house and found we had locked them away? It seemed extreme, but it also seemed right, and I had to tell myself it didn't matter what other people thought. There weren't a lot of things we could do to protect her at that moment, but if getting rid of the knives was taking a stand in keeping Sarah safe, it was a good move. I didn't need to explain myself to anyone else in my efforts to protect my child. I would learn to tell myself that many times in the future.

Neither of us considered taking her to the hospital. It seemed we could take care of the situation on our own. Dale and I returned to our barbecue, with Sarah in tow. We tried to put on an, "everything-is-just-fine," face, but I don't know if we did a good job. We experienced a kind of out-of-body moment as we led our now zombie-like daughter around with us.

People began acting awkward and asking if we had a problem, but Dale and I had already decided we would not mention what had happened to Sarah because we didn't know if talking about it would make the situation worse. We were trying to be sensitive to Sarah's needs, but she was kind of acting as if she were on the fringe of the situation anyway, so maybe it wouldn't have mattered. We quickly realized word had gotten out and it became the unspoken proverbial elephant at the party. The barbecue soon ended, and Dale and I were left to brainstorm what we could do to protect Sarah.

We tried not to panic as we discussed what could have happened. Neither Dale nor I had any indication Sarah harbored destructive thoughts other than her typical angst about house rules and being bugged by Taylor. But that was normal; her drama was our normal; managing the daily simmering pot of emotions was normal; we didn't see beyond what seemed to be every day for us. We decided we would keep track of her over the next two days, and then I would call for some type of crisis intervention on Monday. Sarah appeared to be quieter than usual and acted withdrawn and clingy. We knew we needed to be gentle with her no matter what she said, strange or otherwise. She couldn't tell us a reason she was struggling, and she became frustrated with us the more we asked. Being nine can be hard for normal things, but at that moment, being nine became an awfully big job.

On Sunday we kept Sarah quiet and near us. Even Taylor seemed more subdued than usual. Sarah didn't seem to be an immediate threat to herself anymore, but we still didn't know what to expect, so we continued to plan to find someone for her to see as soon as possible. When Sarah seemed better on Monday, I sent her to school. I didn't even wonder if it was a good idea or not. School seemed like the place she should be, but if I had been a little more thoughtful, I might have considered how much additional stress she would have at school. I didn't question my decision until later when I picked her up and she collapsed into the car emotionally exhausted. If she had the flu I would have let her stay home, but I guess I didn't think having suicidal thoughts ranked high enough to miss school. I berated myself for being so stupid and unfeeling to make her run the gauntlet of school when her mind was under such stress. But how could I have known better? I found myself unprepared to know how to deal with the situation on anything more than my instincts. I didn't have a roadmap to follow, and I certainly didn't have anyone in my life who was struggling with a similar situation. I tried to remain calm as I wondered how Sarah had gotten herself in such a state and I hadn't even been aware?

I got an emergency appointment with a child psychiatrist our doctor recommended. We tried to prepare Sarah for her visit, but it was hard since we didn't know what to expect. Dr. White was very kind to Sarah and to us. We had to fill out a lot of paperwork, trying to remember developmental milestones and recounting Sarah's suicide attempt. Sarah had to wait for us to complete all the paperwork, which frustrated me. We were wasting time when Sarah needed attention. Finally, Dr. White took Sarah to her office by herself, and we anxiously waited, hoping Sarah would be honest and not overly exaggerate her situation. They were gone for a long time.

When we met with the doctor by ourselves, she told us she diagnosed Sarah with Early Onset Bipolar Disorder, Type 2, which is the milder form of bipolar disorder. Initially, I remember being relieved there was a label that described Sarah and her emotions. But it was also as if I had been punched in the stomach; I didn't want it to be bipolar disorder, because I knew what it would take to help her. It seemed hard to believe that something I thought was only an adult illness could manifest itself in my child. We knew what this looked like for me, but we were naïve to what this would mean for Sarah. Separately and together Dale and I pushed the shock of the diagnosis aside and focused on what needed to be done.

We had a ton of questions, which Dr. White patiently answered. But more and more questions would come over the next few days. Overwhelmed by what I didn't know about childhood bipolar disorder, I wondered where to begin. Dr. White sent us off with a prescription for Depakote. There seemed to be so much to process in such a short amount of time. We were trying to figure out what a diagnosis for Sarah would mean to her and to us. I found we were more effective in our problem-solving and in dealing with Sarah's recent suicide attempt and new diagnosis when we kept to the facts and tried to keep fear and emotion on the sidelines.

As soon as Sarah got to the car, she fell fast asleep. The appointment with Dr. White had taken a toll on her emotionally and physically. We were glad she fell asleep because it gave Dale and me a chance to discuss all we had just heard. I was anxious to research childhood bipolar disorder as I've always believed information is power. Having tangible information that I could touch, and process meant not having to deal with the panic and other emotions inside.

One decision that needed to be made immediately was whether we wanted to give medication to Sarah. Psychotropic medications were never to be taken lightly, and we struggled with the fact Sarah was only nine. It was a difficult ethical decision considering children were not allowed to participate in drug study trials yet were given adult psychiatric medications all the time. Dale strongly rejected giving her the Depakote, stating doctors didn't know how it affected children. Would it affect her in puberty? Would it take away from her good attributes and mute her emotions? It was a contradiction, but sometimes these untested adult drugs could stabilize a child or even be lifesaving. I agreed with him, but I also knew that Depakote, despite its side effects, helped in treating my bipolar disorder. Reflecting on Sarah's short life to that point and watching her vacillate between happy and sad had been emotionally difficult for both Dale and me, but especially Sarah. If medication could even out her moods, I considered us obligated to give them a try. I told Dale if I could have taken a pill that would have helped me manage my emotions and depressions when I was an adolescent and young adult, I would have taken it in a minute. He still had his doubts but deferred to my experience, and we agreed to a trial run. Our expectations weren't high but considered after a three-month trial we would be able to better make decisions on what to do. We were shooting in the dark.

Sarah loved to go to Dr. White's office and lie on her couch like she saw people do on television. One of the hard parts of her going to therapy was not knowing what she talked about, because we were not included in the sessions. We didn't know how Sarah felt, what stresses she reported about home, or what types of things we should be doing differently. As a therapist, Dr. White was vague but stated she thought their sessions were productive. What did that mean? Was Sarah being honest about home life and her contribution to our environment, both good and bad? We didn't know, and it seemed insane that our newly diagnosed child would be the only voice speaking for what our life was like. The focus was on Sarah, and we all wanted to see her get better, but we wished we were more involved. Our first experiences with the mental health system were not friendly to the parent, even when the parent ultimately had responsibility to care for the child's needs. As we learned over and over, that fact would never change.

NEEDING ANSWERS

In the fall we decided to put four-year-old Taylor in preschool. We wanted him to be able to get along with other children and looked forward to him having a place to learn his ABCs and numbers. We knew that his play could be aggressive, but his teachers communicated other concerns to us. They saw Taylor as extremely independent and not frightened to venture out on his own; he didn't seem concerned for his own safety at times. He would play alongside other kids but not *with* other kids, like playing cars by himself near a group of kids playing cars with each other. He never said he was lonely. In his mind he had a lot of friends, however, many of the kids were hesitant to play with him. Sometimes he would get rough, but it seemed his aim was to get the other children's attention, not to hurt anyone. He didn't like it when this happened and seemed sad but didn't seem to realize his behavior was the problem.

A fast learner, his impressive verbal abilities made it enjoyable to listen to him talk about his beloved horses to anyone within arm's reach. We had absolutely no concerns for his academic learning as he already excelled. We were glad he enjoyed going to preschool and hoped he would develop the social skills he needed. We knew we needed to figure out ways to deal with his aggression at home, but we wanted to believe he would get along at school.

In the months since we had moved to our new home, Taylor, now almost five years old, became increasingly aggressive and out of control. He had taken the claw part of a hammer and repeatedly gouged chunks of wood out of our new redwood deck. He had made long, deep scratches on the new kitchen table, ripped wallpaper off the wall in his room, roughed up some of the walls and broken some of his toys. This was just the first few days we moved in. It was hard to stay one step ahead of him, and he didn't seem fazed when we punished him. He didn't cry when we got mad but instead became more determined to do whatever he had in mind. When we asked why he broke things or acted rough with us, he would tell us he didn't know and then return to what he was doing. One time while working in the yard, Taylor threw the large tree pruning shears at my back, barely missing. He said he wanted to kill me.

We didn't always know why, but sometimes it was because we weren't paying attention to him. He would get so intense his whole body would shake, and he would yell loudly. He almost never cried, so his strongest emotions came out of his body in the form of hitting, biting, and kicking. The person most often in his way happened to be me. I was grateful he never went after Alex. Sometimes Taylor would hug Alex so hard it would hurt him, but not intentionally. He seemed to know Alex was off limits. But all bets were off when Taylor and I were home together while Dale worked.

Taylor's behaviors became more difficult and unpredictable. Situations where I could divert his attention to avoid a confrontation or tantrum were now difficult to diffuse. It wasn't as if he was purposefully looking to be angry. The simplest thing could set him off—not being able to find the book he wanted, or me telling him to turn off his video so we could eat lunch, or if his toys weren't working the way he thought they should. He would start to yell and throw things as if in a blind rage. I would have to quickly assess the situation and try to calm him down enough to talk about the problem. Sometimes we would do a good job working together. He would be distracted and soon be happily playing again. Taylor's unpredictability was exhausting for me.

Usually I had to be prepared to intervene quickly. Sometimes he had already gone too far in his meltdown and I would have to try to get him to his room to ride it out. Unfortunately, Taylor wouldn't typically go to his room voluntarily when he raged. I would have to try to move him, restrain him, and clear a path for him, all the while trying to avoid his biting, punching, and kicking.

Taylor's raging and meltdowns were not the same as a simple temper tantrum. His meltdowns were as different from a tantrum as a thunderstorm to a tornado. His meltdowns were total mind-and-body reactions to something intensely overwhelming. A meltdown could be rather sudden, but the rumblings were probably simmering for some time. Taylor's meltdowns or rages could be physically violent and verbally and emotionally traumatic; both for him and for those who were his targets.

I recall a particularly long day. We were all tired. When Taylor realized it was not his turn to choose the video for family night, he was unable to do anything but react. I felt the air change as he began his stand-off with me. Taylor's fists balled up, knuckles turning white. His breathing became shallower and shallower and his eyes narrowed as his feet dug into the beige carpet. I quickly turned Taylor so his back was against my stomach and I crossed his arms across his body, grabbing his hands to his sides so he couldn't hit me. As I started to move him down the hall to his bedroom, he kicked back into my shins as hard as he could. I knew the bruises he would leave would join the bruises he gave me yesterday, but I held on until I got him into his room. "I hate you," he screamed. "I hate everyone."

A meltdown or rage could last for hours. Then, as the rage wound down, everyone was exhausted. Taylor didn't seem to be able or want to talk about what had happened. He only wanted to be alone. I also wanted to spend time alone, but I had to take care of the aftermath left behind for Sarah and Alex.

Sarah and Alex knew this was scary. They knew Taylor was not all right, and luckily, they knew to stay out of the way when I dealt with their brother during a meltdown. But a meltdown could change the mood and balance of our home and our emotions for a long time. While Taylor would eventually brush it off, the rest of us would be left with raw emotions of fear, anger, and helplessness.

As Dale and I looked back over a course of about six months we started to see more disturbing behavior building and becoming more common. Previously, we'd thought it was enough to give Taylor space and appreciate that he had more energy than most kids, hence the big yard and his own room. We tried to find ways to get his energy out and gave him some boxing gloves with which he could punch his pillow and bed. He had a basketball, a jump rope, and balls to kick. But we realized it wasn't about Taylor having extra energy. We really struggled to redirect his rages and his aggression. We were fearful he had emotional problems.

After what we had just been through with Sarah, we decided to take Taylor to The Children's Center to see a child psychiatrist. I hated going to the center because I knew it represented some of my greatest fears for Taylor and another uncertain future. We had only come through Sarah's new diagnosis months before, and I became suspicious of what would come of this evaluation. Yet I needed answers. Prior to the evaluation I received a huge packet of information and questionnaires. The questions they were asking were frank and very direct. Questions regarding my attachment to Taylor, and if I had disappointment in our relationship, made me realize what I already knew deep down—I struggled with feelings of resentment about how much chaos he brought to our home. I was supposed to love my little boy, and I did, but I was also scared of him, frustrated in knowing how to deal with him, and wanted some relief. I had to admit to the reality of our situation.

Detailing years of aggressive behavior Dale and I had chalked up to quirkiness looked discouraging on paper. Dale also admitted disappointment in his relationship with Taylor and a desire to improve their interaction, but not to the level of mine. Listing all the symptoms and behaviors Taylor exhibited was eye-opening. There was a definite pattern of aggression, mood swings, and long-term problems. We resolved to be open-minded to what the professionals told us, and we hoped they would be able to help us understand Taylor and what made him tick.

The evaluation, conducted by three different professionals, was comprehensive and long, Taylor was cooperative, even showing his anger and oppositional streak with the evaluators when he didn't like the questions. It was a thorough assessment conducted by specialists in child development and childhood mental illnesses. In the meantime, Dale and I were asked about all of Taylor's developmental milestones and the specific concerns we had. Afterward, we all went home, and

Dale and I spent the next week determined not to second-guess the results. Therefore, when we returned the next week without Taylor, we were prepared to hear whatever would help us know how to help him.

Early onset bipolar disorder, type 1, the most severe type of bipolar disorder.

I needed them to repeat it again. What were we going to do? The professionals at the center, based on the information we'd given them, and through interactions with Taylor were confident with their diagnosis. Testing showed Taylor to be exceptionally bright, and the specialists hoped his intelligence would help him learn strategies to get better. They stressed this diagnosis was significant and recommended we start treatment as soon as possible. They recommended family therapy to get us to build a nurturing connection with Taylor and to help him bond to us, to solidify our family. They talked about possible medication and an excellent day-treatment program in our county. We hoped the program would help him therapeutically and socially, but we knew we had a long road ahead.

So, there we were. Three out of five. Me, Sarah, and Taylor. I didn't want us all to be in the same bipolar club, but there we were. When I heard my children's diagnoses, I experienced a wide range of emotions. Finally having something to call it; knowing it was tangible and not just our imagination was such a relief. I now believed there were people that existed who didn't blame us for an illness we never wanted. I realized that with a name, something could be done, and we could finally take some action.

Although feeling profoundly guilty that I had "given" them bipolar disorder, logically I knew it wasn't something I planned or something I would do on purpose. Dale and I didn't know about the genetics of bipolar disorder, because science didn't know a lot about it. How could we have known those many years before when we first talked about bipolar disorder on our honeymoon that it would be such a huge part of our lives? Parents were supposed to pass down traits like dazzling blue eyes and amazing intellect. What had I done to my children? I thought of the times they would blame me when bipolar disorder impacted their lives, when they wanted someone to blame because chalking it up to genetic chance wouldn't be enough.

I had a unique glimpse into their future, about how it would be for them, and I felt bad. I struggled with guilt about how I had parented them. At times, instead of thinking their behavior might be due to a deeper problem, I thought they were being willful and naughty. I would have been less stringent had I known better. Maybe I wouldn't have given Sarah such a hard time for being so dramatic and emotional had I realized it was an illness. Being able to claim ignorance to the situation didn't mean I didn't have guilt about how I had handled things.

A gut-wrenching grief consumed me when I realized that the dreams I had for my children were forever changed. They were too young to know their dreams would need to be different too, but I knew. Someone later told me I would have to dream new dreams, but before I could do that, I wanted to sit and embrace the images of what I thought my family would be. The whats, would-haves, and could-have-beens plagued my mind. Things I looked forward to, like Taylor going on a church mission might not happen now. What if they decided not to have children because they didn't want to pass the illness on? Would they be able to manage their illness enough to allow them to go to college or get good jobs? Would they fall victim to suicide? These thoughts broke my heart.

Now they had something tangible which set them apart, and they were going to have to struggle with whatever this illness brought. I realized they would be set even farther apart from others if their illness was chronic and severe. I grieved for all of us, because it seemed like part of our family and individual potential had been taken away. With a heavy heart I found it difficult to manage even the daily tasks that kept our family functioning. I didn't want to be sad in front of Sarah and Taylor because I didn't want to give them the impression that the problem was them. I wanted them to know this was something that had happened to them, not because of them. Dale and I grieved apart and together, but we both committed to move forward, determined to set aside any second-guessing that would not be helpful as we tried to meet this challenge.

I reached deep inside and found that the biggest thing I had going for me was my resolve. Now I had something I could fight and focus my energies on. I could now do something, make a difference in their lives. Instead of being at the mercy of Sarah's emotional meltdowns or Taylor's aggressive rages, I could look for answers on how to parent them and gather tools to structure our home life. Working with Dale, I resolved to educate myself about the decisions we were going to make in their lives. I knew early treatment and intervention were key to getting the help we needed while they were young. I would do what it took to find the resources we would all need to overcome this new diagnosis. I would read books, search the Internet, and conference with our treatment team to keep up with the new developments on children's bipolar disorder. I was determined to be a good example of how to care for one's self in the face of bipolar disorder. I resolved to focus on the future, so we could make a difference now, so we could put Sarah and Taylor in a place where they could take advantage of opportunities that came into their lives. We would teach them to be advocates for themselves despite bipolar disorder.

Regardless of all we had been through, we would not be overcome by this diagnosis. Early on I believed there had to be a purpose. I only needed to navigate the million emotions and problems in our way to get to an answer. I wasn't naïve enough to think the road would be easy. I had already come a long way on my own journey and knew better than anyone my cost of this illness. Finally, I had the chance to do something with my frustration and angst regarding the kids. I had something else to focus my anger on, and I could move away from the passive place where I only reacted.

We needed a game plan. Both Dale and I knew treatment would give us the best chance of managing a household of incredibly strong and vacillating emotions. One thing Dale learned from my crisis in Alaska was to address issues early on, to be aware of changes, and to anticipate ways to lessen stress. He was a good example of how to manage an illness and family at the same time. We decided we didn't want to only focus on this new diagnosis for the kids but on ways we could help our family cope with the diagnosis.

I started my research and learned that early-onset bipolar looked different from adult bipolar. Bipolar disorder was a brain disorder that affected how one thought, felt, and acted. I recognized the more rapid mood episodes that came with the kids, and I also better understood the unique symptoms of the mania and depression. I was surprised to realize that though the three of us had the same diagnosis, our symptoms and presentation of the illness looked very different. Sarah acted more emotional in both her highs and lows. She seemed more sensitive to anxiety and stress, and more verbal in talking about her feelings. Taylor was more aggressive and physical, and seemed to have a lower frustration threshold. He showed his emotion through his face and body. Taylor had a much more prolonged mania with a lot of agitation and short depressions, while Sarah's mania was more creative and happy. Sarah, like me, would more often be in a depressive mood, but she would swing out of it easily. My illness was more predictable and had clearer episodes of normal mood, but I struggled with longer depressions. I would cycle through episodes every twelve to eighteen months whereas the kids, especially Taylor, could cycle within a matter of days. I kept my depressions private, and I believed I hid my symptoms well from everyone except Dale.

Life at home consisted of managing our three miniature bipolar fires, and it was Dale's, and later Alex's task to figure out who had the highest flame that day and how to manage it. We found bipolar disorder to be on a continuum ranging from mild to severe at any given time. We all seemed to be on different schedules in our cycling. We enjoyed stretches of time when all three of us were stable and we lived a calm family life. Those were blessed times.

We learned the disorder could be genetic and having a parent or sibling with bipolar disorder exponentially increased the risk of having the same diagnosis. I was mildly comforted to know children could also have a bipolar diagnosis without any family history. I would always wonder how much of a contribution my DNA had in their unique gene pool, but I could do little to change anything. We later mapped a clear, strong bipolar disorder history on Dale's side of the family which further underscored the genetic risk for our children and future generations. Mental illness became an equal-opportunity occurrence. We had to accept we had it and move on.

I knew medications could be effective, but Dale and I were hesitant from the start to give medications just for the sake of giving them, and so we took a "start low and go slow" attitude. Medications could be tools to help manage their illness, but they'd never make it go away. It would still be hard to trust the medications when we couldn't see any benefit, or when we would see a strong reaction that scared us and made us wonder what we were subjecting our children to. It was always a fine line to walk.

An early diagnosis of bipolar disorder was helpful for the most effective treatment. However, the earlier a child receives a diagnosis, the worse the course of their illness may be. Because their moods could cycle more often, they would have prolonged symptoms over time and less periods of normal, stable mood. More bipolar disorder cycles meant there could be less amounts of time of wellness in between episodes. Essentially my five-year-old little boy could spend much of his young life cycling in and out of symptoms with little healthy time in between. Taylor was so young, and yet the professionals had confidence in their diagnosis. Taylor fit virtually every symptom of bipolar disorder. It meant a long road for him, with a disease he would never have a recollection of living without. It became so important we start treatment right away, and I continued to scour the Internet looking for ways to help my family adjust to our new reality.

I came across a few discussion boards hosted by parents of children with bipolar disorder. It was absurdly exciting to find people with stories that matched what we were experiencing. I appreciated their tips on how to work with the school, and what to do with medical insurance. However, the detailed posts about specific incidents some young children were having with police, violence, and suicide became very bothersome. For some, it seemed, the disorder had taken over their family's functioning, with everyone living in lockdown mode and held hostage by the child with bipolar disorder. This greatly disturbed and confused me. This was not our reality, and I didn't know if I should prepare for the worst, or if these incidents were the worst for these specific families. I cried in fear and worried about how we would handle these types of things. Finally, after about two weeks of following these posts, I deleted the addresses from my browser. It was as if all hope for a future for my children was being squeezed out of me, and I felt stunned by the possibility of so much destruction. I didn't want to put my head in the sand, but I preferred to look up and out at the vistas ahead. My life would be different, and if it was not, I wouldn't be paralyzed with fear, just watching it happen. From that time forward, I proactively chose a "We are bigger than this" attitude. I have never regretted making a conscious decision to harbor hope, but I was unprepared for the path of heartache ahead.

MOVING FORWARD

We never hid the bipolar disorder diagnosis from the kids. It didn't make sense to have this serious lifelong illness and not know what was happening to you. I had a friend who still hadn't told her child about his bipolar diagnosis, and he was a teenager. I couldn't understand how they could keep that information from them.

By telling the kids about their diagnoses early on, we developed an atmosphere of understanding. *Bipolar disorder* was a sickness you had in your mind, shown through behavior. We connected the word to a visual behavior reminder. *Mania* looked like Taylor when he flew as high as a kite, bouncing from place to place and topic to topic. Mania for Sarah generally included loud giggling and dramatic behavior, which included music and sweeping movements as she went from room to room. Mania for Mom created a rush filled with intense talking and lots of focused energy. *Depression* looked pretty much the same for all: sad, withdrawn, tired, and hopeless. Teaching the kids to "see" the symptoms around us helped to normalize behavior and not be frightened of the illness.

Labeling our behavior helped us understand what we were looking at. Every medication we took had a name to it. The kids eventually had to recognize their *meds* by sight, know the meds' names, and remember how much they took. That took a long time to learn. *Therapy* was what we did with a therapist and shouldn't be confused with the conversations we had at home around the dinner table. Therapy had a mental health treatment purpose, and our home conversations were what we did to learn the social skills necessary to get along in life and to bond as a family. At home we joked around and talked about everyday things such as friends, family plans, and manners. Dinnertime would often include laughter and teasing. We genuinely enjoyed spending time together and had good memories that had absolutely nothing to do with mental health or bipolar disorder. Sometimes our home conversations could be therapeutic, but they were not the same as therapy.

Even Alex had a label to explain his different, more typical behavior. He was a "*sib*." Being a sib meant he had a perspective and experience unique to him. *Psychiatrist* was the med doctor nobody liked to go see, though he was vital for our health. *Contract* meant you were grounded as a consequence and in much more trouble than usual, and you had better turn it around quickly. *Red flags* were what you got on your way to contract.

For the kids to understand bipolar disorder, it was something to be experienced and viewed. We needed to make it tangible. We needed to make it real for us as a family, so we had a basis to work on when we had to make it real for them as an individual.

Trying to teach normal boundary limits to children can be difficult at best, but to do so with a child who has serious problems getting along with others, acts aggressive, or overly emotional was hard. Both Sarah and Taylor would do better behaviorally and emotionally when we set clear limits and boundaries, but they often fought our efforts to help them. At times it seemed like we were living a life of kill or be killed between raising the two of them.

As mentioned previously, Taylor refused to be calmed by touch; in fact, touch made him more out of control. When I'd have to restrain him, it would get physical fast and I would have to almost carry him to his room as he head-butted me in my throat or kicked my shins. At the back of my mind was always the worry of what would happen when I was no longer able to contain him because he was bigger than me.

Realizing that this situation was extremely difficult then and would be nearly impossible later, I started to brainstorm for a solution. He seemed to love the feeling of being out of control. I watched him and tried to see if there seemed to be a pattern to his behavior. He acted wild in the morning, would calm down when he got to watch a video, read, or take a drive in the car, and was revving again the rest of the night. Then he would start to wind down as we got the kids ready for bed. He seemed almost relieved to go to bed, and, frankly, so were we.

I decided we needed consistency. Bedtime at 8:00 p.m. for all became our goal. I showed Taylor what 8:00 p.m. looked like on the clock and gave him the job to be my reminder of what time it was. Because Taylor would latch on to certain ideas, he took this responsibility very seriously, often badgering Sarah and me to keep to the schedule no matter what. He became the perfect timekeeper. Next, they were to put on their pajamas and come to the front room for at least one story. I tried to keep story time flexible, because once you told Taylor something, it was forever cemented in his head and he had no flexibility to see the situation any other way. So, I built in a choice of books to read, and sometimes we could read two. He balked at first, but upon realizing I was serious, he backed off. Family prayer followed, and then they were sent off to bed. I then came through with a quick hug or kiss, and they could choose which type of cassette tape to listen to while falling asleep. Sarah liked music, and Taylor always chose action/adventure stories. He would often complain about going to bed, but eventually they would both sleep soundly.

We did this consistently every night. I cherished this routine for years because it became so predictable and nobody needed to fuss. It could even be duplicated if Grandma came over and put them to bed. It was also one of the only times Taylor would let me hug or kiss him, which went a long way to resolve any difficulties we might have had that day.

Since it worked so well, I decided to implement other routines around getting up in the morning and after school. When we started to add chores to their after-school routine, there were a few hiccups. They weren't difficult chores—emptying the dishwasher, sweeping the floors, or taking out the garbage—but it was no easy feat to get them on track. As they did the chores and we followed them immediately with a small reward, all three kids came to accept their responsibilities. But linking the chores consistently to the routine made it easier to track, and helped the children not overreact when everything didn't go according to plan.

It wasn't easy at first, but I saw changes in Taylor specifically as time went on. He didn't seem to be so ragged at the end of the day, and he listened better after school. He still liked living on the wild side—that didn't change for a long time—but at least he was more pleasant to live with. We had to work with him to accept that the schedule might possibly change and that it would be all right. The meltdown could be big, whether it was because he had to deal with something he didn't expect or because he had to deal with something he didn't want to do. We had to prepare Taylor for the contingencies in his world, which proved difficult as we didn't always know what unexpected event would occur. This behavior would add to Sarah's anxiety as she was so sensitive to Taylor's moods and how they were going to affect her world. It was a dilemma, to be sure.

Dale and I tried to preserve our routines as much as possible. Sometimes we were frustrated because we had very little we could be spontaneous about for fear of upsetting Taylor. However, by having the structure as a backup when everything was chaotic and uncertain, we had something familiar to hold on to. It became a valuable tool for everyone.

We once wanted to do a surprise trip to Disney World with the kids. We planned to tell them the morning we were leaving to pack their bags and we would be on our way to the airport. Then we remembered who our children were. Taylor would never be able to spontaneously go along with an airplane ride to a place he had never been. He would have to talk ad nauseam about what to expect on the plane, where we were going to stay, how long we would spend at each theme park, and what we would see, what we would eat, and if we would have a big enough rental car. That was just for starters. Sarah would be so nervous she wouldn't know what to pack, she would be teary until we arrived at our hotel, and she'd wonder if we were going to be safe on the plane. Only three-year-old Alex would be excited to go with the flow. It definitely was not worth the surprise, and in fact, took about a month to talk through to prepare the kids to go. Then they were excited.

As an adult, Taylor continued to use structure and built it into his daily life. Establishing black-and-white guidelines allowed him to be prepared for what was expected. This also helped him know when he had reached his expectations and goals. Structure kept his life consistent and made it easier to manage responsibilities. He made better decisions, was happier and excelled. If it helped him function better as he grew up, it was worth all the work.

As our family moved from day to day, we became accustomed to life with mental illness. My mood swings were less harsh, my depression more manageable. I'd been given well-maintained medications and now had better problem-solving skills. Dale still had to step in during bad times. After the crisis in Alaska, he had developed a second sense of knowing when I started to feel depressed and would encourage me to get enough sleep, which was crucial to my wellness. Dale gave me emotional support, and spent time with me, even when I wanted to isolate. Dale became my reality check. He would ask me to describe my depression so he would know if we needed more intervention or crisis help.

Our relationship wasn't always perfect, and I recognized even in my funk I sometimes took more effort than he had to give. But Dale was the epitome of commitment, even in the face of unpleasantness. I don't know what he did to let off steam or if he cried into his pillow at night, but we counted on him to be there, and he was.

I often felt overwhelmed with basic parenting, and I knew the kids sometimes took advantage of my depression to stop doing chores, had selective hearing when I called them, and argued with me and each other more often. Sarah's and Taylor's interactions with each other became more intense, resulting in increased meltdowns and opposition. Even though I knew I wasn't up to par, I wanted to maintain the structure we had established to keep their behavior in line. We tried to stick to chore charts, strict bedtimes, and activities they could do on their own, so they didn't have to interact as much when unsupervised.

I could have never parented the kids alone. I can still remember one day waiting anxiously for the garage door to go up, which was my signal Dale was home from work. It seemed it was taking forever. The garage door was all I was listening for; and when I finally heard it, I immediately stopped what I had been doing to rush to meet him. I circled around the van and caught him as he got out of his car. He greeted me, but I didn't answer. He looked up into my face and asked, "What is the matter?" I needed to be held right there in the middle of the driveway. I didn't care who saw me looking frantic and emotional. As soon as I touched him, I began to sob. He held me in his arms, giving me a soft place to land. He didn't say anything for what seemed like a long time, just let me cry. He finally pulled away and quietly asked me what had happened. I didn't know where to begin.

Caregiver stress was real, and at times it was overwhelming to deal with Sarah, Taylor, and Alex, especially when I wasn't feeling well. Having a partner to help carry the burden, and both a tangible and figurative shoulder to cry on, has been a lifesaver, literally. I had read research that parents of children with a disability were at risk for depression, anxiety, and divorce. I wholeheartedly believed Dale and I were at risk. Tag teaming at our home was a necessity and quickly became an art. I generally served as the warden during the day while Dale worked, and it was understood that when he came home, he was in charge. The last responsibilities I had were to fix dinner and do the bedtime routine. The kids behaved differently for Dale than they did for me. Not better or worse, just different. Miraculously, Dale and I were almost always on the same page in terms of discipline, responsibilities, consequences, and rewards. It was uncanny. I don't know how else we would have functioned.

The kids weren't always having meltdowns and being oppositional. On the contrary, we were often like a typical family who only needed extra structure and resources to keep moving forward. We enjoyed activities together and loved to laugh with and tease each other. Sarah and Taylor would start to riff about random Disney movie dialogue. Sarah would start with lines from a movie, performing with drama and pizazz. Taylor would follow up with dialogue, perfectly mimicking a character in the movie. This went on for a good ten minutes, both lightning fast in their parts. There was such positive energy and we loved watching them interact with each other. We almost always had dinner together, television and distractions turned off, and shared the favorite parts of our day. We went on fun vacations, made a big deal about holidays and birthdays, and enjoyed a sense of unity in all we did together. Some days were better than others, but when we did have a problem, all our attention had to be focused, and we would go into problem-solving and sometimes crisis mode.

RACING DOWNHILL

The financial stresses of our mental health treatment seemed to stretch out forever. Medications, therapy, social skills groups, and more. There was always more need than resources. We had not recovered from the large mental health debt created by the cost of my medications and the treatment I'd received when we'd first arrived in Utah. Even with Dale's hospital administration job, we were barely making it.

Every month we would thank heaven we could cover our responsibilities, but we had little extra. Dale would work on the bills late into the night trying to figure out how to make a little bit here help to pay what we needed over there. He did an amazing job. I remember asking him one morning if he had enough to pay the bills. He paused, and nodded.

"Really? Was anything left over?" I said.

With a grin he said, "We are blessed. We have $1.96. Don't spend it in all in one place!"

That's how it was almost every month. Sometimes $1.96, sometimes $1.25 and sometimes $3.50. We were barely making it, but we were always blessed.

Then I learned about and applied for insurance for the kids through a program run by the state. We were thrilled that, unlike many other health insurance plans, mental health coverage was included.

I'd never wanted to be poor, but our income was low enough for us to qualify for programs. The system seemed to be messed up, but we were grateful to have a hand-up to help us. Without this help we would never have been able to pay for what we needed. No wonder some people are afraid to earn more.

We were grateful for those times things went well for us. But it always seemed something was around the corner that would make us adjust our game plan. Sure enough, after only three years on the job Dale was laid off. We were devastated. He remained out of work for eighteen months. Things had finally been better, and now we were again financially overwhelmed with the cost of treatment. Where would we find the resources to maintain treatment for the three of us? Even as Dale worked a variety of part-time jobs, our mounting mental health debt continued to be our reality. Our mental health needs were as critical as any medical or daily living needs. Having access to public and later private insurance became a standard we knew we could not give up. We knew we would always have to find ways to pay for life-saving medications and treatments. We quickly learned through every move or job change that we had to base our decisions solely on the type of mental health care we could get. Dale had opportunities we couldn't take advantage of because we would have lacked the necessary insurance for our family. It was just something we had to do. It was a sobering situation.

After months and months of managing the family's increased treatment demands, caregiver stress, and the ongoing financial difficulties we experienced, I found that my mental health skills were being pushed to the limit. I soon found myself in a quick and resounding descent into depression.

I kept up with the basics, but inside I was numb. I didn't want to get dressed, and even took Sarah to her appointments in my pajamas not caring if anyone saw. After sending Dale to the store, I would open the pantry to the kids and let them eat whatever and whenever they wanted because I didn't have the brain power to make a decent meal. Just a lot of being numb. I started back into therapy in the hopes of identifying ways I could get better. But I only felt sadder as I realized what a mess my life was and that it wouldn't get better soon.

After about a month of this horrible existence, I decided to take my brother Keith up on his offer to have me come to Seattle to visit. Dale and I hoped it would brighten my mood to be somewhere I loved. My therapist wanted me to take the time to journal all my thoughts and emotions while I was gone in the hopes that being away from the stresses of home I would be able to miraculously identify the answer to my misery. I was so depressed I was willing to give it a try.

Flying into the Seattle airport, I was surprised to find myself teary as I glimpsed the beautiful green colors and the city I missed so much. I got myself settled in a hotel in the area in which I had previously lived and had dinner at my favorite restaurant, feeling reminiscent and even sadder than before.

The next morning, Keith picked me up, and we went to the Hoh Rainforest on the coast of Washington. I told Keith about the struggles that were bringing me to see him, and he was sensitive to my emotional exhaustion and sadness. I had mountains of stuff in my head that I was worried and sad about and I finally had a place to put it. Keith was an excellent sounding board, talking when appropriate and knowing when to be still. Our stop at La Push Beach was so peaceful.

119

The time in the Hoh Rainforest was almost spiritual, looking toward the heavens through the huge, ancient trees. I loved every minute of it. However, I realized the day was coming to an end, and we needed to head back to the ferry to go home. Any peace I had previously felt inside slowly and painfully drained out of me.

It was late when we got on the ferry back to Seattle, and we were parked on the edge of the upper deck. I found myself worn out from talking and just existing. I got out of the car to stand by the edge of the deck. As I looked down at the black water, I realized how much I wanted to jump into the water and disappear. It was an oppressive, blackness to stand at a place of such gloom. I knew if I allowed myself to go overboard, it was too dark, and the ferry was moving too fast for anyone to save me. I was pondering what this might mean to my family when Keith came up beside me. I pointed to the water and told him that if someone wanted to commit suicide, all they would have to do was jump into the water. He agreed but said it would be an awfully cold way to die. I looked him right in the eye and intently told him, "No, it wouldn't. It would be a perfect way to die." He looked at me strangely and got very uncomfortable. He suggested we step back into the car for the remainder of the ride. I didn't want to get in the car but shuffled behind him anyway, discouragement emulating from my whole body. I was frustrated I had not thought and acted on my idea fast enough to see if I could have been successful. It felt like a missed opportunity.

On the drive back to my hotel I cried and told him how scared I was to go home and try to figure out how to even minimally function. I was so frightened by our financial situation and paralyzed to know what to do to help resolve the debt. I loved my kids, but thought I was doing them more harm than good. I knew I was a jumbled-up mess. When we got to the hotel I was exhausted, and Keith said he would come get me first thing in the morning if I wanted him to. I thanked him for his kindness and genuine empathy. He had given a lot of his heart that day.

As I entered my hotel room, I put the Do Not Disturb sign on the door. I went to sit on the bed for a moment and found myself looking at the bottles of my medications I had brought with me. I stared at them as I realized I didn't bring my single-day travel dosage boxes. I brought the whole new refill I just got at the pharmacy. I envisioned having handfuls and handfuls of pills right there and available. There was nothing keeping me from taking as many as I wanted. I reconnected to that moment on the ferry when I wanted to die. I felt panicky and almost giddy with the possibilities of what could happen if I only had the courage to take the pills. I knew I could do it there in the hotel room. Nobody knew me, the Do Not Disturb sign was out, Keith wouldn't call me until the morning, and by then it would be too late. It was real. All the pieces were there.

I thought of calling Dale but decided against it. Our last conversation upon leaving home left me frustrated. Knowing his intentions were good, I was still upset with Dale after he told me how I was overreacting about the debt we continued to carry due to our mental health costs and his extended time of unemployment. It felt like he thought Seattle would miraculously cure me of my depression, and I would return home to pick up my responsibilities again. I felt like he didn't understand. I didn't want to reach out. I paced the room, always ending up back in front of the pills, my heart pounding hard in my chest. Previously, any thoughts of suicide had brought feelings of peace, but this time I became frightened. I realized I was the only thing standing between my life and my death, and I didn't want that responsibility. I laid down, fully clothed, and purposefully turned my back to the pills, and tried to go to sleep. I couldn't sleep at all that night. My heart continued to pound, and I didn't have the courage to do anything. Courage or common sense.

Around 9:00 a.m. I called Keith to tell him I needed him to come get me and let me stay at his house because I was unsafe. I essentially told him I needed to be on suicide watch. He came right away and never left my side until I flew home to Utah the following day. He was amazing and rose to the occasion.

Keith did make me call Dale and tell him what had been happening to me in Seattle. When Dale picked me up from the airport, I was empty, barely a shell sitting there in the car as we headed home. He gently told me we were going to see my therapist first because we needed to talk about my safety to see if I could come home. My brain didn't register where I would go if I wasn't to go home. When we got to the therapist's office, I noticed that Dale and she exchanged a few glances before Dale settled me onto the couch. I repeated what had happened in Seattle, but now, overwhelmingly exhausted, I spoke only above a whisper, with my whole body seeming to fold in on itself. Dale said he had also talked to my psychiatrist, Dr. O'Reilly, and the three of them, with my input, had to decide whether I should be hospitalized or taken care of at home. Frankly, I didn't care, but I decided at least at home I would be around familiar people. Dale and my therapist made me make a contract that said I wouldn't hurt myself and that I would tell Dale if I had any thoughts of self-harm. At that point I would have agreed to anything because I didn't have the energy to do anything to myself or anyone else. I went home to my family, and we did the dance we called "mom's depressed."

A few days later, Dale and I visited Dr. O'Reilly. I was still under contract for safety, and we talked about the dynamic of this most recent depression. Dr. O'Reilly believed the depressive fall had been so rapid and complete I might be helped by adding lithium to my medication regime. I had been trying to avoid lithium for years because I knew it could cause quite a lot of weight gain. In my misery I decided I would rather be fat and happy than thin and dead. The results after only one week on lithium were amazing, and we were so pleased and relieved to have this depression cut much shorter than other depressions.

As the depression lifted and I continued therapy, I had such an appreciation for those moments that people come into your life to save you from yourself, like my brother, my husband, my therapist, and my psychiatrist. They were a nurturing team.

I became a true believer in the benefit of therapy. Unlike the kind seen on TV, which oozes drama, I found therapy to be safe, calm, and methodical. Therapy was the place I went to do the work that I couldn't do anywhere else. It was not easy. One day I envisioned myself standing on a beach in front of a literal line drawn in the sand. I was alone, staring at the thick, distinct line, inching my feet ever closer to crossing over. I knew what the line represented. I had been contemplating it in my mind for some time, and I had finally voiced my feelings about it in therapy. That made it real.

I was ready to cross over the line and acknowledge to myself those pieces of me that were directly connected to my bipolar disorder.

Throughout my life I had actively expended a lot of energy ignoring or downplaying some of these traits, but I always knew they were there. Some were unflattering or embarrassing and came with many painful and regretful memories. I had ambivalent opinions about a few of them, but could not deny their influence. Many traits could be frustratedly present in a manic or a depressive state. Some were difficult to define and my attempts to identify a succinct and accurate label fell short. So, as I lifted my foot over the line, I chose to acknowledge these parts of me: passionate, loud, intense, oversharing, deeply feeling and deeply thinking, loyal, exhausting, resilient, creative, rigid, insightful, impulsive, expansive. I was a lot for me, and I continued to recognize I could be a lot for those around me, particularly Dale and my children. Regardless of how put together I tried to be, there were times my bipolar illness added a significate boost, either positive or negative, to me being me. Not an excuse, but sometimes a reason for who I was to myself and others in my life.

Crossing the line didn't mean I would be able to change a lot of who I intrinsically was, but it was satisfying to take the figurative and literal step forward to at least seeing what was real for me.

WHO ARE YOU

I don't know how I would have survived without the tender mercies we received. While I often was left stymied as to what to do to fix things at home, helping others gave me a sense of satisfaction. An unexpected opportunity came at the local mental health center for me to do some one-on-one advocacy with families entering the mental health system. I wasn't an expert, but I had been around long enough that I could offer resources and useful suggestions. I only worked a couple times a month, and I mostly worked with parents trying to get school services for their children, but it was nice to be needed and to put my experience to use. Working with families in crisis helped me gain a more solution-oriented perspective; to focus on what a child with mental illness could do instead of what they couldn't do.

Around this time, I got a phone call from the producer of the television show *20/20*. Somehow, she had been given our name and was told about our bipolar family. Over the course of thirty minutes, she asked me questions about our family, particularly Taylor. She seemed to be interested in my description of his meltdowns: Did he hurt himself or others? Did he throw things? What types of things did he say? She then offered to have us included on an episode of the show about kids with bipolar disorder. She said they would come into our home and videotape our everyday life. She wanted to know about Taylor's cycles so they might schedule the taping around his worst times. The more she talked, the more disturbed I became. It was obvious her interest was only in getting footage of Taylor at his worst. It was unclear to me if they would present him as a bad kid, or as a kid with a bad disease. Either way, it didn't matter. I told her if she planned to do a show on families who have bipolar disorder, who were doing the best they could to cope and even prosper, then we were the right family for them. However, I would not exploit us, especially Taylor, on a television show that aimed to show kids out of control. We were not the right fit.

About a month later, I got a phone call from our local PBS station, stating they also had heard about our family. I was curious who was going around talking about our family, but they wouldn't say. They were doing a show on the social and emotional strengths in families who had struggles they were trying to overcome.

Now this had me interested. They asked to come meet us and tell us more. When they came to our home, they were gracious and interested in our whole family. The focus of the show was to show the impact of mental illness in our family relationships and the proactive ways we were dealing with it. Their intentions for the footage were exactly in line with how Dale and I wanted to represent our family. It was a message of what to do when bad things happened to good people, and how the choices we made enhanced our ability to live healthy. But before we made the decision to participate, we had a family meeting to talk to the kids about the ramifications of this project.

We tried to explain we would be "coming out" about having a mental illness. We told them their classmates could see the show and give them either good or bad attention and they were going to have to think of a way they wanted to explain themselves. Dale and I had to consider the long-term effects since the program was projected to be on the air for three to five years. There would be a lot of exposure for our family and for the kids specifically. Dale and I decided we would use our first names but not the kids' first names, to put a little distance from the content if it ended up being a negative experience. But we didn't have to worry. The kids were excited; Taylor said if he could help another little boy like him, it would be worth it.

It was exciting to have multiple media vans pull up into our driveway the morning of the filming. Dale and I were not given any previous notice about the questions they would ask, which made me a little nervous. The first part of the day, Dale and I answered questions about ways we helped the kids understand their illness, and ways we managed three very different manifestations of bipolar disorder. We talked about the struggles of each child and our hopes for them as they got older, and their need to take care of their own illness. The producer wanted to emphasize how Dale and I coped and processed caring for a family with bipolar disorder. I spoke of my feelings and insights as one who'd had to both care for myself and the kids' bipolar illnesses.

I liked the focus on how we managed our everyday life in a resilient and positive way. That was the message I wanted to give, not the message about the craziness of mental illness *20/20* wanted.

PBS shot some footage of our family playing in the backyard, doing things any other family would do. The kids were having fun and enjoying the uniqueness of our family. The producer interviewed Sarah and Taylor separately about having bipolar disorder. Both talked about the skills they had learned through treatment. Taylor said sometimes it was a bad thing to have bipolar, but sometimes it was good because you could be smart, run really fast, and do things other people couldn't. Sarah acted mature and poised.

When we saw our segment on the program, I was amazed that an entire day of filming could be condensed into a seven-minute slice of life. We were proud to be a part of the project, and true enough, people recognized us for years to come. But it became a turning point for our kids to be advocates for themselves and for those with mental illness. It didn't need to be something they saw as a bad part of themselves anymore. It could be something special and something we could celebrate as a family.

As we moved forward, internalizing who we were and how we were different, but also more alike from our friends and neighbors, we continued to face the reality of stigma. From the outside we looked like anyone else, but that is sometimes the bane of mental illness. As a hidden disability, you cannot see what is wrong. One mom told me she wished she could wrap a bandage around her daughter's head just so people wouldn't judge her when she was in public. It is a dilemma with no solution.

One of the most difficult things was when you were judged by people close to you. When preparing to move to our new home, I had two women I considered friends visiting me. One suggested I not tell people in my new neighborhood about my children's mental illness. She said by keeping the information to myself, people wouldn't see my kids as different and wouldn't be uncomfortable having their children play with mine.

"What is so wrong with my children?" I asked.

"You know . . . they are different," she responded.

Did having a mental illness make them inherently unable to play with other children?

How could I go into a new neighborhood looking forward to being welcomed as a part of a new group and hide who we were?

The women could see the confusion on my face and hurriedly backpedaled, saying they were probably wrong. "They are wonderful children," they said. "Surely the people in your new neighborhood will recognize that." But it was too late. The words had been said. I began to think twice, and then a third time, about disclosing our mental illnesses.

Kids really didn't play with my children. I don't know why. Sometimes I thought it was because we were new, but then, after living in our home for over four years, I recognized it must be more than that. When there was a birthday party for kids Taylor's age, everyone was invited except Taylor. When kids gathered to play ball in front of the neighbor's house, Taylor was not there. Sarah never got invited to a neighbor's house to hang out. Simply, there was no place for them. Was it because they were different, because they spoke and acted differently? I didn't know. I only knew it was a lonely time for them and just increased our family's isolation.

Beth and I had been friends since junior high school; for almost twenty years. I enjoyed spending time with her, visiting while our children played in the yard. She grew to understand some of the issues we dealt with. One time, things were really tough at our house. Both kids were often in crisis, and in trying to keep up with their needs

I felt I was going crazy along with them. Their necessary treatment became intense and emotionally demanding, but I was managing. I remember talking to Beth one day on the phone and giving her an update on the kids. She went quiet for what seemed a long time and then told me she couldn't be my friend anymore. She said my life was too complicated and overwhelming for her to hear about. That was the only explanation she gave.

Overwhelming? I understood intimately about overwhelming because I lived it every day. But I couldn't believe she, who in my mind was insulated within her "normal" life, would feel like the burden of being my friend was too great. Her friendship had always been a safe place for me to land, and then suddenly it disappeared. I didn't have many people I could turn to, and the loss of her friendship was sorrowful. I wondered if being my friend was too high a cost for others to bear.

As I meet new people, I am better at judging who I can tell about our mental illness. My experience has molded me to be the person I am, much like a parent who has had a child struggle through cancer. You can't separate it from the myriad of other experiences in your life. I don't wear a neon sign that says "Ask me about bipolar disorder" but I am kind and gentle to those who may not understand. Besides, it is always a good opportunity for me to educate people, to help lessen the stigma I have experienced as the parent of children with mental illness.

It was even hard for our families to know how to support us. Sometimes I wondered if I had done something wrong because my children were so different. Even though our families were large, there were few I felt safe with to be totally honest about our struggles. I thought it was because I was private, but I decided it was more because I didn't want to risk being judged. I needed to protect myself.

Our parents listened, even though it was sometimes hard to understand the realities of our situation. In their generation, from their knowledge, children didn't have mental illness. They asked questions and tried to learn about bipolar disorder, but the language of bipolar and the actual behavior of the kids was not what they expected. Both of our moms enthusiastically attended mental health education classes I taught and supported our advocacy efforts. They helped when we asked and stepped in when we were in crisis. They cried when we cried in frustration, and they recognized the accomplishments of the kids. So many times, our lives were blessed when our mothers opened their arms to watch the kids, so we could have a brief respite. They were generous with their time and unfailingly let each of us know of their love and pride in our efforts to be advocates for mental health.

I remember talking to my brother Keith on the phone as I sat in the backyard so I could have some privacy and not have Sarah hear me crying about how exhausted I was in dealing with her current situation. I poured my heart out to him, and when I stopped for his "turn" in the conversation, I heard nothing. I thought we had been disconnected, but he said he was still there. To Keith's credit, all he said was, "I don't know what to say. I can't imagine what it is like."

I didn't know what to say either. I saw myself as obligated to now make him feel better. After the conversation, I believed I needed to protect him and other family members from the raw reality of what happened regularly in our life, so they wouldn't be uncomfortable.

Stigma about mental illness and what that meant made discussion unclear and cautious with Dale and my families. I knew it wasn't a lack of compassion. It was okay if our families didn't have answers for us, we just needed listening ears. But we needed to know we mattered. Our children needed to know they belonged. Sometimes I was ashamed of our needs, and from experience was hesitant to let others in. From the outside it may have looked like we were doing okay, when in reality, we were falling apart. Sometimes it was the not knowing that became the biggest obstacle for people who wanted to help. What we needed was help when we were over our heads and a place we would not feel judged because our kids were experiencing different things than their kids experienced. Surely, they must have had questions, but I rarely had any questions directed to me about our children's mental illness. We weren't always in crisis and we mostly wanted to have a place with everyone else where we and our kids could participate without stigma. We, like them, were doing the best we could. For us it only looked different.

Friends, family—everywhere we turned, we encountered stigma. Once a teacher found out Sarah or Taylor had bipolar disorder, there would be an almost imperceptible change in their expression. It seemed to say, "Oh, *that* is what is wrong with them." Questions and judgment about the children were usually replaced with understanding and sometimes even a sense of helpfulness as they shared what they knew about bipolar disorder. Previous assumptions were now better explained by knowledge of mental illness. But the stigma almost invariably existed first.

What people heard or saw on television about mental illness, especially children with mental illness, often made people uncomfortable. People are scared of what they don't know, and mental illness at that time was a scary misunderstood thing that was not polite to talk about. But there we were, available, and not really that different from everyone else. Our kids went to the same school, and we attended the same church. The sense of being an outsider, drove us to keep even more to ourselves, which in turn gave the vibe of being unapproachable. A vicious circle.

For example, in our religious culture when a family has a medical crisis, a new baby, unemployment-basically a myriad of situations that could cause immediate stress-that family would likely have dinner brought in to help lessen the demands of having to make a meal. Some people were aware of our situation with hospitalization, police visits, ambulance, day-treatment, or outright exhaustion, however, we never received a meal in all the years our children and family struggled with just the day to day. Not once.

I felt sad and isolated, but because I didn't say anything and decided our suffering would be private, nobody knew how to help us. They didn't know how to reach out and they didn't want to make anything worse.

Many years later we found ourselves in a position of needing help to cope with an unexpected depression. I had previously decided to share with some members of our congregation the feelings of loneliness and isolation we felt when the kids were growing up. They in turn expressed their sadness at not knowing there was a need. So, when Dale and I both felt the "here we go again" of another depression, we reached out and asked for assistance. What we needed wasn't huge. Neighbors and friends brought delicious meals twice a week for over a month. When they would drop off the meal, they thoughtfully spent a few minutes with me and sincerely asked how I was doing. A touch on my shoulder, a card in my mailbox, an unexpected text gave me a sense of connectedness I rarely felt in my neighborhood.

What was different? We had to have the courage to put ourselves and my bipolar depression out there, and they heard us and willingly stepped up.

As the kids were growing up the people who became my best friends were those who also had children or family members with mental illness. We understood each other, and it surprised me how many of us were around. We didn't look different, just like our kids didn't look different, but we felt different. There was such comfort in knowing you weren't alone.

Dale and I were committed to have our home and our family interaction as "normal" as possible. Sometimes I would just cocoon at home, safe and comfortable in our uniqueness and sense of family. We needed that sense of solidarity that came from being a part of a family. One of my most favorite things was reading side by side on the couch with each of the kids. They would cuddle close and lean into me. I loved their warm cheeks next to my arm as we read from Dr. Seuss or *Harry Potter*. It became a time where we could experience peace in a world that sometimes didn't give us enough time to enjoy simple pleasures. Some of the best times were when they would request we read from the many scrapbooks I had made for them since they were born. Safely enclosed in each scrapbook were memories of our family the way we wanted to be remembered. We'd smile and

134

giggle as we recalled events that built who we were, in spite of bipolar disorder.

Through our scrapbooks we revisited our trip to Disney World, where Dale smuggled a full-sized griddle through airport baggage so we could save money with the delicious breakfasts he made in our motel room. We were the absolute last people out of Animal Kingdom because Dale wanted to see just one more thing. Taylor got stuck in the elevator between floors at the motel, and Dale and I went into immediate crisis mode, convinced he would freak out and have a severe meltdown once we got him out. However, he merely came to us after being rescued with a gleam in his eye as he told us of his adventure.

There were the trips to the Oregon Coast and to Washington, and campouts in our backyard and in the woods. There were trail rides and campfires and s'mores. And there were the yearly first-day-of-school photos I took in front of the house that showed how much each of them had grown.

But far and away the most sought-out pictures in the scrapbook included the event we made special every year—birthdays.

Admittedly, I was the instigator of big birthday celebrations, believing birthdays to be the only days each year we unabashedly could celebrate the wonderfulness of us. They were the most special days of the whole year. I decorated the house with streamers, balloons, and signs, and served their favorite meals all day long. A specially requested dinner and birthday dessert with lots of candles and singing, and, finally, presents from everyone constituted a perfect day. Our scrapbooks show the kids' lives from the day they were born to the present. Looking at them was a big deal, reminiscing together as we cuddled on the couch and celebrated each of us and our lives together.

Things like sitting around the dinner table talking about our memories or planning a trip to build new memories gave our chaotic lives a sense of normalcy. I couldn't have lived a life focused only on crisis, discipline, structure, and therapy. That would not have been fair to the kids or to us.

We structured our life so that we could move on with the things that were important to us, and so that we could draw on these good memories in times of the crises that were always somewhere on the horizon.

PART II

NO TURNING BACK

We only had a few months after receiving Sarah's diagnosis to wrap our heads around the reality of our family's bipolar disorder. Time was spent managing Sarah's care with Dr. White and coordinating with the insurance company to pay for mental health services they thought were totally unnecessary. We also worked to incorporate ways we needed to change our parenting with Sarah, which took up all my time and then some. She was so needy I knew I had to find the strength to give her the time with me she seemed to be craving. It was hard to go on with our lives when she kept reminding us she had this new thing and that she wanted to talk about it much of the time. She wanted to talk about how she was different from her friends. She wanted to tell others, but we tried to tell her that her mental illness was private and she needed to be careful with whom she shared things. I realized I was already teaching her to be guarded about her bipolar disorder because I was worried how people would see her. Sarah seemed to be trying on her new diagnosis and seeing if it fit.

Some people in our lives didn't believe she could have bipolar disorder and thought we were overreacting. We were told she needed a firm hand when she had a meltdown. We were told kids couldn't "catch" bipolar disorder. Everyone who had an opinion seemed compelled to tell us even when we didn't ask what they thought. Then there were those who silently held their opinions but gave off a vibe of disapproval. To Dale and me, the diagnosis made sense once we did more research and matched the symptoms with behavior we had seen in Sarah for years. We knew we were on the right track. It was hard to listen to the opinions of others and remain firm in the course we were resolute to follow.

Sarah didn't seem to be getting better. Her behavior was chronically extreme. It was hard for Dale and I to identify to Dr. White discrete examples of incidents in which Sarah was struggling. It was the potential mood swings of emotion she might experience throughout a given day that made it difficult to anticipate Sarah's needs. Her triggers didn't always have to be significant or even obvious to quickly lead her to an emotional meltdown.

Sarah hated to be told what to do. Getting out of bed for school was a daily battle, and in the end, neither of us won. Over time I realized the routine of getting up and going to school had to be her idea. I proposed to her she could have her favorite breakfast of Poptarts every school day if she got herself out of bed and was ready at the table at 8:10 am. She wouldn't have any adult supervision, which was probably more motivating than the Poptart. She enthusiastically agreed. She and I went to the grocery store where she chose two boxes of her favorite kind of Poptarts. I thought we were set.

However, Sarah wouldn't totally buy into the agreement until she knew what would happen if she *wasn't* at the table by 8:10 am. Whatever action was connected to not meeting the expectation needed to be clear and unappealing enough she absolutely wanted to avoid it. I told her if she was not at the table by 8:10 am she would eat a bowl of plain Cheerios, and she could not have any Poptarts for the day. Clear, black and white.

With everything seeming straight-forward, the assumption would be the next school day Sarah would get herself up for school and be dressed and at the table at 8:10 am for her Poptarts. No. For the first three days Sarah was not on time to the table and the day began with a long, drawn-out meltdown. Sarah seemed to need to make sure the negative cereal consequence would be followed through. After confirming she could rely on the consistency of the plan, on the fourth day she was eating her favorite Poptart with a big glass of milk at the table.

She was so consistently inconsistent. Sarah later explained the reason she didn't succeed in getting up and getting the Poptarts the first three days of the agreement was because of anxiety. She had so much anxiety over her expectation of what she needed to do, and what we expected her to do, that she was paralyzed to even try. For three days she was too anxious to try. She said on the fourth day she was so mad at missing three days of her Poptarts that she forced past the anxiety and focused on her anger; to let the anger drive her actions to follow through to get what she wanted.

But at ten years old she didn't have the language skills or thinking ability to express or understand what she was feeling or why she was behaving in particular ways. As parents, we didn't know what was going on with Sarah. We were trying to do the "normal" parenting all the while unsure of what "normal" looked like.

She was coping in school but only barely; and she wasn't making friends. She would do her school work but never seemed to get it turned in. One positive happening was she had the lead in the sixth-grade school play. Sarah knew she needed to keep her grades up to keep her role. She was often sad at home, she cried a lot and was easily offended. I had a hard time tracking her moods, but she seemed to cycle in and out of depression every few weeks with some brief spurts of mania. She wasn't horrible, just chronically unhappy and agitated, complaining if things didn't go her way, stirring up trouble when bored or anxious about something, and defiant if she sensed she was cornered. Her sadness was real. It made her out of sorts, but we didn't know how to help her.

I was stubborn in expecting her to behave. She was equally stubborn in doing what she thought was her right. I became increasingly strict with her consequences. She amped her dishonesty even more, knowing it triggered me. Sarah could push my buttons faster than any of the kids, and she knew it. I didn't want to fight with her because we were losing our connection. Confrontations left me feeling like a horrible mother. I seemed to always be angry with her. While I knew she wasn't entirely blameless and seemed to thrive on getting me upset, I recognized I had the responsibility to exercise some level of maturity. There were days I knew I would not be winning the Mother of the Year award.

Just months from turning twelve, and only weeks from performing in the school play, Sarah started acting erratic and emotional. Her moods were increasingly unpredictable, and she seemed frayed. She began making mild threats when she didn't get her way. She was difficult to tolerate because she seemed so irrational. One day she had a friend over. Her friend rushed upstairs and told me Sarah had a safety pin and was digging it into her leg until she bled. I went downstairs and tried to get the pin from Sarah. We ended up wrestling on the floor, each trying to keep the pin away from the other.

With great effort, I pulled the pin out of her grasp and looked at her leg. She had only a superficial scratch on her thigh with barely a mark of blood. She was fine, but she was furious with me. Finally, she gave up after letting fly a few choice swear words, and I left her alone.

Dale and I didn't know what to do. Her very aura was disturbing, and she wreaked havoc wherever she went. She didn't want to be alone, but when with the family, she harassed her brothers and argued with us continually. She vacillated between being aggressive and being sad and repentant. It was a confusing time.

A few days after the safety-pin incident, Dale and I were upstairs on the couch talking when Sarah burst up the stairs and thrust a piece of paper at us. Then she loudly stomped back down the stairs to her room. The paper said, "You die tonight," and was written in what was obviously her blood.

We just looked at each other, stunned. How could this happen? It was surreal. This was more than a stunt for attention; this was her blood and a real threat. What could she possibly be thinking? I didn't know who she wanted to have die, but this message went way beyond anything Sarah had ever done before.

Dale and I both went to a place of logic. With very little discussion, we agreed we needed to take Sarah to the emergency room to have her seen by a mental health crisis worker. We divided the tasks to make that happen. Dale called his parents to see if they would take the boys overnight and he got their things together. I gathered Sarah's medical and basic mental health information.

I didn't know what would occur at the hospital; would they keep her or would they find her safe to come home? I didn't know who to call for information. This felt like our own place of crazy.

Then my mommy heart came out, and I recognized how much pain Sarah was in to go to such drastic measures. We didn't have time to sort out the whys of the situation. Very little made sense. We never considered Sarah could be in such a state of crisis and for us not to been more aware. As I walked down the stairs to her room, I reminded myself to be gentle with her. She was sitting on her unmade bed looking disheveled and wary, and was humming loudly to herself.

"We got your note," I said. "Dad and I are very worried about how you are acting and how you might be feeling. We want to take you to the hospital. Would that be okay?"

Silence. But I knew she was listening.

I kneeled on the floor so I could look at her face. "Sarah, we are asking you not to upset your brothers because they don't understand what happened tonight. Can you do that?" I said.

Sarah nodded.

We looked at each other. I knew we were in for a long night and I knew going to the hospital automatically raised my level of "I can't believe this is my parenting life" a number of notches. But most importantly we needed to face whatever needed to be done for Sarah. We were going into this blind, Sarah was kind of buzzing within her skin. She was not hyper or loud, but was kind of in an agitated performance mode. I didn't know what she saw in me as we sized each other up, but I hoped she knew that I'd be steady and stick by her side. We needed to do the hospital thing to figure out how to help her and keep her safe.

It was well past the boy's bedtime when we left home to drop Taylor and Alex to their grandparents' house nearby. The boys both knew something was wrong and became scared as they listened to Sarah mumble to herself. Taylor didn't want to ride in the van with Sarah because he said she looked crazy, and Alex cried quietly. They both sat as far away from her as possible. Luckily, we didn't have to go far. I didn't know what to say, so I tried to reassure the boys it would be fun to have a sleepover, and we would be by to pick them up the next morning. To their credit, Dale's parents didn't try to ask questions at that moment but opened their home to the boys to keep them safe, nurtured, and away from the situation so we could take care of Sarah.

On our way to the hospital, I decided it would be best if I sat with Sarah in the backseat in case she did something unsafe, like opening the van door. Luckily, I was there because she started flailing around, trying to take her seat belt off, singing nonsensical songs, and talking a million miles a minute. To see her acting this way was like having your child on the edge of a cliff and holding on to the edge of their shirttail, wondering what you could do to keep them from falling. Sarah seemed to be aware of us and what was happening in the present, but at the same moment, she was in her head singing songs and having conversations with herself. The ride to the hospital seemed to last forever. As we approached the emergency room, we realized we didn't know what to prepare for. We just had to have confidence that others would know and help us along.

Everything at the emergency room went slowly for us. We were put into a sterile room that was used for suicidal patients. The room was stripped bare of any instruments or tools that could be used by a patient to harm themselves. That was sobering. After Sarah was cleared by the medical doctor from needing any medical intervention, we waited, and waited, and waited. Sarah had calmed down a bit from being frantic to talkative. Hours passed, and finally a crisis social worker came and heard our story. Everyone kept asking Sarah why she made the note in blood, and she said she didn't know. She wouldn't promise she would be safe and not hurt herself again, and so she was admitted to the children's psychiatric unit. The decision was kind of made for us at that point. Our goodbye to Sarah was brief, and then she was taken behind a locked door to the children's unit. We were left with a mountain of paperwork to fill out before we could go home.

I woke up the next morning and started thinking, I didn't know how to wrap my head around Sarah being in a psychiatric hospital. Truly one of my greatest fears dealing with the reality of living with bipolar disorder was having me or one of the kids admitted to a psychiatric hospital. It had always felt like the worst that could ever happen, and now it had happened; to Sarah.

But I had learned, when I got stuck in the worst-case scenario thinking, I shut down and I hated that feeling. So, I began my self-talk in my head. I began to make plans and started a list of things to manage. I thought about getting ready to go see Sarah. "I don't want to take Alex with me to see Sarah, because I don't know how long I will be with her. I will make a batch of Sarah's favorite cookies. I'll pack a small suitcase since we didn't have time to get her one before we left for the hospital. I hope she wasn't too scared last night sleeping in a strange place. I wonder if it's too early to call her or if she is even up yet. I'll start to get ready and get a sitter for Alex."

I practiced conversations in my mind-speaking with Sarah's nurse, her doctor or other staff-to orchestrate what would happen next. If I could keep a situation-such as my young daughter in a psychiatric hospital-as a predictable, unemotional conversation in my mind, then I felt prepared for what might really happen. I was ready and in control for whatever was ahead. Because if I didn't go into my automatic mode of self-preparation and self-preservation, I feared I would fall apart.

Such was my naïve thinking, because, I soon found out that having a child in a psychiatric hospital was much different than having a child in a pediatric hospital ward. I called to check on Sarah's status and how the night went. I told the nurse the time I planned to come see Sarah. The nurse clearly and firmly informed me that I could only come during visiting hours and that these occurred three times a week for about two and a half hours each time. The next visiting time wasn't until the following day. I would not be seeing Sarah that day. No cookies, no suitcase. No exceptions.

Could I not access my daughter when she needed me? I could only talk to her during specific hours on the phone, and she couldn't call home when she wanted. I was stunned. Here I had admitted my eleven-year-old suicidal daughter in good faith, and I was restricted to seeing her only every other day and for only a few hours. I didn't know if they were going to run any tests on her or who would be talking to her about her episode. I found out that she would be in touch with the unit social worker and the therapist, who would talk to her about her episode. Because she was in a psychiatric unit instead of a medical unit, I had no legal right to those conversations and the things Sarah disclosed. That seemed so messed up. What if my child, who was ill, made up stories and shared information about our family and the circumstances that had led to her hospitalization and there would be no parental input to clarify or refute what she was saying?

How could the psychiatric team establish a good treatment plan based on the rantings of my young daughter, who had a long history of dishonesty? I didn't know the names of the people who were caring for her, so it was difficult to find someone who would act as liaison. If Sarah had been in a regular hospital, I would be welcome to stay with her, even sleep by her bedside. I would receive full disclosure before anything was done to her. I would be a full participant in any conversations held with or on behalf of my child. But most of all, I would be there if she needed me; she was just a child. I didn't like the restrictions, but I had to comply. I prayed Sarah knew of our love for her and wouldn't think we had abandoned her.

In the end Sarah didn't seem the worse for wear. Her hospitalization seemed to give her a break and place to decompress. In the morning she would attend a school they had on the unit, and in the afternoon, she would have some sort of recreational therapy. Her psychiatrist visited with her daily, and with us once during her hospitalization. He diagnosed her with an extreme manic episode, and he wanted to adjust her medications to help stabilize her. We needed to understand why this had happened, so we could keep it from happening again. We needed the "So, what now?" answer before we took her home. Sarah was assigned a new therapist who specialized in behavior such as hers. Dale and I were hopeful we would be able to partner with him to address her needs.

When we finally saw Sarah, she was quiet and apologetic for what had happened. She didn't remember a lot about the incident, only what had happened in the emergency room and after that. I appreciated the insight she shared about her behavior and hoped it would be enough to make sure it wouldn't happen again. I would be proven wrong. The hospitalization became an incident Sarah would later refer to as, "Oh, and then when I was twelve, I was in a psych hospital." Kind of as a marker in her life.

Upon discharge from the hospital Sarah was fast-tracked to enter the children's day-treatment program. She no longer needed to stay in the hospital full-time, but she continued to need intensive treatment. This transition was meant to bridge the gap between urgent care and Sarah's immediate need to learn concrete skills to cope with her illness. She had to be un-enrolled from our neighborhood public school. Sadly, she missed her chance at participating in the school play, but she was not well enough to go back to her home school.

I would drop her off at the facility at 8:00 a.m. for breakfast with the other youth, and then she would attend an abbreviated session of school on the unit until after lunch. Her afternoons were full of therapeutic activities—individual and group therapy, recreation and art therapy, and field trips on Fridays. I would pick her up at 4:00 p.m. every day. Drive time for me was about one hour, twice a day, Monday through Friday.

Key to the philosophy of the day-treatment providers was accountability. Built into their system was a behavior management program focused on areas such as compliance, respect, boundaries, and responsibility. Sarah would have to earn points for complying with expectations in each area to have privileges both at day-treatment and at home. She would achieve levels of privilege that gave her more independence and control over her behavior. However, if she was not compliant, she would lose points and levels, and for more significant issues, she could be put on a half-day hold or a full-day contract that was basically a timeout with no privileges. Sarah tested the limits and quickly learned that her behavior level at home was directly tied to her level at day-treatment, so she needed to be consistently on track at both places.

She eventually figured out how to behave within the boundaries of the program, and to also have a sense of autonomy. She was doing so well we decided to use the same behavior management system for all the kids, adjusted to their age and maturity. Taylor wasn't thrilled with the new system, but he enjoyed the behavior rewards of more TV time or an ice cream trip with mom or dad so much that he started to curb some of his difficult behaviors. Using a formalized system Taylor accepted was a welcome bonus. Alex only knew that you could get a flag if you made a bad choice and he never wanted to be on contract. Although only four years old, we thought it good to expose Alex to the behavioral expectations along with his siblings.

The system only worked if the kids were willing to be accountable and comply with the behavioral goals, and sometimes they were willing to take a consequence rather than do something they didn't want to do. But generally, it was a good way to help them know what was expected of them at home. The moods and episodes continued; no behavior plan could totally change that, but it was a little less edgy, and we could see things start to spiral out of control sooner if we paid attention to the system.

LINES IN THE SAND

Being a teenager was hard for Sarah. Pretty much all her life situations gave her angst or rubbed her the wrong way. She was unhappy at home but didn't seem to know of any other place to go, and she was often bugged by us. Yet at times she would be affectionate and interested in interacting with us on a personal level. It must have been extremely confusing for her, feeling so intensely but not knowing why.

While many teens can be oppositional, for Sarah it was much more. She would hold on to a grudge forever and want to make us pay. Half the time we didn't know why she was so mad. When we got the "look," we knew we were in for it. It wasn't so much that she was vindictive; she needed to vindicate herself. She was miserable and made the rest of us pay for her misery.

Once, around age thirteen, Sarah was grounded for thirteen weeks. Essentially three months! The day-treatment behavior system we'd adopted for all three kids said you could get warnings for being disrespectful, not doing what you were asked to do, being dishonest, etc. The being "disrespectful option" tripped Sarah up the most. She couldn't seem to remember that as a child she did not hold an equal role with the adults in our home. We would give her three warnings, but she often continued to intensify her behavior. Rather than retreating to her room, or participate in an alternative activity she would be more obnoxious, talking louder and sassier after each warning. She steadily increased her volume as she argued over whatever she thought she was being restricted from doing. Sarah was intensely focused on fairness and equality.

When she mimicked either Dale or me, she always got a quick final warning and she understood there was no tolerance left for her behavior. After the third warning she received a short timeout, but if she got another warning or if she were "over the top" in her offense, she went on "contract", which was the same as being grounded. Being grounded usually lasted one day but could increase according to behavior. Often when Sarah got on contract, she would throw a temper tantrum, stomp, cry, and be mean. Her behavior got her additional days. She hated it, and I hated dealing with her behavior when she got so defiant.

Sarah got on contract, got mad, went to her room, and started banging around. She wouldn't stop and continued to escalate and quickly started racking up contract days. That made her angrier, and the cycle went on and on for weeks. She would steal food from the kitchen and lie about it. One day grounded. She would call her brothers names and try to get them to fight with her. Another day grounded. When we tried to reason with her, she became belligerent and upped the ante. After about three weeks of this constant battle she had declared on us, we were tired out. Everyone was on edge and avoided her. She noticed, her feelings got hurt, and she became even more defiant. We were tired of the yelling, so instead of trying to talk it out, we started throwing more contract days at her.

We were much more punitive than we needed to be. Dale and I didn't want to relax our expectations and so we got caught up in the emotion with her. It was definitely not our finest parenting.

We had never dealt with this type of behavior and found our emotional resources wearing thin as we tried to maintain some level of peace in the home. Her brothers were also angry and would tell her to do what she was supposed to do. We would sit and watch her spin her wheels, getting upset when we weren't interacting with her. We were embarrassed at not knowing how to handle what seemed manageable at first but now was like a huge snowball gathering us all up and plowing downhill.

We tried to turn it around with positive reinforcement when she did what she needed to do. We rewarded even the smallest efforts. We tried to find the most basic ways she was positively behaving and made it a big deal by rewarding her. But Sarah thought we were trying to trick her and dug in her feet about almost everything. She convinced herself she had to prove a point, day in and day out. We didn't know this, but we could see she wanted to stop but didn't know how.

Fortunately, the solution ended up being rather simple. We went into Sarah's therapy session with her and told her how sad we were to see her so unhappy and how being at our house was not very pleasant. We asked her what she wanted to do. She started to rant again, and we let her. She was mad we had turned our home into a substitute day-treatment facility. She didn't like the structure and believed she was old enough to be on her own and manage her behavior. She went on and on, and as she continued, she kind of lost steam and became quieter.

"I guess I've been stuck," she admitted.

"I don't want to be in trouble anymore. I hate when everyone is so mad at me."

Sarah took a deep breath as she looked down at her hands. She was quiet and very still for a while. Nobody spoke as we waited for her to continue.

"I don't like it when you guys always think you're right and you win," she said with emotion. "I mostly stay mad and don't obey because I don't want you to win."

Dale asked her, "Did you think we were trying to win something from you? Did it seem you would lose if you started to follow the rules?"

Sarah nodded.

"We never told you that. Why would you think that?" Dale said softly.

"I know that's not what you ever said," Sarah explained. "But that is how it felt if I gave in and did what you wanted me to do,"

"But now I'm tired of being on contract, and it scared me that it might never get better."

The concept of winning and losing was a big deal to her. She never wanted to find herself on the losing end because it affected her sense of worth.

Her frustration now spent, she started to physically wind down before our eyes. When she seemed to be finished, we apologized for our part in things getting so bad and said we wanted to start over. No more contract, no more winning or losing, just her being a part of the family. That was it; that was all she needed to know. What a long battle she waged against herself. It ultimately lost her nine weeks of what she called hell. We were glad to have a breakthrough, but Sarah would still get stuck drawing lines in the sand throughout the years.

Sarah continued to struggle at school and especially at home. It was a gradual but steady descent. Sarah was again chronically irritable, oppositional, and difficult to parent. She particularly struggled when she turned fourteen. She acted disobedient at home and wanted to be anywhere but where we were. Sarah couldn't seem to explain why she was so unhappy, but her behavior became increasingly confrontational.

Anticipating the start of ninth grade only increased her moodiness. School had already been a source of conflict for us at home, but ninth grade seemed to make everything worse. From the inauspicious third day of the school year, I started to get automated phone calls from the school relaying she had missed one or more class periods.

When I asked her about missing school, she said she had gone to the class late, and instead of marking her tardy the teacher had marked her absent. This explanation worked a couple of times, but I received absenteeism calls at least three times a week. Even faced with evidence she was cutting class, Sarah would lie and say she was sick in the bathroom, visiting the counselor for emotional support, helping a friend in crisis, or other such excuses. Arguing about her cutting class only made her more secretive. Dale and I emphasized our expectation she be in class every day, every class, period. We were convinced this was not the time to be heavy-handed, but the bottom line was she needed to go to school every day.

This continued for the first month of school. The absenteeism calls now became daily. I refused to excuse any of her absences, especially when she wouldn't tell me why she cut class or what she did during school. I hoped the school would initiate its own consequences to help get her in class, but they did nothing. We would ask Sarah what the problem was. Was she being bullied? Was she sick and needed to go to the doctor? Was there a specific class she avoided? Sarah wouldn't, and evidently couldn't, give us an answer other than all she wanted to do was stay in her room. Why was she willing to risk being in so much trouble?

One day I received a phone call from a friend who, in dropping her son off to school, noticed Sarah sitting on the bench at the bus stop outside the school parking lot during school hours. I got in the car and went the back way to the bus stop, so Sarah wouldn't see me. I parked and sat in the car for a few minutes, just watching her. She sat reading a book, not paying attention to anyone or anything around her. She didn't appear to be stressed or anxious. When I got out of the car, she startled and then sheepishly looked down.

"Sarah, are you waiting for the bus?" I asked. She looked and before she answered I continued, "Where did you get the money for the fare? Where exactly are you going?"

I could see the wheels turning in her head as she considered what to do. She began to lie about needing to go downtown but seemed to recognize how ridiculous that sounded and admitted she was avoiding school. It seemed as if she got stuck in her head and didn't know what led her to be at the bus stop. She knew what she was supposed to do, what she wanted to do, and what she wanted to avoid, yet when given the opportunity to problem-solve she shut down and did what her instincts dictated. She usually knew what she was doing didn't make sense, but she saw no other way. When I told her to get into the school and to stay put, she dejectedly walked across the parking lot with me watching her from the car.

This same type of avoidance happened at home. Alex went to go to school one day and came back in the house to inform me he found Sarah sitting up in the pine tree on the side of the house. I went outside and looked up into the tree. Sure enough, I could see Sarah's legs dangling as she sat on a high branch. Alex and I started to laugh because it seemed so absurd to think she would hide there.

"Sarah, why are you in the pine tree and not in school?" I called to her. "Come down from the tree, now."

She slowly climbed down, looking crestfallen. I asked her again why she would be in the tree. I tried to work with her to figure out what she needed, but I was admittedly frustrated with her being up in the tree. She kept saying her brain couldn't do school. Without what I considered a valid excuse, I made her go to school anyway. I didn't consider it was her bipolar brain as being the reason she was in the tree. She seemed stuck between not wanting to go to school and being willing to be in trouble. At that time her history of defiance and trying to get out of school colored my understanding of what she was really saying: "Mom I am not feeling well, and I need your help." I needed to see the behavior was only a symptom of the problem, not the actual problem. But that was a much more global perspective than we were able to grasp at the time.

Dale and I had come to the uncomfortable realization that we couldn't force Sarah to do anything she didn't want to. Our only way to influence her was to set consequences that would either entice her to obey or encourage obedience to avoid something she didn't want. We finally gave Sarah an ultimatum—she had to stop cutting class and attend school, or she would have a consequence to make her go to school. Sarah never did well with ultimatums, maybe because she didn't believe we'd follow through. That reasoning didn't make sense because we always followed through, especially with Sarah. Having the possible consequence be vague and unexpected must have bothered her. She pompously acted like there was nothing we could do that would change her behavior. She had it all figured out, and there were no options for us or the school. It was maddening.

Sarah started hanging out and "dating" boys from school— the type we did not approve of, and she knew it. They were immature and unkempt. They were easily led by Sarah to do what she wanted, and she enjoyed the attention. She knew she had chosen to break a major family rule in our home by dating before age sixteen and seemed to revel in the fact that she was getting away with something. We wondered if it was the boys she was hanging out with who were contributing to her cutting school.

We came to realize that Sarah needed more intense help than what was given at home, through weekly therapy, or through the school. Her therapist, Samuel Frasier, suggested she go to day-treatment once again.

Having Sarah in day-treatment sounded like a good deal all around. Sarah would be in a school environment where her bipolar disorder and her mood cycling were understood. She obviously had significant issues with Dale and me, which needed to be discussed, in addition to her own personal demons. Therapy might be a safe place where some headway could be made. Group therapy could be helpful if she were exposed to solutions and skills. We were concerned she would be subjected to issues and negative behaviors of the other teens, but we had no control over that.

On the other hand, this committed me to five days a week, morning and afternoon, transporting her to another city, days of family therapy, and a major change in family structure and discipline. It was going to be intense, but since this would be the second time she attended day-treatment, we knew what we were agreeing to. The only difference was that Sarah's sophisticated manipulation far exceeded her previous day-treatment stint; we shouldn't have underestimated her.

Sarah did not want to go and couldn't believe we were making good on our threat. Like a blindsided deer in the headlights she was stunned to find herself back on the road to day- treatment. But she was signed up, and we took her to and from day-treatment starting the first part of October. We could tell we were in for a long haul.

Like before, Sarah had to participate in a system of rewards and consequences at day-treatment. She fought the system from the beginning and often found herself without the rewards that made treatment easier. She didn't like the fact the level she was on when she left day-treatment would be the same level she would be on that night at home. She felt trapped. But Sarah had been down this road before.

She realized she would do better if she made the system work for her, so she kicked into overdrive and outperformed expectations.

If her daily goal was to earn five positive merits, she would make it eight. We told her we were proud of her effort and happily rewarded her at home with privileges and special treats. She came home pleased with herself because she could finally access privileges she hadn't had in a while. She maintained this intensity for about three weeks, then suddenly crashed because it took so much energy for her to maintain the good behavior while fighting against her anxiety. She would start at the bottom level again and work her way up. It was all or nothing for Sarah.

Her misery during this time led her to begin cutting her arms and wrists. She sometimes marked up her hands, too. At first, we weren't aware of the cutting, as she kept to long-sleeve shirts and was very protective of her body. I think she wanted us to know, though, because she started leaving razor blades on the shelf in her bathroom closet, or a random blade in her bathroom garbage can. I knew the significant dangers of cutting and the importance of addressing it as soon as possible. Sarah's emotions were raw. We didn't want cutting to become a way of emotional escape for Sarah. We did our best to remove all sharp objects from her, but in reality, almost anything could be used as a weapon against herself. She also had access to other girls in day-treatment who were cutting so she could get information on how to get what she wanted.

Luckily for us, Sarah's cutting was superficial, and she didn't plan to kill herself. She said it just made her feel better, that it made her feel something when she was so numb inside nothing seemed to matter anymore. I was hyper-vigilant every time I entered her bedroom or bathroom to seek out evidence she had been cutting. Sometimes it was a long time in between incidents, but often it was at least once a week. We didn't know how to deal with it more than talking about it in therapy, setting boundaries at home, and trying to keep her close to us so she didn't have the opportunity to cut. We tried to let her know how much we were concerned for her.

One time I went looking for Sarah and peeked my head into her bathroom. I found her sitting with her left wrist exposed from under her hoodie, her right hand gently holding a razor blade. She had a few fine lines of blood on her wrist where she cut just before I walked in. I wanted to scream that this had to end, but instead I became instantly calm. There was a pregnant pause as I tried to gather my thoughts and Sarah sat in anticipation of what I would do. I told her she would need to put the razor down so we could wash out her wound and see if she needed stitches. If she did, we would immediately go to the hospital, and if not, we would bandage her up and move on. Although I was calm, I flashed to the memory of me gouging my arm in my own form of self-harm so many years before. That sense of being out of control and not knowing how to get out of the situation was eerily familiar. My heart was sad for her and I felt compassion for her situation. I needed to tread lightly.

She stuttered incoherently and looked angrily at me and said, "Why are you not freaking out?"

It was a good question.

I told her, "One of us has to keep from freaking out, and I figure it needs to be me. Now wash your arm, and let's look at what we need to do."

Her cuts were superficial, and after we silently and efficiently cleaned her wounds, I left the room. Sarah seemed to be taken a little off-kilter with my unexpected response and her lack of consequences. I figured she was in enough turmoil that she didn't need heavy-handed consequences on top of her angst. Dale and I realized part of Sarah's cutting was a cry for help and a demand for attention, but we didn't know what more we should be doing.

This all-or-nothing attitude was exposed during her therapy sessions. Sarah revealed she knew she would be in trouble for making bad choices like cutting school, lying, and talking back. She told Samuel she hated being in trouble, but she couldn't let down and let us "win." To Sarah, it was like playing a high-stakes poker game, one we were unaware of, and she had to win at all costs. It seemed truly unacceptable for her to give in to our house rules, our family activities, school attendance, church, or anything she considered was being forced upon her. Instead of talking about these problems, she let her behavior get her deeper and deeper in trouble until she could not get out and believed she would literally break. While amazed at the level of internal strength she had, it saddened me she had to be so destructive to herself and others.

Part of the day-treatment program was a mandatory parent class I attended once a week, run by the director of the teen day-treatment program. Each parent would, in turn, share their child's progress or difficulties in the program or at home. As we went around the circle, I learned about the troubles and mental health diagnoses of the other youth in the program with Sarah. I was sometimes shocked or saddened by the burden other families had to bear, burdens which seemed worse than ours. Sometimes I was jealous when I learned of a youth who seemed to be so much healthier than Sarah. We all sat in our self-imposed isolation each week, wishing we were somewhere else but committed enough to our child to be there anyway.

After our roll call we were taught one of the therapeutic skills the day-treatment staff had also taught our children that week. For instance, one of the hardest things for Sarah was accepting "no" for an answer and not arguing back. Through her day-treatment program she would be introduced to this skill, taught ways to use it, practice it with the staff, and then be assigned to do it at home. The therapeutic techniques were a part of Dialectical Behavioral Therapy, or DBT, and had been found to be effective with people with mental illness, especially bipolar disorder. By using DBT, Sarah learned how to develop skills or strategies to use when she was stressed, having conflict, or when she wanted to negotiate for something she wanted. She also worked on the skill with Samuel. The parents learned the skill, and we were told when it would work best, but it was up to us to try it at home.

Sometimes I didn't always understand what we were taught, but I shared the information with Dale, and we did the best we could. We needed to cultivate our relationship with Sarah, so we could use the therapeutic techniques that would help her accept "no". We wanted a way to interact in a positive, wellness-based manner. When we asked Sarah to teach us more about the skill, she seemed eager to show what she knew, and then we would have a positive conversation that wasn't so charged and difficult. Sarah later shared she appreciated our efforts to learn the DBT techniques as she worked on them.

I recall one specific week during the parent group when I listened to all the other parents report on their weekend successes. It then became my turn. My brain screamed with discouragement and with shame because I knew I couldn't report a good weekend. As I listened to each parent sharing, I believed I failed Sarah and the boys because we had so much contention in our home and nobody was happy to be there. I was aware of how totally inadequate and powerless I was to be raising children with bipolar disorder. Swallowing my sense of intimidation at sharing my thoughts in front of the group I decided to own it and be honest about my frustrations.

I lifted my head and in a loud voice said, "I have been a horrible parent. I didn't use the level system all weekend, I was angry and frustrated with Sarah, and I didn't try even one DBT skill. It was a bad weekend, but I endured it and am now making myself sit through this depressing group."

After a slight pause, all the other parents laughed.

I didn't mean to be funny, but my words struck a chord in all of us. We all had so much pressure to do everything right and to have our child move out of day-treatment, and it was maddening it took so long. We were all so tired of investing a huge chunk of our lives driving our children every day regardless of what the rest of life demanded. We had to do this foreign level system and attend a parent group that sometimes made us believe we would never be a good enough parent. But we did it for our kids because we loved them, plain and simple.

I am confident not one of our children understood the commitment we had to make to place them in treatment. Sarah and I both believed we were being punished. We had to learn some things the hard way. Even though the program worked, at least for a little while, it was hard to do.

Sarah attended treatment through October, November, and into the first part of December. One Monday I went to pick her up and stood at the desk waiting to be checked out by a staff member. I overheard two of the staff talking about Sarah's discharge party on Friday.

"Discharge? Who said Sarah is going to be discharged?" I asked.

"Well, she has been talking about it for at least two weeks. Didn't you know?" they replied.

"I don't think Sarah is going to be discharged this week," I told them. "There has been a mistake. I need to talk to her therapist."

Samuel said he had not ordered her discharge; in fact, he saw little progress with her. Samuel and I both smiled as we appreciated what an amazing person Sarah was. She had the gift of persistence and focused determination when she had a goal. Getting out of treatment was her goal, and she would find a way to make it happen. She'd been so close to getting away with it. While not specifically the way I wanted Sarah to use her talents, it certainly became evident she was a force to be reckoned with.

When the therapist talked to the day-treatment staff, the real story came out. Sarah had decided herself that her time in day-treatment would be over, so she simply convinced the staff she had a discharge date, and nobody thought to double check with her therapist. In fact, when I overheard them, they were trying to decide what treat to bring for her going-away party. She didn't want to get anyone in trouble; she only wanted to get out of the program. Now she became stuck again, and trust was lost.

PLAN B

About a week after Sarah's attempted premature escape from day-treatment, I was in Bethesda, Maryland, at the National Institute of Mental Health (NIMH) with Taylor for his yearly visit. I had to cut short a meeting with the team to take a conference call with Sarah's day-treatment team in Utah. When I briefly explained Sarah's situation with day-treatment and her home difficulties to the NIMH team, they became curious about Sarah's current mental health status and treatment.

The next day at the NIMH debriefing for Taylor's visit, the team offered the opportunity for Sarah to come to their hospital as an inpatient and participate in a research study. They thought that based on her current poor prognosis and problematic behavior, they might be able to help her. The study involved slowly tapering Sarah off all her medications. During a two-week period in which she would be totally unmedicated, Sarah would participate in testing. The data gathered from the testing would be studied by the team and used to help them recommend what might be the best medication regimen for her. This had to be done as an inpatient to help her be safe while tapering off meds and to provide her twenty-four-hour support. They estimated this hospitalization would be between eight to twelve weeks. I told them I would talk to Dale and Sarah and get back with them.

I trusted the NIMH team, but this was a big decision as we were moving Sarah from day-treatment to inpatient hospitalization without a plan or timeline for getting her back to some sort of normal life. Sarah would be across the country in Maryland for two months with only a few visits from either Dale or me. This was unlike anything we had ever done before, so we really had to think it through.

We had worked with this NIMH team for years and knew they had Sarah's best interests in mind. Dale and I were familiar with the type of tests Sarah would be given as they were basically the same comprehensive tests given to the kids when we came for their yearly visits. The procedures were clear, and they assured us they had worked with many youths in Sarah's situation and would attempt to make it as homey as possible.

We weren't concerned with her physical care but with her unstable moods and emotional distress. The only apprehension we had was when we were told Sarah would not be able to have any psychological counseling or therapy while there. We were assured there would be staff to talk to Sarah if she needed it, but they were nursing staff, not psychologists or therapists. We knew how much good came from Sarah having access to therapy, and it would be hard for her to lose that support for the time she was at NIMH. However, we could see Sarah had stalled out at day-treatment and could not attend school. Her behavior was poor at best, and she was always angry with us. Upon discussion, we all decided it would be a good idea to do the study. Sarah acted especially excited, treating it like a long vacation.

We checked her in on January 4. The process was quick, and since we knew the protocol, we had no problem understanding what was expected. The study would allow one parent to fly out to see Sarah every other weekend and stay for two days. Sarah would be allowed short phone calls each night if she wanted. She would go to school on the unit each day for as long as possible as her medication schedule changed. The teachers there would provide support to help her make up credits. There would be recreational opportunities and other activities on the hospital unit. She had her own room, which she could decorate with posters. We brought her comforter and afghan from home, along with some pictures and other personal items. The team included a social worker who would check in on her, and she would always have a shift nurse available. She anxiously wanted us to leave and assured us she would be fine.

The doctors started weaning her from her medications the second week. We didn't expect much change initially. At first Sarah had a lot of attitude when we had our phone calls. She had little patience, so our calls didn't last more than five minutes. She seemed disinterested when I talked about home. She didn't want to share much about what she did except to share she enjoyed playing the Dance, Dance Revolution game. I called and talked to her nurse every few days to get an update. They said she struggled with her emotions and would put herself in isolation, but after she would talk to her nurse, she'd be okay. The report basically stayed the same as Sarah went through her hospitalization, with only a little more emphasis on how reactive Sarah seemed to be and how long it took her to come down from her emotional meltdowns.

I got the first trip out to see her for the weekend. I was excited to see Sarah, but I thought it best if we kept our time together low-key. It ended up that our time together was rather subdued. Sarah was angry with me. I tried to talk to her about the issues we had at home, and she thought I wanted to pick a fight with her. She didn't want to talk about negative things for the time I was there. I could understand that, but I thought we needed to discuss changes so things would be better when she came home. Sarah didn't want to process anything that had to do with home. She only wanted to live in the moment.

At about four weeks, when Sarah was almost totally off her meds, she became very emotional, crying on the phone every night. The nurse reported she could be defiant at times, showing attitude about having to abide by the rules, but was most often teary and needed a lot of reassurance. Each phone call I made from week four to week seven became more difficult. Sarah started calling me Mommy and asked me to come get her. That was a problem because she was only through half of the study and the team needed to get her back on medication. It had to be a slow process for her. She begged me to come home and promised she would be good. She was more upset than I had ever heard her be before.

My heart was sad for her. My fourteen-year-old daughter was across the country where I couldn't hold or comfort her. She may have acted mature and had attitude, but in the end, she was just a kid. She had few people she knew she could talk to. She missed having someone there to engage with the therapy skills that helped her cope. I started to doubt the wisdom of our decision to have her there. I knew there were other mothers of kids on her unit who got to stay at National Institute of Health (NIH) full time while their child was at the hospital. I decided I also needed to be there full-time.

I was coming up on my next weekend visit and decided I would try to pull everything together at home, so I could stay at NIH until Sarah was discharged. Dale agreed that Sarah needed the support.

We didn't want Sarah to think we had abandoned her. I didn't know if the study would pay for me to stay at the Children's Inn on campus. I decided I would contact someone from the local congregation of my church in Bethesda to see if there was someone with whom I could stay. It was awkward to ask for help, but it was critically important for Sarah that I be there. Before I called the church liaison to finalize my plan, I needed to call the doctor to let him know I wanted to stay with Sarah.

I shared my concerns for Sarah's emotional well-being and talked about her sense of abandonment. It sounded as if Sarah was falling apart more than keeping it together. I was convinced Sarah would have a sense of security knowing I was on campus, even if we couldn't spend a lot of time together. I shared my plan to get help from people from my church but asked for permission to stay on campus at the Children's Inn if possible.

There was a pause. He said, "May I be perfectly honest with you?"

"Of course." I said. I had a lot of respect for this doctor.

"I cannot keep you from coming to the hospital, that is your choice." he said. "However, I see your relationship with Sarah as an emotional trigger for her. Don't you think it would be best for you to stay home so she doesn't become upset? We want her to complete her program, don't we?"

I was too taken back to answer much more than, "Okay, I understand."

But I didn't understand, dazed by the implication that I was the root of Sarah's problems and her inability to be well. Whether that was his intended message or not, it was perceived that way. I came away from that conversation with a sense of parental inadequacy I had never experienced before. I truly believed she would have been comforted by my being there with her. It didn't seem right.

I was not bad for Sarah. Sarah became triggered by things all around in her environment, as we later discovered, not only me. Having someone judge that I could be a detrimental trigger to Sarah was disturbing and threatening. I felt degraded and unfairly judged. We certainly had a lot of conflict, but I loved her and would do anything for her. I was still the person she came to when she needed to be brought close.

Being invested in Sarah's well-being had been my focus throughout her life. I was confused and hurt. I didn't know how to reconcile what I was told and what I believed to be my real relationship with Sarah. What made the doctor think he knew all our story? He had only glimpses of our life. Questioning my role in Sarah's recovery, I didn't return to see her until she was discharged.

The NIMH team reviewed all the data from Sarah's testing and behavior while she stayed there for nine weeks and gave her an additional diagnosis of generalized anxiety disorder along with bipolar disorder, type 2.

It seemed we finally had our piece of a miracle. This answered the questions we had for years. We now understood the whys of Sarah's illnesses and behaviors much better, but she would continue to be very complex. She had so much anxiety, almost all the time. She was easily overcome and behaved in a negative way to avoid anything that made her anxious. It was anxiety that ruled her emotions, thoughts, and feelings, which then in turn triggered the bipolar disorder moods and behaviors. Both went hand-in-hand, and for all of us, especially Sarah, was incredibly difficult to separate out. The behavior had been our focus, but now we could look behind the behavior and act accordingly.

She didn't like confrontation with us because it triggered anxiety about how we would interact with her. So, she would shut down and push us away. She worried about possible consequences at home, so she misbehaved to avoid them. She feared people wouldn't love her, so she did inappropriate things to get their attention, not always knowing it would end up being negative attention. She worried about looking dumb or incompetent, so she would avoid anything which might make her feel that way. Her anxiety would often shut her down, making her seem inflexible and noncompliant. This increased her irritability and the intensity of her emotional behavior. She didn't have the language, emotional maturity or sometimes desire to express what she was feeling, which lead to a rather unhappy state, but we didn't always know why.

It was as if a lightbulb had gone on. We had to aggressively address Sarah's constant heightened state of fear if we were to hope for a more normal life for her. The medications would help but learning coping skills and strategies to manage her generalized anxiety would allow her to enjoy activities and relationships.

The team put Sarah on Prozac. It seemed to be the right drug for her. It was the first-time medication had a direct effect with Sarah.

With Prozac, she could more honestly and accurately share her feelings. The nursing staff could see the medication's effect, she was less intense and more flexible. She attended school on the hospital unit and got some of her credits made up for junior high. Sarah received academic testing and was diagnosed with a math learning disability called dyscalculia. Understanding some of the accommodations that could be done to help her math difficulties gave Sarah hope to return to school when she was discharged.

When we came to pick her up at discharge, she was more herself and better able to communicate her needs. She thought ahead and realized she was going to come home soon, so she became more open to talking about a plan. When she was discharged, she was proud of the hard things she had done and had a sense of closure.

Dale and I had high expectations for Sarah's behavior for sure, and we never wanted to blame her bipolar disorder for her choices. But now we understood about her anxiety. Now we realized that not knowing about her level of anxiety really impacted how we previously dealt with her. Even validating her irrational thoughts and feelings would have helped to avoid so much conflict and confusion. The diagnosis made a lot of sense, though it didn't make the problem go away. Sarah still struggled with limits, but at least we were more aware of issues that had likely been lurking behind her actions. It allowed us to start to speak the same language when talking about her mental illnesses.

Dale and I had been talking about how we should reintroduce Sarah to home and school once she was discharged from the hospital. She had been gone from school from the first week of October to mid-

March. We knew from experience that after a hospitalization there needed to be a transition time to avoid a mental health crisis. We couldn't let her jump back into school, so we looked at our home schedule and rearranged some of Sarah's responsibilities and needs. Then we went to the school.

Many of her teachers were supportive, but some didn't get it. We tried to explain Sarah's needs during her transition back to school. We requested she receive extended time to do tests and assignments, breaking some assignments into smaller chunks, grading her on a pass/fail, and not making her do the work which had already been given. Obviously, she wasn't going to be able to catch up with the work her peers had been assigned. She was still sick and needed to have all the school services and accommodations under her special education plan. We found we had to use the comparison of a child who had undergone cancer treatments, or a child who had been in a serious car accident with the teachers to illustrate the magnitude of Sarah's illness. If the school would accommodate a child with a life-threatening illness or one who'd been involved in an accident, surely, they could understand mental health was as vital as medical health and that she needed accommodations.

Some of her teachers were very understanding and some were oblivious to the impact her mental illness had on her daily life. The worst was her English teacher. His eyes glazed over as we asked for accommodations. When pressed to extend her time to do work, he said he would give her three extra days to catch up. That was it—Three days to bring Sarah up to par after a six-month absence from regular school. No wonder she often lived in a state of hopeless despair at school.

Sarah finished out her ninth-grade year. We were cautiously relieved when it ended. She stuck with school when she came back from the hospital, even when it was hard. She reentered therapy and learned new techniques to help control her anxiety. She also started to make amends with the family for her past behavior. We all cheered her on as she continued to show progress. She was willing to take her medication, but she kind of kept to herself and spent a lot of time sleeping. I figured she had gone through a lot in nine months and needed some rest. We all needed rest.

A NEW PLACE TO BE

Though she'd anticipated a positive, fresh start as a sophomore in high school, Sarah struggled to even get through the first few weeks. Going to high school meant becoming familiar with a new building, a new set of administrators and teachers and a new schedule. Being one of 2,200 students was overwhelming for her. For Sarah, getting up for a 7:30 a.m. start time was torture. Soon I was again receiving truancy phone calls and wondering where Sarah was during school hours.

Was she safe? Who was she with? What was she thinking? It was only first term, and she was tanking fast. I only knew I continued to drop her off at the front of the school every morning and anticipated I would eventually see her later in the afternoon. We would ask her repeatedly to talk to us about her day at school, her friends or problems she was having. She was good at deflecting and ignoring our questions and told us everything was fine. Or she got mad and told us to leave her alone.

I became so frustrated I made a call to the vice principal in charge of Sarah to ask him to help me get Sarah to class. I started calling him once Sarah had accumulated twenty-seven truancies. He referred me to Sarah's counselor.

The counselor only said, "Mrs. Greenwell, we have far more students worse than Sarah. I am concerned with the kids who are doing drugs and other things, and Sarah is only missing school. I'll consider it, but I don't think she is much of a concern."

Furious, I said, "I don't care about the other students, Sarah is my daughter and I expect you to care about her too. Something needs to be done at the school level."

We were deeply troubled and arranged for Sarah to have a conversation with the principal. The principal was a neighbor of Sarah's grandparents and we hoped he might have a firm but positive discussion with her. Sarah giggled as she later reported how the principal had only asked her to do better and; gave her a Snickers candy bar; and a school pin. There was to be no follow-up, attendance tracking, or referral to the truancy program. I was sickened by the response we received from the school staff and wondered what type of recourse we had to get Sarah in school. I wanted the school to follow their own policy and refer Sarah to detention or other available resources. It seemed like nobody was taking this problem seriously.

Sarah realized she had everyone at the high school fooled into allowing her to take the path of least resistance. The message she got from the school was to keep her head down and stay out of trouble and there wouldn't be any consequences. However, Dale and I had a different opinion. We reminded her of how long she had come in her journey to manage her anxiety and moods. Sarah needed to be her own cheerleader when things were tough to keep herself on track. We were doing the best we could to support her, but she knew she was the one who had the final power.

I could not just let it all go. I kept track of each of her truancies, writing letters to her vice principal and special education teacher, stating that she'd missed classes without permission. I sent letters for thirty-eight truancies, fifty truancies, then sixty-three truancies. It wasn't until Sarah had seventy-three truancies in her first term that we received a letter from the school stating she was considered a student-at-risk. I begged the school to send her to the school district truancy court, so the judge could help us set up a plan to help Sarah, but nothing happened. Sarah watched from the sidelines, enjoying the struggle we were having at keeping her on some forward track.

Sarah willingly continued to attend therapy, and we received reports she made progress there, but what could we believe? We saw her behavior at home and there didn't seem to be progress there. She stopped taking her medication. Sarah failed most of her classes apart from a passing grade in subjects she loved, like creative writing, choir, and English.

Sarah was beautifully expressive in writing and in singing. Grateful she had some positive avenues in which to excel, we encouraged her in her talents. She happily performed with the school choir and received praise and attention for her efforts. We knew she could be successful in school, we just didn't know what the carrot was to make her want to do well.

As the school year went on, Sarah again became more secretive, and her behavior became much more withdrawn. I searched her room to discover any clue as to what she was doing while away from home. Everything looked the same, with her graffiti covered jeans tacked to the wall and her innocent childhood mementos in her small ballerina jewelry box. Haphazardly strewn across her dresser and folded into her cubby spots were random snippets of poetry about suffering and death. There was graphic picture after picture of Goth-like drawings of girls with huge, haunting eyes who were cutting, crying, and looked empty. I found razor blades, which confirmed what we already thought. But I didn't find any evidence of drugs or any firm indication of what she did with her free time. She would burn scraps of paper she'd written on, probably to make sure we didn't know what was troubling her.

We sat down with her repeatedly trying, even pleading, to get her to let us know how we could help her. She knew we expected her to follow the rules of our home, but she did that only marginally. Sarah knew how far she could go before she got in severe trouble. She yelled at us to leave her alone, to quit asking so many questions, and to let her stop going to school.

By the spring of her sophomore year I was again exhausted dealing with Sarah's behavior day in and day out. We weren't any closer to knowing how to help her. She started to stay away from home long after school got out and then into the early evenings. We told her if we didn't know where we could find her, we would have to call the police and report her as a runaway. Of course, she didn't think we were serious, and the glint in her eye told us she thought we were the stupidest adults she had ever encountered. The next time 7:00 p.m. rolled around and Sarah was not home from school and we didn't know where she was, we called the police.

We still always hesitated to call the police because of the attention we would receive, but we were committed to follow through with our decision. We spoke to the policeman in our front yard, so Taylor and Alex did not have to be involved in the situation. Dale and I shared our long-standing concerns about Sarah and the impact of her

180

mental illnesses on her behavior. We had been talking to the officer for about ten minutes when I glanced behind him and saw Sarah walking toward us from the opposite side of the street. She slowed her walk and stared ahead at us. Her face went pale and she looked scared, and yes, she knew then that we would follow through. We couldn't help but laugh when we saw she was wearing her "Witness Protection" T-shirt, which boldly said, "You don't know me." But now she would become known to the city police.

We left the officer and Sarah alone so he could talk to her. After they spoke, Sarah came into the house and went to her room, very somber and quiet. When Dale and I again spoke to the officer, he commended us for how we were handling a very difficult situation and assured us the police would keep an eye out for Sarah in the community.

Instead of things getting better, they got worse. Sarah hardly attended school, and the school refused to consider her a dropout. She rarely spoke civilly to us and hid any information or clues that would have allowed us to help her. She acted dark and moody, wanting to dress in Goth-like clothing, and isolating herself when she was home. Dale and I did our best to maintain our home structure for the boys and to continue to establish the type of behavior expectations we had in our home, and for Sarah, in particular.

One day in May I got a phone call from Sarah who said she would be home late and asked since she had called would I refrain from calling the police. I told her I needed her to come home right then. I expressed deep concern about her and sensed she needed the safety of being home. I knew something was very wrong; every part of my maternal instincts warned Sarah was in serious trouble.

She started to sob uncontrollably and handed the phone over to her friend Jordyn. Jordyn then went on to boldly tell me she had Sarah and would be keeping her for the night because coming home upset Sarah and she didn't want to talk to us. She said Dale and I were the ones who were making Sarah sad and that Sarah was happier away from us. She was incredibly disrespectful and arrogant as she conveyed that she had power over Sarah's actions.

I was furious at this Jordyn, whom I had never met. Who was she to talk that way to me? Who was she to Sarah? I demanded to speak to Sarah to find out her location, but all Sarah said was she'd be home soon and then hung up.

The waiting was terrible. When Sarah finally came home, she was sobbing so hard it looked like she would be physically sick. She wouldn't let me comfort her or understand why she was so upset. She stayed in her room all night. I even put in an emergency call to her therapist, but he couldn't meet with us. The next day I dropped her off to school as usual and told her how much we loved her. I wanted her to know how important she was to our family. I didn't know how to open my heart and visually show her how much I hurt for her and how Dale and I would do anything to help her in the situation she'd found herself in. I knew she desperately needed help.

That afternoon Dale and Taylor went camping on a scout trip, and I was left alone with Sarah and Alex. I had been working downstairs in the office most of the day when Sarah came home in the late afternoon. I was so frustrated with her and the ongoing conflict she brought into our home, I ignored her when she came into the room. She sat against the wall behind me, and I heard her sniffling and crying. Soon she was crying harder and harder. I continued to keep my back to her, waiting to see if she would interact with me.

She finally said, "Mom, I am in real trouble."

As I shut the door and turned to face her, I had the sickest feeling. Her face was splotchy from crying so hard, her posture screamed defeat, and her eyes looked haunted. I instinctively knew it would be bad, but I also knew it would finally bring to light the reasons for Sarah's behavior.

"Everything is a mess and I am so scared," she began. "I don't even know how to tell you about what's been going on, but I am scared something bad is going to happen."

"Are you hurt? Do we need to go to the hospital?" I asked. She didn't seem to be injured, but she looked so worn out and tired. Since I hadn't had much interaction with her during the previous week, I didn't know what shape she was in.

Sarah shook her head. She said, "A girl named Jordyn was in my art class the first of the year, and we became really good friends. She is a senior. I like hanging out with her."

Her words hung in the air challenging me to question the meaning of her intentions.

I didn't say anything. I knew if I interrupted, she would retreat back to not sharing anything personal with me. I tried to show nonconfrontational body language and wait her out.

"Jordyn is different from the other kids in school," Sarah stated. "She's cool. She likes the same things I do and it's like we are so connected."

As Sarah spoke, she looked down at the carpet, seemingly not wanting to make eye contact.

"Oh. Why haven't you brought Jordyn home so we could meet her?" I asked. "If she is such a good friend, we want to get to know her."

"Jordyn isn't the kind of person you guys want me to be friends with. I didn't want you to meet her."

I was getting annoyed with the conversation because I knew the issue was about more than us meeting her friend. I struggled to maintain my patience to allow her to tell about her situation in her own way. I wanted her to figuratively "rip off the Band-Aid" and move forward.

Finally, she took a deep breath and began to tell the truth. "I was skipping class with Jordyn a lot, even since the first term in school. Sometimes we would just get a drink and drive around. Sometimes we would meet up with people she knew. These were other kids our age or older adults. I knew some of them, but there were a lot from outside school that I didn't know." She paused to quickly glance at me, then looked down again.

"I could tell they were what you and dad would call a "bad" crowd," she said. "But that's kind of what excited me to be with them. I liked that they were different and they accepted me. I liked that you wouldn't like them."

Sarah told me after hanging out with Jordyn through the first of the year, Jordyn started to invite her to spend time with some members of this group after school. Youth and young adults would gather to spend time together at a given location and would come and go with each other with what seemed to be at random to Sarah. She didn't really question the situation because it gave her a chance to be away from home and she felt accepted. Acceptance was something Sarah had never experienced. She also liked the fact we didn't know where she was.

Slowly over time, Jordyn revealed to Sarah they all belonged to a kind of secret gang or group that encouraged and participated in illegal activity. Sarah said she didn't know the name they called themselves, but they were involved in ritualistic practices and interests within the gang. Sarah knew very few details about these activities. She felt as long as she stayed as far on the fringe of awareness as possible, she could almost deny the existence of these happenings, even to herself.

Up until that day. After school Jordyn took Sarah for a ride and proceeded to tell her the whole, detailed story of the gang with whom she had been affiliated. Sarah had not been totally aware of the magnitude and depth of the group's activities. Jordyn had only hinted and revealed a little here and a little there as she'd spent the better part of a school year grooming Sarah to become a part of them. Now that Sarah fully understood what was going on, she was truly frightened and trapped.

"I always knew the things Jordyn said about you and dad weren't true," she sobbed. "I sometimes felt like you didn't want me here, but that was because I knew you wouldn't want me if you knew what I was doing. I know you and dad love me." She paused to catch her breath before continuing, looking me in the eye. "I didn't do any of the things those people did. I don't want to be a part of anything to do with them, ever."

But it had been daring and different to be with Jordyn and her group. She'd become scared when she realized that the gang's activities had nothing to do with how she was raised and who she wanted to be. She wanted to get out but didn't know how.

My head was spinning as she shared details of what Jordyn had told her. The activities were so evil. It was near impossible for me to comprehend that people lived and participated in such destructive behaviors right in our "safe" neighborhood and community.

We could not have protected her. She had effectively placed herself outside of our help. The fist in my stomach came when Sarah said she had recently been contemplating running away from home to be with them. That was the reason she had been sobbing so hard the previous day, because she had told Jordyn she no longer wanted to live at home. Jordyn told her their group had a sort of "underground railroad". Sarah could use it to run away and hide in places throughout the country. Jordyn assured Sarah we would never be able to find her. When Jordyn said this group had the power to hide her from us, Sarah realized she was in way over her head. She said she was unhappy at home and had been for a long time, but she knew the responsibility for her unhappiness mostly had to do with her.

We talked for many hours. Sarah mostly shared her sorrow for getting involved with Jordyn, and how she was starting to grasp how messed up everything was. She said some of the people she had met were scary and she knew she couldn't trust Jordyn anymore. None of them had cared she had a loving, committed family who worried about her well-being.

I secured an emergency appointment with Samuel the next day. Sarah committed to come clean with everything so we could figure out a solution. Samuel, who had dealt with clients in gangs, talked to Sarah about how she had been groomed to become a part of this group early on when Jordyn targeted her to be her friend. Samuel also shared that now she knew intimate details about the group, in order to protect themselves, they would not want her to leave. He said it would not be as easy as Sarah telling Jordyn that she didn't want to hang out anymore. Sarah had to take a stand and be firm until Jordyn and the gang finally understood that Sarah was not a threat to them. Sarah committed to Dale, Samuel and me that she would be honest and accountable as we worked through a plan to get her away from them.

We absolutely believed everything Sarah told us regarding the illegal activities of the group and we knew her fear was real. Our fear for her was real.

Jordyn had been extremely cautious to conceal and distract Sarah from being aware of names of people of leadership within the gang or places in which they met. Jordyn controlled when they met, with whom they met and what they did. Unfortunately, because everything Sarah shared was hearsay through Jordyn, we had no direct evidence or locations of their activities. Although extremely frustrated, we did not believe we had anything we could report to the police. We were focused and most concerned with Sarah's well-being and immediate needs.

Sarah started attending extra therapy appointments to implement her plan and regulate her moods and mental illness. Dale and I talked about what we needed to do next. We were frightened at how close Sarah had been to leaving our home and how little control we really had over her. We recognized Sarah returning to the high school, where Jordyn attended as a senior, would be difficult and probably unsafe.

We talked at length with Samuel about placing Sarah in a residential treatment center. The residential treatment center had many advantages for Sarah and for us. Sarah had been off her medication for almost a year, and her anxiety levels were frequently maxed out. This would give her the chance to get things regulated. Nobody from the group would know where she had gone, which would help her make the separation clean and safe. I, for one, wanted Sarah to go away for a while. As much as that sounded nonmaternal, I had been dealing with Sarah's dishonesty, emotionality, behavior, and contention for so long, I was done. Dale was tired of trying to maintain both his work and support my efforts, and the boys were tired of the drama. We all needed a break, and admitting Sarah provided respite.

Sarah didn't know of the plan to admit her as we didn't know how likely she would be to run away. As a family, we celebrated Sarah's sixteenth birthday as normally as possible, but we knew we would need to tell her before the week was out. When we told her the night before she was to be admitted, she was teary but willing to try it. I think her biggest concern had to do with how long she would be away. We didn't know. During the intake interview the next day, Sarah's emotional instability and difficulty with thinking through her answers clearly demonstrated she should be in intensive treatment. When we left her, she seemed to understand this arrangement was best.

My expectations of Sarah's treatment were low. I wanted to see her get better, but she seemed like a different person, one I didn't know. During our first visit with her, we brought Taylor and Alex to see where she was living. At first, she seemed happy to see us, and we tried to play a board game together. But soon she accused Taylor of cheating, and she started to yell at him and then at all of us that we didn't love her. Angrily, she accused us of leaving her in residential treatment so we could get rid of her.

Dale and I gathered everything up to leave. We decided she needed time away from us. We all needed to have time to recover from the destructive influence she had in our home. We knew her actions were a result of her long association with the gang, and we knew her bipolar and anxiety disorders needed attention. The problem was way bigger than we were. We weren't giving up on her, but we knew she needed professional expertise.

Sarah went to school at the residential program and had therapy groups throughout each day. Sarah's new therapist, James, met individually with her at least once a week. Dale and I also had family sessions with Sarah. During our appointments with Sarah, she had an attitude and acted entitled—not at all the contrite child I thought I would find. She criticized us for the strictness at home and for our use of consequences. She claimed we never listened to her and she perceived we always considered her to be the bad kid. Admittedly, there was some truth to this.

After a few weeks of this dialogue, I wondered if residential wasn't really helping her to move forward in accepting responsibility for her actions. I frankly told Sarah and James I wasn't ready for her to come home until she could live by our rules and respect the members of our family. She would stay in treatment as long as it took. I didn't want her home only to have the same behavior manifest in a matter of months. We had been living this situation for too long. Dale agreed, but he held more hope she could come home sooner than later. I thought she had a lot to learn and process related to her behavior, her involvement with this horrible group, and about where she was going with school.

Part of our responsibility having Sarah in residential treatment was attending Dialectical Behavioral Therapy or DBT therapy classes with the other parents. We had already been exposed to DBT when Sarah had been in day-treatment in ninth grade, but the DBT therapy in residential was extensive and more involved. DBT was particularly effective for people who showed intense emotions, manipulative behavior, cutting, difficulty forming relationships, and difficulty managing their feelings. All things Sarah experienced. The therapeutic focus was to teach Sarah to better tolerate her emotional distress and proactively utilize positive techniques to build relationships. Sarah would learn tangible coping tools to solve and create wellness for herself instead of always reacting after the fact to emotional turmoil and its consequences. Simply put, to deal with her life in a healthier way. Sarah received the same therapy daily and was expected to put her best effort toward learning these skills.

If Sarah had to do DBT, I was required to do it too. But I had been so angry with her I found it hard to hope that DBT skills would make a difference. I attended my parent group each week and participated, but grudgingly, almost daring the therapists to prove Sarah would change.

As we continued to attend sessions with James and Sarah, and as Sarah started to take her overnight home visits, I had to admit she really was trying. She hadn't made the big changes I envisioned, but she changed nonetheless. She made good progress in making up her school credits and no longer had a bad attitude about being placed in the residential program.

One day I had to go to the parent group alone. We were talking about love languages, and we were supposed to try to define our child's "love language." What was the love language Sarah used to give and receive messages of love and acceptance from the people around her? As I reflected on Sarah's needs from Sarah's perspective, I had a powerful realization.

I took my love language tendencies and needs out of the equation and only focused on what seemed to make Sarah respond. I realized she was a physical touch, emotional-validation communicator and had been her whole life. She had always loved to have me tickle her arm or rub her back or play with her hair. It calmed her, and she ate up the attention. She wanted a physical connection, a literal closeness. She checked in with me and Dale to see how we thought she was doing, needing validation she was on track. She wanted us to notice her and tell her why and how proud we were of her. She needed to have her efforts recognized and praised often. She needed to have us verbally acknowledge and empathize when she had a bad day. She had needs to be fulfilled in ways that spoke to her.

Sarah wasn't a needy person. Although I had felt her pull on my emotional reserves in her efforts to get her needs met, it was not because she was intentionally trying to "suck me dry" as I used to often feel. She was rather effectively communicating in her way and in her language the way things made sense in her world. But in her intensity, it was often a foreign language to me. She had tried to show us this love language without knowing what it was, and we didn't always understand what it meant.

That was the beginning of me seeing Sarah in a different way, in the way she needed to be loved and the way she showed love. Wow. I was faced with a whole new paradigm of how to love Sarah. I thought I was doing a pretty good job, but now I realized I had fallen very short. Tears filled my eyes as I sat in the group. I was trying to communicate with her in all the wrong ways. My love language was to show love by doing for someone, to invest time talking and exchanging ideas, and generally be less emotional. It wasn't that I was not a loving person. We were sometimes incompatible in how we showed love to each other. She didn't hate me, nor did I dislike her. We were just out of sync.

Guilt washed over me as I realized I had unintentionally parented Sarah in ways that made her feel invalidated and unloved. I thought, by being emotionally in control and emotionally calm, I could help Sarah develop a sense of calm. What she needed to see was my emotionally vulnerable side. I had never been very demonstrative physically, as growing up in my family didn't include hugs or arm tickles. In my family we weren't physically or verbally affectionate. Growing up I felt jealous of families who would express their love through physical touch. As a result, I consciously made the decision to have a home in which our family would know and hear affection through a hug, kiss, or an "I love you." I was comfortable with being able to receive and give affection, it just wasn't always my preferred way. I also did physical, functional things for the kids to show my love.

I thought this type of mothering showed I would be available for them and a steadying influence in their lives. For Taylor this would be a good message of love. Alex knew he could depend on me. But this mothering did not fill Sarah's needs. She needed to know she was cherished and appreciated. I could trace this problem in our communication back to Sarah's early childhood, when I always considered Sarah and myself like oil and water, unable to mix. I needed to communicate in the way that touched her heart and gave her the assurance that I loved her and was on her side. I needed to change.

With this realization, I attended our weekly therapy sessions with James with a new focus. We talked about Sarah's absolute need for validation in all parts of her life. Sarah and I discussed ways we could come together, and I apologized for not knowing how to do better. From then on, therapy progressed quickly as we determined what needed to change at home, so Sarah could return and what she needed to continue to work on. We practiced love languages and talked about situations where each of us, Dale included, would need to be flexible and tolerant of each other's differences. We brought Alex and Taylor in for a family session that included Samuel and James and allowed the boys to tell Sarah how her behavior affected them and our home life. They were angry with her for the stress she brought home but were willing to forgive her.

Sarah began to better understand how her chaos impacted the whole family and how we were not willing to live that way anymore. Sarah needed to understand that, although we would listen and validate her better, she would be held responsible for her actions and her decisions in our home. Even though we had a more enlightened understanding, that did not give her a free ride, just better parenting from us.

Dealing with Sarah's continual crises left me feeling emotionally empty. It made me reflect on how difficult growing up with bipolar disorder could be, with its up-and-down emotions and skewed thinking. I told Dale I was saddened because I knew from my own experience that Sarah and Taylor would have to go through life with bipolar regrets and painful realities. I wished more than anything I could change that path for them and make it easier, kinder. Yet I didn't know what I could do except be there for them when life was confusing and the effects of bipolar swept over them in never ending cycles. The only thing I could offer them was love, treatment, and a willingness to share my experiences to soften the blow.

PANIC AND PEACE

As Sarah left residential treatment behind, she worked to identify what kind of life she wanted to have. After her close call with Jordyn she became more consistent with her behavior at home, more open to communicating with us, and not being so secretive. Dale and I began to "get" Sarah and her needs better. But sometimes she continued to be such a mystery. She still had difficulties with strong, unexpected mood swings and anxiety. Working with her to manage her emotions was a daily effort.

One day after school while waiting to pick Sarah up, Alex came rushing out to the car.

He said, "Mom, you have to go into the school right now. Sarah is freaking out!" But he couldn't tell me why Sarah was freaking out, just that she needed me right away.

Dread washed over me as I approached the high school wondering what I would find. There in the vestibule of the front doors, Sarah had pressed herself against the far wall and was looking at me with frantic eyes. Her boyfriend stood at her side distractedly patting her arm and looked like he would rather be anywhere else.

I took an inventory—her breathing was shallow; her face was drawn; and her color was off, kind of red and patchy; her eyes darted back and forth; and she was tense, tense, tense. She was in a full-blown panic attack and didn't know what to do. She didn't even seem to be aware of her surroundings.

195

I moved closer and touched my hands to both sides of her face to force her to look only at me. I started to breathe slowly so she could hear the rate of my breath. Nice and easy. I spoke softly, slowly, and calmly. She was still panting and looking frantic. I told her she would be okay and that I would help her. I told her to breathe slowly with me, and a few minutes passed as she tried to get her breathing under control.

Then she began to relax as I gently massaged her arms and put pressure on her shoulders. She started to make a mewing sound, as if she were stuck between crying and talking. She noticed her brother and boyfriend as they stood quietly nearby, and she started to get upset again. We went back to the breathing, and she began to calm down. Everything had to happen so slowly for her to be able to get rid of the tension and open up again. But we were patient as we worked together. I continued to tell her she would be fine, that it must be a hard thing, and that I was sorry she didn't feel well.

Then I backed away and looked her over. Her color returned, and while her breathing continued to be faster than normal, it was within an acceptable range. Her body became slack, and she looked at me. I could tell that all she needed was rest, to sleep it off. She was on the verge of tears and I knew she didn't want to cry in front of anybody. I knew she wouldn't want to talk about what happened right then; there would be time for that later. For the moment she just needed to go home.

Later we talked about triggers, physical response and interventions. I tried to teach her what she could do to help herself, to empower herself in the face of such scary situations. I let her know I would always be there for her, so we could work on it together.

Meanwhile, life with Sarah and Taylor was calmer, usually. Both were focused on school, and they'd come to a sort of truce with each other. While symptoms still flared, we were taking care of them as they happened. Alex excelled in his activities and in developing his own sense of self apart from mental illness.

The current behavior plan and reward system worked well enough that we could rely on everyone to follow expectations generally. By now all the kids knew that consequences, good and bad, followed actions, and they knew we were serious about upholding rules. It was as if the years and years of therapy had finally jelled and we were all using our skills at the same time. We were hesitant to acknowledge, even to ourselves, that we were seeing progress largely due to our hard work. Nobody was in the hospital, nobody was in day-treatment, and nobody was in residential care. Things looked good for us. It seemed like too much to hope for, so Dale and I didn't talk about it for fear of jinxing our peace.

Sarah had a beautiful singing voice since she was a small child, and we knew she wanted to have professional voice lessons. We also knew she had a long way to go to get herself enough credits to graduate. So, we agreed to pay for voice lessons if she would work hard to get all her credits on track and obey house rules. It was an expensive carrot, but we knew we needed something big to motivate Sarah to change her past behavior. She agreed, and we made her sign a contract, and she began a special interest that brought her a lot of joy. Instead of hearing the rantings of a morose, angry child, we would hear snippets of lovely music coming from her room while she was getting ready in the morning.

Sarah showed her commitment with practicing and follow-through, which was wonderful to see. I enjoyed attending her voice lessons and noting the progress she made as she prepared for her recitals. Sarah loved to perform at recitals, where she had an engaged audience wanting to hear her special gift. She looked beautiful and content as she sang. In those moments it was easy to forget the years of angst and pain. It was so wonderful to see her happy. The validation and compliments she received at these recitals motivated her to keep moving forward.

Sarah continued to lag behind in school as she started her junior year. She hadn't been acting the part of a real student since seventh grade, and she didn't know where to start. Her special education teacher, Susan, seemed to understand what made Sarah tick and took on the task of mentoring her toward graduation. Sarah lacked confidence in herself and we had to continually give pep talks and small rewards to help her. She also participated in her IEP meetings, where she learned to write effective goals and actively advocate for her own needs.

One area in which Sarah was absolutely resolute was her refusal to get her driver's license before she graduated. We all talked of the importance of driving as a life skill, but she would not consider it. It confused me that someone who acted so fiercely independent wouldn't want to have access to the freedom driving could bring.

Sarah had been in choir all through junior high and high school but had not been interested in school clubs. Then she heard of the

LARPing, or "Live Action Role Playing," club. With LARPing she would dress like a medieval character, such as a knight, and with handmade weapons would battle or joust with other members. The clothing was basic, as were the weapons. They would take pieces of PVC pipe, foam, and carpet padding and cover them with duct tape for swords, lances and shields. It was fascinating to see these creative kids take such simple materials and make rather effective weapons.

Sarah liked LARPing because the members were guys and she got along better with guys. There wasn't as much drama. She also fit in better because the club members, like her, were kind of outsiders and had alternative attitudes and experiences. But the thing Sarah liked the most was being able to do battle with the other kids. She insisted the guys not back down from fighting with her. She wanted to be treated as an equal and developed strategies to increase her likelihood of winning against any opponent. She was aggressive and took a lot of hard hits, but she loved it and stayed in LARPing through the rest of high school. It was a cathartic experience to have a safe place in which to have conflict and where she became empowered at a time she didn't feel empowered in other aspects of her life.

It was "crunch time" as we began Sarah's senior year. I knew she, and later Taylor, could receive educational and financial resources from the state Vocational Rehabilitation Program. I got Sarah's vocational rehab counselor involved in school meetings. Susan continued to mentor Sarah, praising her with every positive step. By the middle of Sarah's senior year, Susan was confident Sarah was on track to graduate. But Sarah had to make it happen. Her IEP team came together to write her final goals and discuss her transition into the real world. Sarah thought she might want to be a pharmacy technician but found out the field required a lot of math, and with her math dyscalculia learning disability decided it was not for her. I had empathy for Sarah as I remembered the stress of having everyone asking you what you wanted to be when you grew up. For Sarah, it was enough to just grow up and be healthy. The vocational rehab counselor suggested Sarah go to school to be an American Sign Language Interpreter at the local technical college. For the first time in a long time I saw Sarah get excited about something in her future. She wanted to pursue the interpreter avenue. All she needed to do was make sure she walked across the stage with a high school diploma.

Sarah had two days till graduation and still had three credits to make up. Susan found a humanitarian project Sarah could do—making and tying a quilt for the local senior center. Successfully completing the project would give her the last three credits she needed. Sarah had never done anything like this before, and the caveat was she had to complete it without any help.

She gathered the materials from Susan, and we set the quilt up at Dale's mom's house. For two days I sat on the couch reading and watching television while supervising and watching Sarah struggle to complete the quilt. She didn't complain and seemed resigned it was something that absolutely had to be done. On the second day, she had about a third of the quilt left to finish when she hit the wall, crying and emotionally spent. Her meltdown was brief, like when she was younger and would get overwhelmed and cry to get the tension out. After a spell, she bounced back and moved on. I was so proud of her when she called Susan exactly the night before graduation and reported she had completed the task. Sarah was going to walk!

Oh, the joy and satisfaction any parent must experience to see their child graduate. For us it was magnified tenfold. Dale and I sat in the audience squeezing each other's hands and reviewing the past six years of Sarah's life. She had such a history of hardships, some not of her making and some brought on by herself. To see her huge smile as they called her name was rewarding and memorable. It seemed like we were all graduating that day. She had a plan for her future and hoped she would be successful.

She was amazing not because of her struggles with mental illness, but despite them. It was a good moment.

PART III

MISUNDERSTOOD

As a family with three of us trying to live with bipolar disorder, we had a myriad of real-life experiences to remind us of the true nature of the illness. For Taylor, however, his bipolar disorder "looked" different than ours. From his very beginning he was intense, self-focused and relentless to express himself.

Taylor's explosive meltdowns could, and did, happen anywhere. Once, at the mall, Taylor wanted to visit the toy store. While a typical request, I knew he was too keyed up to do well in the store. All it took was a firm "no" from me, to go ballistic, right there in the middle of the walkway of the mall. He kicked, hit me, and screamed profanity at the top of his lungs. His switch had been triggered, and his immediate response to a simple "no" became catastrophic. He wouldn't calm down at all, and I knew the best place for us was the car, so he would at least be contained. Unfortunately, I had parked the car at the opposite end of the mall. Taylor, at five years old, was still small enough for me to carry and restrain. Kind of, anyway. I picked him up in a football hold and started marching toward the car. Sarah and I had experienced this type of meltdown in public before. We had previously worked out that when I gave her a signal, she could walk away from us so she wouldn't be embarrassed, as long as I could still see her. So, Sarah quickly moved to the other side of the aisle, glancing over at us with a devastated look on her face. I know she prayed for me to have enough strength for the long walk before Taylor would break free. I tried not to notice the people coming out of the other stores to see what the ruckus was. I saw the disapproving, judgmental looks I invariably got as I tried to manage Taylor in public.

Once we were in the car, I released Taylor to the back of the van and let him scream his heart out at the perceived injustice of life. As usual, it took him a long time to calm down. This was good because it took me just as long to be able to want to be with him again. I always got the short end of the stick with these meltdowns—I was emotionally and physically drained and had to fight the justifiable feeling of how much I didn't like this child right then.

Dale and I always knew there was a risk of taking Taylor in public. People would think what they wanted, but they never asked if they could help. I had a rule that if Taylor got violent in the car, I would pull over somewhere safe and he would have to get out and stand by the curb until he could calm down enough for it to be safe for me to drive.

One day he had gone over the top, kicking the windows and seats of the van and very nearly kicking Sarah and Alex. Sarah shrank in her seat, trying to make herself as small as possible, and Alex wailed in distress. I pulled over to a safe location and stopped the car. I thought of how crappy my life was and wondered where in the cosmos I had gone wrong. I demanded that Taylor get out until he could get it together. He finally did and stood next to the car fuming and mumbling to himself. After about fifteen minutes of sitting there, a car pulled up behind me. A woman got out of the car and went to Taylor and asked him what was wrong. Taylor, in his precocious way, told her he had a mean mommy, and shared with her how he believed he was picked on. When the woman came to my window, I tried to explain Taylor had a mental illness, that this behavior was part of it when he got angry, and that stepping outside the car helped him calm down.

Unbelievably, she accused me of child abuse, and stated she would be calling the police. What! This was Taylor abusing us, not the other way around. She went to Taylor and asked if he wanted to come sit in her car until the police came. That scared Taylor. He immediately pulled himself together and jumped into our car with an apology and an urgent request to drive away, fast. For once I did exactly as he suggested. I hated the way the woman thought she knew better than I did how to manage my son.

Where were her hard-earned credentials from years of raging, violence, and fear?

While I knew on an intellectual level that his explosive behavior was a symptom of his illness, and while I didn't blame him, I still had to deal with it on an emotional level. It was difficult to know if I was doing the right thing. I always had a fear that one day I might find myself sitting across from a police officer who would also question my judgment.

We followed The Children's Center's advice and got Taylor into the children's day-treatment program at our local mental health center within a month of his diagnosis. Three afternoons a week, Taylor attended therapeutic activities, social skills instruction, recreational therapy, diagnosis-specific activities, and fun activities with about eight other kids who also had mental illness or behavioral problems. Once a week, Taylor would have individual therapy with the program therapist. The program would pick him up from school, and I would get him a few hours later at the mental health center. He loved it, kind of seeing it as a special camp, but not relating it to any mental health treatment. The program didn't make him feel weird or uncomfortable with who he was.

Taylor learned some of the social skills he lacked—not mastering them, but at least he was exposed to the skills. He also developed self-confidence and began to use his words to communicate. Progress was slow, and I had to accept realistic goals as I defined what it meant to have him "get better." Instead of daily meltdowns, he might have two days without one, or they would last thirty minutes instead of an hour. Instead of being rigid in his thinking and chronically argumentative, he would sometimes be flexible or try to compromise. He was less agitated, less hyper, and wouldn't hit all the time when frustrated. Sometimes he could "keep it together" long enough to have someone play with him at recess. Getting better didn't necessarily mean *being* better, but any progress was noted and enjoyed. Dale and I began to accept that getting better would never mean being cured.

Once a week, we had a parent activity with the kids at the day-treatment program that included dinner and a sort of workshop with the program therapist. Being with other parents who understood what we were going through was like a breath of fresh air. We had a sense of someone else "getting it" and bonded in our frustration, fear, and confusion. We also enjoyed a time of positive energy as we talked. We saw our children progress through the program and become more stable through the treatment they were receiving. How wonderful it was to have hope.

Then the leadership of the program changed about four months into Taylor's program, and Taylor received a new therapist. Taylor complained he didn't like him, but we encouraged him to give it time. Taylor wouldn't share specifics about what he didn't like; and we had to admit when we met with the therapist once a month that we were also bothered by his demeanor and attitude about our son. We were pleased with his program, but we were not pleased with his therapy. At all.

From the beginning, Taylor's new therapist didn't seem to understand him. He saw Taylor as a boy with dangerous, aggressive tendencies he believed would follow Taylor his whole life. He envisioned a future of detention and jail, no friends, alienation from family. A dead-end future was to be Taylor's destiny. He predicted Taylor would find himself in prison if we didn't do something drastic. Where was his data? Was this from information Taylor was giving him? To whom had he been speaking? Taylor was only five! Who can decide a child's future at five?

Dale and I weren't blind. We recognized there were many times Taylor's aggression was intense and sometimes destructive. That was one of the reasons we sought treatment for him in the first place. However, we also knew behaviors could be changed and that Taylor had already made progress. We knew there were solutions, supports, and things we could try. Despite this therapist's prognosis, we determined we would do whatever we could to help Taylor and believed in a bright future. We believed that eventually Taylor would learn to control himself and that with support he would be successful in anything he wanted to do.

After a few months of working with this therapist, we'd had enough and stopped therapy altogether. We had to be firm and brave in our decision, as we were told we couldn't fire the therapist and remain in day-treatment. It didn't matter; we were doing it anyway, and so we ran, almost literally, away from that therapist, knowing there was a better match for Taylor. We were fighting for his future. How could we allow this horrible, unfounded information follow Taylor? Oh, I wished the therapist would have seen Taylor later in life—independent, accomplished, well-spoken, poised, and blessed with a remarkable gift that drew people to him.

Dale and I knew Taylor's participation in the day-treatment program was a critical piece of his treatment. We were vocal about our therapist experience to the center's administration, and Taylor stayed in the program. From then on, we were careful to ensure a better match between our family and those working with us. Taylor graduated after participating in the program for almost a year. It was a perfect start for what would be years of treatment for Taylor's bipolar disorder.

After Taylor's graduation from his day-treatment program we were faced with the daunting task of finding a new child psychiatrist for the kids. We were thrilled when we connected with Dr. Flint. A charismatic and compassionate man, he worked magic with both Sarah and Taylor. He confidently diagnosed six-year-old Taylor with ADHD; Combined Impulsive and Hyperactive Type and went on to help us understand how we could help Taylor. Trusting Dr. Flint's recommendation to put Taylor on a stimulant medication, we saw immediate results. Once Taylor received the right medication, he was a different child. We were grateful Dr. Flint did a thorough medication evaluation. A diagnosis of ADHD made sense immediately.

It explained why Taylor always acted and reacted without a safety net. Impulsivity had been a problem for him since kindergarten, continued in first grade. What Taylor thought was funny was usually his impulsivity causing him to react inappropriately, often at the expense of others.

One Saturday morning I was playing with Taylor. After a while he wondered where Dale was in the hopes Dale could join us. I told him his dad was sleeping and Dale's eyes were tired and dry since he had worked late the night before. I teasingly suggested it would be helpful if Taylor spit in Dale's eye to help wake him up. I was kidding and thought Taylor would know that. However, he turned and marched into our bedroom in search of his dad. When I realized he was actually going to spit in Dale's face I desperately tried to stop him. But I was too late. Dale was awakened to Taylor hovering by the bed. Once Dale looked at him, Taylor spit directly in his dad's eye! Oh, I couldn't believe he had done it! I was laughing so hard I couldn't begin to give an explanation to Dale. Taylor saw me laughing and wondered why Dale was so angry with him.

Another time he dumped an entire water bottle over the top of a classmate's head and laughed himself silly while doing it. He had no ill will to the boy, he just thought of doing it and then did it.

He was curious about a peer's hearing aid. One day in class he walked by the boy, flicked the hearing aid out of his ear, and went to the corner to examine the expensive piece of equipment. He was adamant he needed to figure out how it worked.

He never understood why he got in trouble when he was only doing whatever popped into his head. He had no filter and no forethought. He seemed to always be loud, loud, and loud. He laughed loud, he talked loud, he cried and argued loud, and no matter what we tried to do, he could not seem to whisper, ever.

Given this new diagnosis, Dr. Flint prescribed Taylor a stimulant named Concerta, along with a more effective combination of mood stabilizers. As always, we were hesitant and protective of Taylor trying new meds, but we knew he wouldn't be able to progress unless we had medications which worked for him.

The first twelve hours after we gave him the Concerta, he developed facial and upper-body tics, which Dr. Flint had said might happen. Even knowing the tics were a possibility, it was disturbing to see my little boy struggle with this new side effect. We even videotaped Taylor that first day so we could show the doctor. But the following day he behaved like a new child. The tics were completely gone, and he said he felt good. We were hopeful we could manage the extremes of his behavior. The beautiful thing was, it didn't take away from who Taylor was, like so many other meds did. It just evened him out and made him more enjoyable to be around. Taylor, then six, said that before he went to Dr. Flint, he was a "bad kid," and after he saw Dr. Flint, he became a "good kid," and people wanted to be around him. The continual administration of Taylor's Concerta was important to him functioning at home and at school. As a family, we always knew when Taylor had missed his dose of Concerta because his behavior was so erratic.

BACK TO SCHOOL

One of my favorite childhood memories was playing school in the basement of my grandma's house. I loved the musty piles of leftover spelling and math worksheets she saved from the time she taught elementary school. As we created beautiful, colorful art projects out of crepe paper, string and old glue paste she regaled me with stories of teaching children of all ages how to read and write. Pretending to teach my own class I used her old, dusty textbooks and beginning readers, especially savoring her hardcover Dick and Jane books with their bright colors and simple stories. She told me it was hard work to be a teacher, and I believed her. Coming from a family of educators had taught me to value the art of teaching and I wanted to be a part of that profession too.

I was not surprised to find myself wanting to become an elementary school teacher. It felt like a natural career choice. Always interested in the learning process, I thrived in my education class in cognitive learning which opened a whole new way of thinking. Understanding and examining how motivation and intuition relate to learning was as fascinating as were the whys we sometimes find ourselves unable to learn certain concepts. Figuring out how to educate the mind was exciting.

Though I loved teaching my students, once I had Taylor, I never went back. I struggled at times wondering about the usefulness of my degrees in psychology and elementary education, but I later realized I used my degrees virtually every day as a mother and tried to keep up on my own learning as I could.

It was because of these experiences I assumed my interactions with my children's teachers and their schools would be positive. Sarah excelled in school from the beginning, especially in reading and writing, and had a positive attitude about school until the third grade. Her learning progressed, but her attitude changed. School became difficult for Sarah for a lot of reasons, but she was talented in many ways. Being an exceptional and voracious reader, she was curious about many things. She struggled with math around fourth grade and, as evidenced by her standardized testing, showed a math learning disability. We didn't even have to request her school services; they were set up automatically based on her scores. Our experience with Taylor's schooling was a difficult and painful polar opposite.

Getting help for Taylor became, hands down, one of the most difficult things I have ever had to do.

For Taylor, school became a daunting place where he didn't fit in. He fought to understand and to be understood. Before kindergarten even started, Taylor had a letter in a file from his psychologist stating he had been diagnosed with bipolar disorder. It stated the types of behavior and problems one might expect from Taylor because of his illness. It gave recommendations for helping him succeed in the school system. It was a terrific letter, informative and precise. I thought I had it covered. I wanted to be proactive. Dale and I decided it would be best that the staff at the school know of his illness, so we could all work together to help him. I don't think anyone ever looked at the letter or understood what it said as to the implications of Taylor's illness.

Kindergarten wasn't too bad because Taylor had an excellent teacher who kept him engaged. He was smart and inquisitive, so he kept himself busy. But there were problems with his impulsiveness and not respecting other kids' body space. Sometimes he would refuse to clean up his materials and seemed not to mind the consequence of a timeout. He would grab crayons from other kids and blurt out answers when they were in groups. But kindergarten was forgiving. He learned what he needed to learn. We hoped the problems he had would improve with maturity and additional support.

From kindergarten through fourth grade Taylor didn't have any friends. None at all. He didn't seem to mind as much at recess because he played group games like soccer or basketball or kept himself busy in his own world. But he became upset when he came home and shared how nobody ever picked him to be on their team. Even with us role-playing and teaching him how to get along with others, he didn't seem to understand how to interact without being too forceful. He would be unnecessarily physical and didn't know when to stop. He would want to talk about his most recent interests, like horses, even after the other kids grew bored of his endless facts. He wasn't being included in any neighborhood activities either, so there really wasn't any place Taylor could practice being a friend or how to play in a group. Carrying such a sense of loneliness he would withdraw when we would suggest outings in which he might invite a peer. He didn't know of anyone he could invite. He felt defeated.

As first grade started, Taylor had a hard time adjusting. His behavior was inconsistent, and he often acted angry with his schoolwork because he didn't always understand what was expected of him. He could be a great worker once he understood the instruction, but he didn't always get it. Overwhelmed, he didn't have the skills to resolve his frustrations. To distract himself he would lean across his neighbors' desks and play with their papers and pencils. He didn't seem to have the concept of "my space" versus "your space." He was loud, and he constantly interrupted others. These were the exact behaviors outlined in the letter we had given the school before kindergarten. But no one put the information together, and no one listened when I tried to tell them. Taylor's behaviors were exactly what would be expected of a first grader with bipolar disorder and ADHD. However, since he could read and write, there was no proactive emphasis on how his behavior affected his school day.

I didn't want to hover over Taylor or make his teacher uncomfortable with my over-involvement, but I wanted to help the school understand his diagnosis and his needs so he could be happier in school. I realized Taylor needed some formal school services to give his day the structure he needed to behave and learn. I had attended a parent support group that talked about Section 504 plans or special education with an individualized education plan, or IEP, for kids with disabilities. The school was required to provide Taylor with specific accommodations or services if his bipolar disorder and ADHD were keeping him or other students from being able to learn. We talked to his teacher whenever there was an incident, and she agreed she needed more help with Taylor. I knew from experience that until we resolved the behavior and learning issues with Taylor, he would not be able to progress at school. I knew there must be a solution somewhere for Taylor to get help; I just couldn't figure out what it was.

Thankfully, I connected with an advocacy organization for children with mental illness and they assigned an experienced parent advocate to help me navigate the school system. She listened for hours about my frustration and my thoughts on how to get the school to take me seriously. Her empathy, expertise and commitment to both me and Taylor was key in keeping me focused amidst the confusion of the school system. She told me one of the best and least threatening ways to communicate with the school was through letters, so I became a letter-writing mom. When Taylor got suspended in first grade for hitting another student, I wrote a letter to the principal asking for a meeting. In Taylor's mind he'd hit the kid because the other kid butted in front of him in line. The unexpected suspension embarrassed me, and I was unsure of what would happen next.

I decided the situation would serve a useful purpose to help Taylor understand boundaries and the importance of not hurting others. The principal shared that Taylor had had other incidents on the playground where he'd acted rough with other students and didn't think he was in the wrong. I explained that due to Taylor's bipolar disorder and ADHD, he was prone to be impulsive and not understand the reciprocity of interacting with other students, but the principal inferred Taylor was just being naughty and willful. She said Taylor could converse about these incidents in such a way that she knew he was intentionally causing problems.

She used one of Taylor's greatest strengths against him. Taylor has always had superior verbal ability, using big words and being described as a little professor. These were the skills Taylor used as he spoke to the principal about his behavior. He may have been able to talk about the incident, but he didn't always understand the implications of what he was saying. Dale, Taylor's therapist and I spent huge amounts of time trying to teach Taylor what was appropriate when being with others. Taylor knew exactly how to parrot back what we had said. The problem was he didn't really know how to implement it, and now he would be the one to pay the price.

First grade ended with an unhappy boy, a frustrated teacher, a dug-in principal, two desperate parents, and no supportive services.

The summer before second grade, Taylor suffered a significant mental health setback and was in outpatient day-treatment five days a week. However, once school started, I wanted him to have some time in his school classroom with the other students so he would be considered as part of the class. I got special permission for him to attend half-day at the elementary school three days a week. I tried to convey to the school team that Taylor being in day-treatment was a big deal; it emphasized that his illnesses truly did affect his whole life, including his time at school. With the standard for admission into day-treatment quite high, it was clear he really did have a severe mental illness.

I offered to have Taylor's therapist come to a school meeting to give a training on bipolar disorder and ADHD, and how it impacted Taylor, but the school, including his teacher, said they knew all they needed to know from Taylor's file. When I asked to see the file, I was told it was confidential. I wrote another letter asking the school to consider him a student-at-risk and to have him tested for special education services. I was told no. The school considered him to be like any other second grader. How many other second graders had spent part of the summer in a psychiatric hospital?

I wrote another letter as I pressured the school to take actual data regarding Taylor's behavior both in the classroom and on the playground. With this data I hoped to have tangible and objective information about Taylor's behavior. Then when we met with the school team we would be looking at and discussing the same concerns. At first, they wouldn't gather any data, but then they assigned a parent volunteer to watch him on the playground during recess. This volunteer had not been trained to know how to gather data or what behaviors relating to bipolar disorder might look like. After only a few days the school reported to me Taylor was, again, like any other second grader at recess, going from play area to play area. If I had known about the conclusion of the data, and if Taylor had been questioned as to his behavior on the playground, it would have been obvious that Taylor's play was not that of a typical second grader. According to Taylor, the reason he moved from play area to play area was because he perceived other kids were trying to hurt or kill him, and that had become his strategy for keeping safe. He was frightened at recess but believed there was no one he could trust to talk about his fears, not even us. I unknowingly sent him off to school each day fearing for his own safety. Was this the play of a typical second grader?

The teacher said Taylor had absolutely no problems in the classroom. How could this be? Was this the same kid we saw? The school acted as if the child we described with his mental illness and difficulties outside of school was not the same child who got dropped off every day at 8:30 a.m. I told the school it was as if, according to them, Taylor would shed his bipolar self and hide it behind a bush and enter the school to act like any other kid. He would then stop after school and pick up his bipolar self and go merrily on his way home, so we would be the only people who saw or dealt with his illness.

It seemed incredible, and yet the person who suffered most was Taylor. When pressed, his teacher did consider him to be unwilling to make efforts on his work. The work samples I gathered clearly showed that Taylor's unwillingness to work or do quality work was directly related to his mood swings. When he was in a depressive state, his work was sloppy and incomplete. When in a manic state, he would be more productive and complete his assignments, but in a hurry. When manic he would be loud, impulsive, and have pressured speech, often talking as if he were compelled to get information out faster than his mouth and mind could keep pace. Did they not recognize this?

Suddenly I realized that what was lacking was a knowledge of what bipolar disorder was and how it could affect Taylor, or any student in school. I didn't believe the teacher had the information she needed to see Taylor's work in a truthful light. So, another letter. I asked the principal again to have a training or information given to this teacher, but I was refused. The principal said Taylor showed no evidence of having a disability. Unfortunately, she acted as the gatekeeper of all services. She held all power and wielded it freely.

I continued advocating for Taylor throughout second grade, but nothing came of it. He finished second grade without any positive experiences. There was no meeting of the minds, but Taylor did learn most of what was taught. It was maddening. By the end of the year, I had developed a reputation as a problem parent and experienced increasing hostility from the principal and Taylor's teachers.

But I wasn't going to go away and just let things happen. Not only were Taylor's social skills an overwhelming disability for him, but he had begun to fall behind in his math and science. His IQ scores predicted him capable of performing at a higher level. What was happening? I began reading everything I could get my hands on about special education and disabilities and ways Taylor's learning problems would affect him in school.

If necessary, I would be the parent who marched alone in front of the school each day with a picket sign demanding an education for my son. I vowed I would not go away, and I would not back down until Taylor received the services to which he was entitled.

I kept going back to my experience in education. Why did Taylor's teachers not care to understand him, to know why he learned and acted as he did? Where was the steadfast commitment to help a child who had been struggling for three years to be successful within the school environment? Where was the appreciation of his innate gifts and talents? What would they lose if they recognized his challenges and provided the services he needed? I tried to relate to them on the commonalities we shared as teachers, but that seemed to make things worse. Whenever I brought up the fact I had been a former elementary school teacher, I would be told that being the mom of a student wasn't the same as being the teacher of a student. Of course. But couldn't they see I could relate and even empathize with them due to my background? It had become a no-win situation that only hurt Taylor, and I didn't know how to resolve it. Sometimes I cried out of frustration, but I would not give up.

The principal placed Taylor with a male teacher for third grade. This proved to be a good thing because Taylor developed a positive relationship with this teacher. At back-to-school night, I approached his teacher and told him of Taylor's illness and how it might impact him in school. I asked his teacher if he knew anything about bipolar disorder. He said he did not. I asked if he would like to have information about the illness, and he said he would. Wow, finally. This was literally the first time in nearly four years that someone wanted to know more. I was thrilled to get him basic information about bipolar disorder, ADHD, and how Taylor might perform in the classroom. He got back with me a few days later, asking insightful questions and was positive about Taylor as a student.

I think this particular teacher had a connection with Taylor because he might have struggled with being different in school as well. He had empathy for Taylor. Taylor enjoyed talking to his teacher and was comfortable going to him for help. This proved to be especially helpful as it was during this time Taylor started to show significant signs of being unable to understand math. His math struggles to that point had been easily brushed aside when compared to his behavior issues, but he had always fallen behind in math and found it to be extremely frustrating. Taylor's teacher started to keep track of Taylor's math work and tried to supplement his learning with extra instruction.

Unfortunately, Taylor still struggled with the behaviors he had exhibited in previous years. His school performance was erratic. According to my mood charting, Taylor cycled about every eight days. During this time, Taylor began to report a lot of bullying by two boys in his class, Jesse and Derek. He said they were bullying him separately, and he couldn't get away from them. He had reported them to the teacher, and the playground aide, but the kids kept giving him a hard time in line, at recess, and when walking the halls. Taylor came home and told us about the bullying. We then relayed this information to the principal, but she said they didn't see anything going on, so they would just wait and see what happened. I told her this was unacceptable from a school that claimed zero-tolerance for bullying. She said there was no evidence of Taylor's claims. Taylor became more and more scared about these boys and felt threatened throughout the day. This, of course, only intensified his symptoms. Finally, he shared that he believed Jesse was going to kill him at school. When I asked Taylor how we could help him feel safe, he said he wanted a personal appointment with the principal.

The principal was impatient as we sat down in her office. She asked Taylor to explain the bullying and when it happened. She tried to point out that perhaps his perception was flawed. She told Taylor she had already called both boys into her office and both denied they were bullying Taylor.

When Taylor heard this, he became upset. "You don't understand. They are going to kill me. They told me they would kill me." he said.

"Taylor, what do you want me to do?" the principal asked.

"You need to make both Jesse and Derek go to another school. You can choose which one, but it has to be away from here," he said. His voice was shaky, and his face flushed. He looked her directly in the eye and whispered, "That is the only way I will be safe."

Taylor believed she would really do it. When she said she couldn't, he became visibly deflated. He looked so hopeless and mumbled he would have to figure out a way to protect himself if she wouldn't help him. She curtly dismissed us and said she'd keep an eye on things. Concerned about his emotional state, I let him come home for a while.

Later, when we returned to school and checked in at the office, the principal called me into her office. She stated she had been disturbed about the meeting with Taylor because she could see he really believed he was in danger and he really believed she had the power to remove the boys from the school. She now realized how this thinking affected Taylor socially and academically. To my relief, she suggested he have a temporary IEP put into place immediately. She even had one filled out on her desk.

What a turn of events. Here was the service plan for which I had worked tirelessly for almost four years, and now after only one conversation with Taylor she discerned he required an IEP? She told me she had written a letter to the school district immediately after her meeting with Taylor. In her letter she stated her concerns about Taylor's potential for violence, his paranoia, the possible need for a classroom aide, and she'd requested a special staffing of his case. It seemed she was suddenly concerned about something that had been in front of her for four years. I quickly signed the forms and thoughtfully went on my way, amazed that my son had to go to the edge of hysteria for someone to notice he had strong moods, inappropriate perceptions, distractibility, and an intense demeanor—all direct symptoms of bipolar disorder and ADHD.

Fourth grade was when the rubber met the road for me as Taylor's advocate. I had gone to Phoenix to attend a special education law conference to learn more about how to more effectively advocate. I read special education law and became familiar with the Supreme Court cases dealing with similar issues. I attended community workshops, read articles and blogs online, and became thoroughly educated on the issues for kids with bipolar disorder, ADHD, and math learning disabilities. It was a new day; and if I was going to fight for my son, I would have to learn the language of the school. When fourth grade began, they didn't know what hit them.

Once, in a school meeting, Taylor's principal stopped the conversation and said, "Karen, you are the most highly functioning bipolar person I know." Was that a compliment or an insult? From that point on, the sting of stigma followed me in almost all our interactions.

Taylor's fourth grade teacher was experienced and kind. Once she understood that my issue was not with her and I would be there to support her in teaching Taylor, we had no problems with each other. Both the principal and special education teacher, on the other hand, seemed to return to the stance of discounting my son and his need for services. Understanding their resistance to services for Taylor was a mystery to me. Did they just dislike him? I knew they disliked working with me. It was as if I were playing tug-a-war trying to inch over the line that would finally help the IEP team see the whole picture of how we could all work together to make Taylor's school experience productive despite his disability.

I wrote letter after letter, asking for team meetings to talk about IEP goals, to follow up with accommodations not being made in the classroom, and to clarify my understanding of the team's position on some of the services we were requesting. I provided well established research on the benefits of the behavioral supports and accommodations Taylor needed to be successful. I asked for and analyzed data about Taylor's performance in school. I was a force to be reckoned with. When the school didn't agree or didn't follow up on what they had promised, I went to the district. Not in anger; I was just done waiting to see what would unfold if we didn't do something for Taylor. Waiting had gotten him four years of nothing. It was a rough year for me, but for Taylor it was a great year because by the end of the year his plan was comprehensive and complete, and he finally got the help he needed. Increased math and social skill instruction and adjustments to how he was instructed when he was cycling with his bipolar disorder were services and accommodations that were well received by Taylor and helpful to his overall school experience. Best yet, Taylor made a friend, his first ever, and didn't feel bullied anymore. He especially progressed in math, catching up for a lot of lost instruction, and did an outstanding job in every other way. He was, for the first time, happy to be in school, and I was elated.

The following year a new principal came to the school. I was anxious because I could only guess what she had heard about me. There was no love lost between me and the previous team; in fact, the special education teacher told a friend of mine she had wanted to transfer schools partly because she couldn't stand to work with me anymore. With much trepidation, I set up a meeting between me, the new principal, and new vice principal before the school year began.

Taylor now had a thick file, undoubtedly filled with my letters and other paper trails. I introduced myself and told them about my Taylor and what a wonderful kid he was. To my relief, not a word was said about the past. We were given a clean slate, and they were on Taylor's side. I hardly knew how to react. It was as if I had received a stay of execution and now, I could go back to being Taylor's mom.

We still had a hiccup here and there as Taylor moved through school, and I still wrote letters and stayed on top of his IEP plan and the type of services he needed. But the issues were small, and most of his teachers were anxious to know more about his illnesses and what they could do for him. Wonderfully, Taylor eventually learned to be his own advocate. He turned out to be conscientious, hardworking, honest, academically inclined, willing to try hard things, ask for help if he needed it, personable, dependable, and an all-around good student. He never used his disability as an excuse or a way to gain sympathy. Once he had the support he needed, his natural abilities could shine. As Taylor navigated his way through junior and high school, he became accomplished with some pretty impressive goals in academics, leadership, and debate.

On his high school graduation day, as they called his name and he walked across the stage, I was so proud, not only of what he had accomplished, but of myself. I had learned so much and was now helping other parents of children with mental illness work with the schools. I had also graduated from the world of special education and could let go of the responsibility that had weighed so heavily upon me.

After the ceremony, Taylor looked for us in the crowd, and when he found us, I asked for a hug. He gave me a good, long hug and said, "We did it, Mom. We did it."

911 EMERGENCY

Although we managed with things like behavior charts, chores, consistency, and expectations, sometimes the reality of the disorder would take over and knock us upside the head. We knew it was important to prepare what to do in the case of a fire or earthquake or other natural disaster. What we didn't think about was the need to have a crisis plan revolving around our family's mental health.

We had one rule: you could not harm yourself, another person, or property. We figured that about covered everything. We had the structure we needed to teach the kids about boundaries and consequences. Sometimes the concept of harm would be sketchy to the kids when they were younger. But with time and maturity, this one rule helped to set a standard we all could live with.

Taylor, at age nine, was the first to take our rule to the next level. He had been consistently cycling for about three weeks. He swung from one emotional state to another in a split second. Dale had often been working overtime, not getting home until after 11:00 p.m. Day after day it was just me and the kids and we were all getting sick of each other.

It had already been a particularly long day with Taylor for me. Taylor wanted to be the center of attention and went rapidly from one activity to another. He was loud and intense, short tempered, and he and I had already had two physical bouts with me restraining him and putting him in his room.

Getting him to his room was what finally set him off. As I forcibly moved him down the hall to his bedroom, he was breathing heavily through his teeth, spit spraying in the air. Beads of sweat had formed on his forehead, and his face glowed cherry red. He pounded on his door and walls. He swore and yelled at me and threatened to hurt all of us. He made no attempt to get out of his room to actually do anything, but I inherently knew something felt different. I didn't know what he would do, as he had never been that bad before. As his raging went past the one-hour mark, I got the sinking feeling it was only a matter of time until he became totally unglued. I thought of what Dale and I had informally discussed we would do if Taylor got violent. We created a crisis plan with basic steps to take if his behavior was out of control. I decided this might be the time I put our plan into action. I just had to have the courage to follow it through.

I first needed to protect Alex and Sarah. They, of course, usually heard all the ruckus and, being a part of our home, weren't often surprised by it. But this time it seemed different for them too. Taylor had upped the ante with his threats, so I asked Sarah to take Alex downstairs to her room and, if necessary, lock the door. They were instructed to stay there and not come upstairs. I didn't want them to hear any more of his threats or rantings; it wasn't fair to them. This scared them because they didn't know what would happen, but they knew to stay put. They were left with the job of comforting each other. They barricaded themselves with some furniture behind the door and tried to distract themselves. At ages five and thirteen, they were left to care for themselves in a situation where we were all running blind.

As I went to Taylor's room and knocked on his door, I said a quick prayer I would be calm and sensitive to his emotional state. He let me open the door, but he kept shouting angry, mean, and vulgar words at me and about me. He said he wanted to kill me and was rather specific about how that would come about. I couldn't calm him down. I backed out of his doorway but left the door ajar. I stood outside his door and I modeled deep breathing until I almost hyperventilated.

When nothing seemed to work, I left him, went to my room, and shut my door, but he continued to yell threats. I could hear him through the walls, incoherently ranting to himself. I thought he would eventually tire out. I sat in my room preparing myself for anything and trying to remain calm. I became rather offended at the things he said and irritated we were having to listen to him at all. I just wanted him to stop and sleep it off.

After a time, something switched for Taylor, and instead of threatening to kill me, he said he wanted to kill himself. He rambled on, alternating between crying and yelling.

I opened his door, but kept my distance. He was laying on his back on his bed with tears streaming down his cheeks. I couldn't get a clear answer from him about his specific intentions. I slowly moved a little closer to his bed and looked him in the eyes. It was as if he wasn't there, His pupils were huge and black. He seemed to be functioning from another emotional place. That scared me because I didn't know how to connect with him.

"Taylor, it's mom. Is there something you'd like me to do for you?" I said.

Nothing. He just continued to moan, and talk and sometimes yell about wanting to die. He sounded like he would really hurt himself or one of us. I knew it was time to implement the next step in our safety and crisis plan Dale and I had discussed only in theory. I took a deep breath and held the phone in my hand. The reality was it was going to be up to me. Dale was at work and could not be contacted. When we made the crisis plan, we never considered another person as back-up for me if Dale wasn't home. We were shortsighted and didn't really want to believe a crisis in which I would need outside help would occur. I had to trust myself. So, truly concerned for all our safety, I decided to call the police.

Calling in the police was a big risk for me. I had no idea how they would treat a nine-year-old with bipolar disorder. I knew he wouldn't go to jail, but I didn't know what other options they had. I worried about scaring Sarah and Alex even more, so I went downstairs and told them what I was doing and that the police would help Taylor to be safe and calm down. They were so scared they only stared, wide-eyed, as I explained I would get someone to take care of them. I hoped it would turn out that way. I called my friend who also had a child with mental illness and asked her to come get Sarah and Alex. She said she would come right away. At least I could protect the other kids. I could put the worry about caring for them away at least for the short term.

I was surprised I was so calm when I called 911. I guess I knew I had to be in charge and I could fall apart later.

"My son is nine years old and he has bipolar disorder," I told the dispatcher. "He is saying he wants to kill himself. Calling 911 is part of our safety plan."

The dispatcher asked my name and address. She asked if Taylor was hurt or bleeding. I responded he was not. The dispatcher asked a lot of questions about Taylor's danger level and if he had any weapons. That question seemed so bizarre. I laughed loudly.

"His room is full of potential weapons. He collects rocks, he has heavy toys and even the end of his hangers can be sharp," I said. "If he wanted to hurt himself, he could." She didn't think it was a funny question, so I made myself stop laughing right away.

I told her, "I need an officer to come and take Taylor to a hospital since I can't safely drive him myself. Please don't have the lights or sirens on, so it won't scare him. Please, I need you to come right away." Then I hung up.

I went into Taylor's room, and tried to sit next to him on his bed. He didn't even flinch when I touched him. He seemed to be very disoriented. He was still yelling on and off. I hoped Sarah and Alex couldn't hear what he was saying. Making sure to speak calmly and slowly, I explained how I had called someone, so we could get him to the doctor. I didn't know if he heard me or not.

Two big, burly city policemen came to my door. I didn't know what they were expecting, but they heard Taylor moaning and hysterically crying as soon as they came in the house. I briefly told them what had happened, that my two other children were safe downstairs, and that our focus would be on Taylor only. By now

Taylor was crying loudly and begging me to kill him so he could stop feeling so bad. I will never forget the sound of his pleading to die. It broke my heart and made my head spin to be so powerless.

While the policemen tried to calm him down, I went into my other-world state, thinking of what I needed to do. I became eerily efficient as I distanced myself from Taylor's misery. I gathered his medications in a big plastic bag, got the insurance and psychiatrist information, and kept checking in with Taylor so he knew what we were doing for him. I called Dale and left a message letting him know where he could find Sarah and Alex and that I was taking Taylor to the hospital. We told Taylor he would be riding in the police car, not as a punishment, but because I needed to drive separately. This would be the safest way for him to get to the hospital. I don't know if Taylor understood, but he didn't fight or argue. At the last minute I asked him if he had anything, he wanted to bring to the hospital that might comfort him. He wanted to bring Hector, his stuffed animal. My last picture of him was as my frightened little boy walking beside a burly policeman with Hector tucked under his arm. The whole situation felt surreal.

At the hospital, we went through the long process of getting mental health crisis triage. Hospital staff came and went, asking the same questions, but not offering any answers.

I wanted to yell at the hospital staff, "You may see this every day, but this is my little boy! Stop staring at us."

We just waited and waited, wondering if something was going to happen. The ordeal lasted into the early hours of the morning. In the end, Taylor recovered enough that he could go home. He was too exhausted to be a threat to himself or anyone else. For several days, he seemed to be emotionally and physically spent. Me too. In fact, everyone in our home seemed to be in a bit of shock to realize how destructive bipolar disorder could be.

Later, after years of bipolar cycling with Taylor, I came to realize that whenever he threatened to kill me, he would always progress to a point where he threatened to kill himself. He didn't know how to directly express his suicidal thoughts until he went through all the depths of emotion and ended up with what he thought was a final solution—to kill himself and stop feeling so overwhelmed and so bad. At that age he didn't know "dead" meant dead forever.

We decided to have comprehensive neuropsychological testing to better assess Taylor's emotional and cognitive functioning. The extensive testing was through the day-treatment program, and we normally wouldn't have been able to afford it. We were looking forward to getting the results to see if we could better understand his illness. When we met with the neuropsychologist and got the results, I remember reading them and thinking, "Now what?" "What does this information mean?" I understood that the results showed he had a high IQ; we already knew that. Of significance was the difference between Taylor's verbal IQ and his performance IQ—a full 43 points. He was so verbally advanced his whole world revolved around language; other skills like visual, spatial, and math were low. We came to understand we needed to set up his world around his verbal skills to help him be successful, and work on his areas of weakness to support his understanding. Interpersonal skills were a challenge for him as he didn't understand body language or things like sarcasm. He was a concrete learner and took what you said literally. The other results indicated a range of difficulties Taylor would have as a result of his illness, some of them severe. A nonverbal learning disability, which I had never heard of, answered some of our "Why does he do this?" questions.

Some of the projective tests were alarming regarding Taylor's tendency toward violence. Even with the aggression we had at home, I never considered Taylor to have the potential to hurt himself or others as he grew up. I was living in the here and now. To me the future seemed too hard to visualize how an older Taylor could be so impacted by his bipolar disorder. The doctor's explanations gave me no comfort or even understanding of what the test was saying. I knew Taylor needed powerful behavioral skills to help manage his anger, but was he doomed to a truly violent life? We just could not see that being a reality. They snatched away the hope that I held on to every time I had to deal with Taylor when he was ill. In my heart I wondered "How can I parent this child?" I then recognized that this represented only one person's subjective opinion and there could be other explanations and opinions from professionals who worked with Taylor. They didn't know him; they had only spent a few hours with him. Were any of these recommendations right for Taylor? We weren't even sure if we understood what the recommendations were.

After receiving the test results, Dale and I came home and were sitting in the car in front of the house. I was stunned. We were drained by the parental responsibility weighing heavily upon us. We remained quiet for a few minutes. Then Dale began to cry and with great compassion said, "He is just a boy, and he isn't broken. He came here with everything he needs, and we don't have to fix him and change what his plan is. It is not up to us."

He continued. "Who is to say that if we do this intervention it won't take away some of the great gifts he has? We don't want to mute who he is."

This insight was powerful. Taylor wasn't broken; he was only a child. Our job was to help him maximize his strengths, to build him up. We realized we probably wouldn't know until he got older if we were making the right decision, but the realization that it didn't have to be fixed stayed with us as we faced the many decisions of what to do on behalf of the kids. We needed to parent with confidence and have faith we would know what we needed to do. Ultimately, we had to have faith in who and what Taylor would become.

RAGING ENERGY

Taylor had always dreamed of owning a horse. At age two he could name breeds of ten horses from a book he always kept at his side. We have a picture of him at almost three, on top of his grandpa's horse in an oversized cowboy hat, gloves, and boots, with a huge smile on his face as he holds the reins. He even walked with the lopsided gait of a cowboy as he wore his cowboy boots, sometimes to bed.

Horses were a part of who Taylor was from as long as any of us can remember. He got to spend some time at Dale's parents' house helping Grandpa feed and sometimes groom the horses. Occasionally, Taylor would go for a ride with Dale on a Saturday afternoon. He was not fearful at all. He had many books on horses, and as he got older, he would regale us with every fact about horses imaginable. Sometimes he would stand outside the pasture and watch the horses for hours.

When Taylor was eight, he was accepted into an early onset bipolar disorder study at the National Institutes of Mental Health (NIMH). I had been searching the Internet for different treatments and researching childhood bipolar disorder, when I found myself on the NIMH website. The study was for children and adolescents who had either been diagnosed with bipolar disorder or showed symptoms of the illness. The study looked at the differences between children with bipolar disorder and those without it: was there a difference in how they thought, performed, processed information, dealt with stress, and how they interacted with others? We wanted to be a part of the study to see if we could get more cutting-edge information on Taylor's illness, and for the excitement of doing something unique with it. We felt very cool to be participating.

Dale, Taylor, and I were flown to NIMH in Bethesda, Maryland, where Taylor spent three days going through screening tests, IQ tests, computer tasks, and MRI scans. In the end he fit the category of "gold standard" bipolar disorder. I figured you couldn't get more bipolar than that. He matched the criteria for the long-term study, and they wanted him to take part in it. Taylor would visit NIMH four times the first year, then once a year thereafter until he turned twenty-five. He was excited, and we were thrilled to be a part of something that would add to the knowledge of bipolar disorder and hopefully effective treatments.

Taylor was motivated by more than just the intrinsic good feeling of helping generations of other children with bipolar disorder; he was going to get paid for his participation. He knew it may not have been a lot, but at age eight, it was a lot more than he could earn any other way. From the beginning Taylor told us how he would spend that money; he would buy himself a horse. Absolutely, for sure, no wavering. As Taylor participated in different testing tasks, including MRIs and other unusual tests, he did so without complaint. He knew that the more testing he did, the more money he would earn. All the members of his NIMH team knew of Taylor's goal to get a horse, and we all excitedly watched his savings account grow. The first year of the study, Taylor and I went to NIMH five times, and by the time he turned nine he had saved about $600.

Taylor talked to Dale about how to buy a horse, how much it cost to feed one, and what would be the best age of horse to buy. First, he thought he wanted a stallion, then he wanted a foal to hand raise himself. For a minute he thought of buying a pony but then realized he wanted to keep the horse for a long time, and at nine he would quickly outgrow a pony. After talking to Dale and to Grandpa, Taylor decided it would be a good idea to attend a local horse auction to see what types of horses were available and how much a horse would cost. Taylor, his dad, Grandpa, Alex, and I all went together on a late spring afternoon to see what we could see. We didn't expect to buy anything, especially because we didn't bring a truck and trailer.

Taylor was kind of quiet except when asking questions to his dad about particular horses he saw. He seemed drawn to sorrel or brown horses and ones that seemed to be relatively calm and well behaved. We sat in the auction area watching horses filter through, some sold, and others did not. Taylor kind of perked up when he saw a few mares with their new foals for sale, but Dale quickly let Taylor know, that combination was more work and money than he could manage by himself.

Among the last horses was a sorrel quarter horse/paint mare being sold for about $1000. Dale and Taylor both looked excitedly at one another. The mare was well behaved, obviously having been well trained. She had beautiful color and looked healthy and alert. Taylor wanted to bid on her. Dale stiffened and said under his breath to himself that we didn't come prepared to buy a horse. But he liked the mare too, so he told Taylor he could bid at $300. The bid quickly rose higher, and Taylor was so excited he bid at $500. Dale started getting squirmy not knowing how high the bidding would go. Taylor had permission to bid to $600, but that was the limit. He only had $600 to spend. It all happened so fast with Dale and Taylor whispering to each other. Dale looked paler and paler as each bid went by, and Taylor looked like he would jump out of his skin at the thought of buying this horse. He looked disappointed when the bidding stopped, and the auctioneer deferred to the horse's owner. The owner didn't think the bidding had progressed enough for her to get the price she needed, so she pulled the mare from the auction block.

Taylor kind of melted in his seat next to me. Dale and his dad briefly spoke, and Dale came and got right in front of Taylor and asked if he was sure he really wanted this horse. He did. Dale took a deep breath and went to approach the owner of the horse. We couldn't hear what they were saying, but Taylor kind of perked up when Dale pointed at him, and Taylor gave her a wave. After a while, Dale came back and told Taylor that if he wanted the horse, he could have her for $600. Taylor was thrilled. The owner didn't really want to sell her, but she needed money for her tuition at school and couldn't afford the upkeep. When Dale told her about Taylor wanting the horse and how he only had $600, she thought about it and agreed.

Taylor grinned from ear to ear. He approached the horse and vigorously stroked her neck and nose. As I looked at him, it seemed as if it were just him and the horse. We asked what he would call her, and he said Mary. From that moment on, Taylor formed a meaningful connection with something that would be an incredibly important part of his life.

Taylor spent as much of his free time as possible with Mary. He proudly groomed her and later got a secondhand kid's saddle. Dale shared with Taylor how important it was that Taylor knew he was solely responsible for taking care of Mary. Dale patiently began to take the time to show Taylor how to meet her needs. Teaching Taylor to put on the saddle alone took some extra time as he wasn't very tall and all the twists and turns of the leather straps proved to be a lot for him to remember. But once that was accomplished, Taylor sat tall and ready to ride, armed with the information he had amassed for years, enthusiasm for the adventure of riding, and love for Mary.

As he grew, Taylor became more confident and competent in taking Mary out by himself around the fields of his grandparents' house. He developed a friendship with Max, a neighbor down the street where Mary was kept. Max was two years younger than Taylor and just as devoted to horses. Taylor and Max would ride all day on a Saturday, racing each other, exploring, and touring the fairgrounds arena. Taylor bonded with Mary during the time they spent wandering. He was always disappointed when the summer drew to the end and he and Max had to return to school.

One time when he was suffering through a significant depression, I asked him what I could do to help him feel better.

"I want to be with Mary," he said, his voice barely over a whisper.

"Do you want to go right now?" I said.

With tears in his eyes he simply nodded. I drove him to the pasture and watched from the car as he slowly walked toward her. Mary walked to Taylor and stopped in front of him. He placed his arms around her neck, and snuggled his face in her coat. Then he stood very still. He stayed that way for a long time. I imagined he was talking to her, telling her about how sad he was inside. He started to

240

brush her over and over, as gentle as I had ever seen him be. We stayed there for a long time; I was in no hurry, and Taylor could have whatever amount of time he needed.

"Did that help you feel better?" I asked him when he finally got back into the car.

Looking over his shoulder at Mary he said, "Yes. Mary didn't even try to walk away. She held still for a long time."

"Do you think she could feel you were sad?" I said.

"I think so," he said.

After that incident, Taylor asked to visit Mary on days when he was especially sad. How grateful we were to know he had something to love unconditionally. Mary always had a place in Taylor's life well after he became an adult.

Slowly, over time, Taylor started to even out a little. His violent rages toward me and his vivid, graphic threats lessened as he began to internalize all the hours of treatment he received. It seemed he was much more receptive to the structure and boundaries we had established at home. He knew what to expect from us, and he knew what we expected from him. As he moved toward being ten and eleven, there began to be more peace in our home.

Taylor decided to have a stand-off with me in the dining room when I asked him to clear his dinner plate at the table. I knew I only had a literal split second to decide if this was a battle I wanted to fight. He clenched the edge of the table and shook his head vigorously.

241

"I don't want to miss my show. Why can't you do my plate?" he said aggressively.

"I did your plate for you last night," I answered. "It's your turn."

He started breathing through his teeth, growling, and shifting his weight back and forth. I made myself very still. Alex turned on the television in the other room. Taylor looked anxiously at me.

"Okay, I'll make a deal," he bargained. "Can I leave my plate and come back for it later?"

"No. It has to be done now," I said. I knew I was being firm, but sometimes it seemed Taylor got his way because I didn't want to deal with his temper. "No show until you take care of it."

He looked wary and almost confused. He looked at me, I think to see if I was serious. Then without explanation or reason, the situation of placing his plate in the dishwasher became the most important and contentious topic to argue in the world to Taylor. For the next fifteen minutes he ranted about the unfairness of him having to live in a home that requires anything of him, the stupidity of parents, and his absolute superiority over all adults in his life. It was amazing to hear.

From experience, I knew as long as he was not violent I would do best to sit in a chair and hear him out. Even if tempted, I would not argue back. As he slowed down, I reminded him he was missing most of his show and if he cleared his plate, he could watch the rest. He paused and then as if remembering why we were there grabbed his

242

plate and roughly put it in the dishwasher. He stormed out of the room.

I knew it was best to not acknowledge the incident until later. The last thing I said to him before turning out his light for bed was "Thanks for doing the plate." He heard me but didn't answer. That simple situation could have been an hours long disaster. Maybe in another home the issue would have not even been an issue. But for us, that was huge progress.

Taylor and Sarah still couldn't seem to manage any sort of interaction, and we still would rarely leave them alone together. We were hyper-vigilant in monitoring them. Sarah would try to resolve a situation by continually tattling, and Taylor got sneakier about bothering her. Sometimes it seemed like I spent most of my day playing referee, judge, and jury. But it was rewarding at the end of the day to know life was basically as under control as possible, and that everyone was happy for the most part.

Taylor started cycling early in April when he was eleven; he was hyper, loud, and pinpoint focused, making elaborate plans for projects that took up all his time. I didn't mind his mania anymore and enjoyed seeing him engaged in activities outside his isolated room. I would also, on occasion, receive a quick, coveted hug.

The thing I hated about mania was what came after. With each meteoric rise came a hard fall. No exceptions. Depression would always follow, and it impacted everyone. Taylor cycled faster than either Sarah or me, so I had to keep track of his moods carefully to try to minimize the effects. But we had enjoyed a long period of relative calm with Taylor, and I wasn't expecting anything extraordinary. Was I wrong?

Unlike Taylor's previous major crises, I thought I didn't need to rely on our old crisis plan. I had turned a little cocky with the many successful incidents I had been able to deescalate and thought I didn't need to follow the plan. It was a mistake I will forever regret.

Sarah, Taylor, Alex and I attended a family wedding at a nice reception center. I knew I would want to stay for a while and visit with family, and I knew the kids would be bored, so I had them pack their backpacks with books and things to do while they were waiting for me.

Early on, Taylor found a quiet place away from the reception and spent at least an hour there reading. But then he wanted to go and became angry with how much time I was spending with my extended family. I told him I would wrap it up, but he got mad and stomped off. When I finally gathered the kids to go to the car, Taylor was steaming. Dale was at work and not able to help; he was not even accessible by phone.

Taylor never seemed to learn how to deal with his anger once it became intense. He could go zero to sixty in the blink of an eye. Before we even got to the parking garage, Taylor started yelling at me. He called me names, called my family names, and ranted about how stupid we were. We had heard these tirades so many times we weren't really paying attention to his meltdown. I was focused on getting to the car, so we could get home where Taylor could calm down. Once he got to the car, I tried to reason with him, but he was livid. Taylor sat in the middle seat of the van and started hitting and kicking both the middle and the front seat. He thrashed and turned his body to kick the long side windows along both sides of the van. He was yelling vile threats about me, and others. Sarah and Alex moved to the back seat of the van to get as far away from him as possible, but we were still all trapped with him in a very tight space. While this was not the first time we had been temporarily stuck with Taylor in a van when he was raging, he had been much younger and much smaller. This was very different.

My happy-go-lucky brother Steve suddenly opened the door of the van and began teasing me about leaving the party so soon. He looked to the back of the van and stopped talking so quickly it seemed as if he swallowed his words. Taylor had abruptly tried to put the lid on his emotions as soon as Steve showed up, but it hadn't worked. Sarah and Alex were mute, frightened about what might happen. With as much calm and urgency as I could muster, I asked Steve to please shut the door and leave me to handle the situation. He started to object, but I implored him with my eyes to please let it be. Although he did not understand the magnitude of the situation, he quietly closed the door and walked away.

As soon as Steve was out of sight, Taylor exploded. It was scary to realize the three of us were trapped in the van at the mercy of his volatile tantrum and that there wasn't anyone who could help us. My mind didn't consider other options than staying together in the van. I tried to wait it out but realized Taylor would probably be best off at home, in his own environment. I didn't interact with him any more than necessary and drove home praying this would turn out better than it felt it was going to. Alex and Sarah huddled together in the backseat, absolutely silent, with Sarah looking at me in the rearview mirror. I could say nothing for fear I would upset Taylor further. Taylor continued to talk, mutter and yell to himself or maybe to me. I didn't answer him.

When we got home, I asked the kids to put their bikes in the shed. Sarah and Alex did as I asked. Taylor got out of the car, went directly to the backyard, and started pacing along the back fence, mumbling to himself. After a few minutes he picked up a large piece of firewood and went to hitting the trunks of the trees.

I was grateful to have Taylor break away for a minute so I could speak to Sarah and Alex.

Sarah said "Mom! He is totally crazy. What is his deal?"

"You're right," I replied. "I don't know what is wrong with him, but I'll take care of it. I want you two to stay together."

I knelt down and gave Alex a hug, "Alex, Sarah is in charge. I will let you know if something happens, okay. But you are not to go anywhere. Stay in the house."

I stood at the edge of the yard watching Taylor get more and more agitated. I hadn't seen him act so frazzled before. His behavior was unnerving. I stayed near the side of the house where I could see him, but I decided it was best not to physically approach or speak to him at length. The only thing I said to him was not to break anything, and please to calm down. That made it worse.

"Kill, kill, kill," Taylor said as he paced the length of the yard in a threatening way.

In a firm voice I said, "Taylor, I need you to stop saying that. I need you to calm down."

That went on for at least ten minutes. Suddenly he diverted over to the barbecue and, with its full tank of propane, picked it up, and threw it across the fire pit and onto the grass. I knew the barbecue had to be heavy, and he wasn't very big, but it seemed like it took very little effort. Where had he gotten that kind of strength? I was stunned and scared and recognized he was way out of control and could be a source of harm to himself or me.

Taylor resumed his now frantic pacing. "Kill, kill, kill." However, now he began listing specific people he wanted to kill. I was top on his list.

I told myself I needed to start the crisis plan and call the police. As I left the yard through the garage, I was apprehensive about leaving him alone in the backyard. I told him I was going to get help because he was obviously out of control. I began debating calling the police. I didn't want the neighbors to see the police come to the house because I was embarrassed for Taylor and our family. I didn't want people questioning whether I had done the right thing by going so far as to call the police. I didn't want to be the subject of discussion in the neighborhood. I didn't want to deal with it on that level, but I knew I needed help. I figured I could think of an acceptable alternative.

Since Dale wasn't at home, I needed a male presence to calm Taylor down, someone who could intimidate him. Obviously, Taylor wasn't scared of me and I instinctively knew I had little or no control at that moment.

But who? I hadn't planned any of this, and I didn't know who would want to help, and whom I could trust. I first called a friend who had crisis experience with her son who had mental illness. I told her I wondered if she and her husband were available to drop by and help with Taylor. I minimized the problem, indicating that if they were busy it was okay, and I'd talk to her later. If I'd have told her the real situation, they would have come right over, but I didn't want to interrupt their Saturday. She could tell by my voice something was significantly wrong and said they could change their plans. Embarrassed she would find out I couldn't control Taylor, I again minimized the situation and got off the phone without letting her know how much I needed help.

I then thought of calling the neighbor over our back fence. Since we'd lived in our home for years, I assumed he had undoubtedly heard some of Taylor's meltdowns and would understand and come over. When I called him, he said he would be right there. I didn't convey the urgency to him. Reassured help was coming, I figured I had a good enough plan in place.

Relived I had figured out a solution to avoid a call to the police I went to face Taylor. I had been gone for about ten minutes. That was ten minutes too long. For a moment I was confused when I couldn't see him in the yard. I found him sitting on the ground next to our tree with a jump rope knotted around his neck. He was pulling on each end of the rope as hard as he could, his face turning blue, and he had a wild-eyed look.

How could I have been so stupid? I drew in a quick breath and assessed the situation. I prayed for guidance to know how to help him.

I needed strength. I walked calmly to him and softly called his name to get him to look at me. I knew to be gentle and aware of his potential not only to hurt himself further but to lash out and hurt me. He was like a wounded animal, making soft grunting noises. He vacantly continued to pull on the rope, his hands shaking with the effort. I told him exactly what I was going to do. I began to take the rope off his neck. He struggled against my hands as I tried to untangle it, and his face got bluer. I had to become more forceful as I moved his hands aside and loosened the rope. I was sickened when I realized I had to tighten the rope for a brief second to get the last knot away from his throat. Finally, he loosened his grip and went kind of limp.

Once the rope was off, his face started to color again. I slowly unraveled the rope from around him and rubbed his shoulders telling him how sorry I was for leaving him alone. He didn't seem to hear me. I know this only took a few minutes, but it seemed like forever. I couldn't figure out why my neighbor was taking so long; it was just over the fence. Taylor began to whimper. I kept rubbing his shoulders. I didn't know what else to do. Finally, the neighbor showed up and kind of stood there, seemingly at a loss for words and not knowing what to do. Taylor quietly lay on his side, his face in some stray grass clippings, weakly crying and beyond the sound of my voice. I asked the neighbor to watch Taylor to make sure he stayed safe while I went into the house to call for more help.

I was finally formulating a cohesive plan. I still didn't want to call the police because an ambulance would also be called. How proud I must have been to put my embarrassment before the well-being of my child! I needed more help to get Taylor to the emergency room before he became dangerous again. I called a friend, a member of our church, who knew something of our bipolar life, and, miraculously, he was home. He came right over. I briefly explained to both men what had happened and that I needed them to drive together to take Taylor to the hospital.

They had never seen Taylor in this condition before and were visibly bothered. They were confused with what I was asking them, and I didn't have a lot of time to be more detailed. I couldn't drive with Taylor alone and keep him safe if he tried to jump out of the car or do something which would jeopardize our safety. I needed them to drive, one of them sitting next to Taylor to keep him safe and follow me to the hospital. I became sort of irritated they didn't seem to comprehend what we needed to do, but I recognized they were seeing a part of our family they were barely aware existed.

Taylor, still feebly whimpering, allowed himself to be led to their car. He was wobbly on his feet and wouldn't look at me. I removed his belt and shoe laces from his shoes for his safety. On the way to the hospital, I called ahead to the emergency room and explained the situation and Taylor's young age. Based on our previous experiences I also requested to be taken immediately back to triage, so Taylor wouldn't have to sit in the waiting room in his deteriorated condition. By the time we got to the emergency room, the two men reported that during the car ride Taylor only sat staring and crying weakly and not responding to them. I was so grateful for their kindness and help in keeping him safe. Taylor walked through the emergency department like a zombie, as if he wasn't there anymore. It scared me. I knew he would hate to have anyone see him in his present condition, so I tried to protect him from the stares of others.

The medical doctor checked him out, noting the rope burns on his throat. The rope burns were red and inflamed, but the doctor felt Taylor was okay physically, and released him to a crisis counselor. The crisis counselor, Taylor, and I had many brief conversations in the ER to determine his state of mind and whether he could safely return home. Finally, she said she wouldn't have a problem admitting Taylor to the inpatient children's psychiatric unit. However, based on her conversations with me, she believed Dale and I had the experience to keep Taylor safe and that we were prepared to manage him at home now he had calmed down.

For the next few days it was like protecting Taylor from himself. He was introverted and swung from being intense to lethargic. He was always in our line of sight, and that first night I hardly slept, trying to be aware of his needs and making sure he was okay. After four days, Taylor stabilized enough for us to lessen the suicide watch and move toward getting him increased treatment and support at school. While protective of him, I had to trust the crisis plan we had established would be effective.

Taylor had had so many meltdowns that this one didn't seem to be very different at first, but if I had looked at the signs— his facial expressions, his body tension, the things he said—I might have seen the crisis coming. It was as if I had failed him. The situation was dangerous enough and I should have quickly called the police before he could hurt himself. I was more intimidated by what others might think. But in the end, I hoped Taylor knew I loved him and that he could always count on me to be there for him. I handled it and was stronger than I first thought.

A few years later, we were having a family discussion where we were sharing good memories of each other. As we went around the room, I noticed Taylor getting quieter. When it was his turn, he looked down and very quietly said that his best memory was with me and the time he hurt himself. He said that the best part of the memory was when I gently came to him to help him be safe when he couldn't help himself. He didn't say much, but it was how and what he said that was powerful. For a moment, we looked at each other as if we were the only ones in the room. We understood how monumental that moment was for both of us. Tears sprang to my eyes. I wondered if Taylor knew he had given me one of the greatest gifts I had ever received. We had come to an understanding and had forgiven each other. What a freeing feeling.

TRANSITION TO SUCCESS

As Taylor moved into junior high, I was nervous about how well he would transition in school. After working so hard to get his school services and accommodations in place during his elementary school years, I was hyper-attentive to Taylor's needs. I worried everything would get messed up. Would he get behind if I didn't stay on my toes to make sure nothing fell off his educational plate?

I really didn't need to worry. I had made friends with Alison, the special education teacher at the junior high, a few years before Taylor started there. We connected through the From Hope to Recovery class I wrote. She was first my student and then became a trusted friend and co-teacher. Alison also taught Sarah when she was in junior high and understood my intentions to help my children. She became my "go-to" person. She was calm, easygoing, generous, and empathetic. She was a perfect balance to my neurotic panic regarding school. I connected on a deeper level with Alison—as mothers of children with mental illness. We shared our grief when things were sad and having a friend who understood made all the difference.

Alison helped Taylor choose his seventh-grade classes as she reminded me, he could now start making his own decisions as to what he might enjoy. She empowered Taylor as much as possible, giving him a safe place to go if overwhelmed. She helped to develop a solid behavioral intervention plan and accommodations to keep Taylor on task without getting too stressed with his responsibilities.

One class Alison and I did disagree on was sewing. I went to the school and met with Alison privately.

"I think Taylor's learning disability will keep him from doing a sewing class. Sewing is about as visual-spatial as you can get and that is exactly what he struggles with." I said. "He is going to be too overwhelmed."

"You're right, it will be hard for him. But what if he can do it? Why not give him a chance to try?" Alison said. "It will be good for Taylor to try and we'll keep track of his work all along the way."

I looked at her skeptically. I knew she was right. I needed to check my attitude and let go of my anxiety over his stress.

"Taylor will do his best, he always does. The hard part is for you to tell Taylor you have confidence he can do this." she said.

On day two of sewing class, Taylor was given a paper drawing of the parts of the sewing machine that he was supposed to use to know how to thread the needle. He tried but said he ended up laughing when he couldn't even figure out where to start. To him, none of the parts of the sewing machine looked even mildly related to the paper. He didn't seem discouraged he didn't know how to thread the needle, rather, he seemed to see it as a challenge. He chose to sew a stuffed football as his sewing project because it looked the easiest.

As the weeks went on, it became more apparent Taylor did not have any inherent ability to do sewing on his own. I spoke to Alison and she acknowledged Taylor could use some help. She assigned a ninth-grade student to act as his one-on-one sewing tutor for the rest of the sewing portion. Taylor appreciated the help, and he appreciated the tutor didn't try to do the sewing for him.

Taylor did finish the football. When he brought it home, he was so proud of himself. It was a handsome football. Upon close examination, however, some of the seams were crooked and some missing, the decorations on the football were backward, and it had some lumps and bumps in its stuffing. That did not take anything away from the awesomeness of Taylor's football. He would always keep that football as a monument of what he accomplished. I was proud of it because it represented an excellent example of who Taylor was becoming—a determined, emerging successful student. Alison teased me about letting Taylor do hard things and being willing to get out of the way of Taylor's forward movement.

That was a hard concept for me—getting out of Taylor's way. I had spent more than twelve years trying to steer him forward in the face of adversity and all the unknowns. I harbored the memory of the trauma of trying to help him at home when he seemed out of control or unsafe. The frustrations of not knowing how to communicate with him. The inability to make him happy. The overwhelming fight with the school system in demanding his services had me primed to be a mama bear. I thought I would always need to be a mama bear with Taylor. But both Alison and Dale helped me see I could back away a little bit, and then a little bit more, and allow Taylor to develop on his own.

It was amazing. In the three years Taylor attended junior high, he became a new child. Under the supervision and sometimes pushing of Alison, Taylor got good grades in all his classes, even in math.

Taylor made friends—not many, but friends all on his own, and he became more socially successful. Taylor took increasingly harder classes, excelled and felt proud of his grades and his learning. He attended his IEP meetings and fully participated in advocating for himself in school. He even won awards for his scholastic efforts and his involvement in school. He came home excited to share what he was doing, genuinely looking for our input and approval rather than just talking at us.

In ninth grade Taylor started debate. He had wanted to be in debate ever since he knew he would be able to take it his last year in junior high. Taylor was a born debater. At home we knew he would be successful because he had been arguing with us since he had words. He could be persuasive and driven. He spent hours researching, writing arguments, practicing his speeches, and giving pep talks to his fellow students. His specialty became foreign issues debate, and as each experience built on another, he got better and better.

We didn't notice it at first, but over time, we found Taylor happier with himself and happier with us too. Taylor continued to be intense; that was how he showed his strongest emotions. His face would get red, and his fists would clench as he spoke through his teeth when he reacted to something that made him especially angry. He was difficult to reason with when frustrated, so we learned to wait him out if necessary. Sometimes we would hear things banging around in his room, but at least he didn't bang them at us. From the time Taylor was young he and Dale had a history of easily triggering anger and frustration with each other. Although not always common, these moments were loud and contentious, which was why I acted as the-go-to person to deal with Taylor when he was agitated.

Taylor learned how to internalize his frustrations enough not to strike out as much. He found ways to calm down in his bedroom with reading, reading, and more reading. Reading became his escape. It was odd to actually ground him from reading when he chose not to do his chores or school work. Reading also meant he spent a lot of time in his room by himself, and we wanted him to want to be with us. He was more difficult to engage, but we tried to bring him out of his own world at dinner or whenever he was around us.

Some of my favorite memories during Taylor's junior high years were when he shared something, he thought was funny at school. He had started to pick up on social cues and interactions, and many of them didn't make sense to him. He would ask us to explain teenager stuff at home, and when he understood it, he would laugh or make a disgusted look and say how dumb teenagers could be. He was always a few seconds behind the punchline, but when he finally got a joke, his whole face would light up and he'd laugh long and hard.

Taylor followed Sarah to high school with an attitude of determination to learn, excel, and be a leader. Almost every part of Taylor's high school experience was the polar opposite of Sarah's. With an intense focus and love for debating he excelled as a member of the debate club throughout high school. With debate he had access to resources and a teacher who led the debate team to first place in the school district for more than ten years. It was exciting to be a part of a tradition of excellence.

As he progressed during his junior and senior years, he brought home trophies big and small, a testament to how successful he had been. His debate teacher relied on his work to manage the foreign extemporaneous resources, knowing Taylor's attention to detail would help the whole team. She allowed Taylor to help train the new students in debate and to run practice sessions before competitions.

During debate season, Taylor was so hyper-focused he seemed to need less sleep even as he continued to perform at top level in his other classes as well. In Taylor's junior year, he won first place in the American Legion Constitution Oratorical Contest for Utah and went on to compete at the national level. As a senior he was awarded many trophies and got special recognition as Debate Student of the Year as voted by the coaches from the other schools and adults involved in the tournaments. He lived, ate, and slept debate for more than half the year, and it was good for him. He had social connections and opportunities and experienced different environments as he traveled to tournaments.

Taylor still had bipolar cycles throughout high school, but they were manageable when he got enough sleep, continued therapy, and distracted himself with activities that took his focus off what he was being ultra-intense about.

Sometimes Taylor would take a time-out from everything and hole up in his room for a few days and kind of unplug from everything and everyone. He maintained a good medication program with the same medications he had been taking since junior high. He would bump from a mild mania to sink into a mild depression but enjoyed longer periods of stable moods.

When Taylor was sixteen, I realized I had to make myself stop seeing and worrying about all the bipolar things in Taylor's life. I needed to shift my vision and see Taylor as he was, a typical kid. He no longer represented my child who had bipolar disorder. My perception of who he was changed. I had to redefine who *I* needed to become as I saw Taylor change. For years I had been Karen Greenwell, mother of Taylor, who'd been diagnosed before he was five with bipolar disorder and ADHD. I was still that, but was now enjoying my role as Karen Greenwell, mother of Taylor, a kid triumphing despite his disabilities. I was ashamed to admit the transition to seeing the cup half full took a lot longer than it should have, but once I did, I thoroughly enjoyed being Taylor's mom. His complexity became a blessing in my life.

Then one day, without us even expecting it, Dale and I looked at Taylor and recognized he had grown up to be his very own self. Having distance and time from the days of raw emotions, meltdowns and trauma gave us the opportunity to enjoy a moment of deep satisfaction. Taylor had evolved into the fine young man we always knew he would be.

PART IV

THE OTHER ONE

As our life often revolved around Taylor and Sarah, we had to be careful not to forget our Alex. He saw, heard, experienced and lived through things most of his peers would not understand. Because Alex was the youngest of our family, he never knew differently. Our home and family were his "normal."

I read an essay titled "Welcome to Holland" by Emily Perl Kingsley shortly after Sarah's first hospitalization. The essay considers what it is like to have a special needs child, or for us, a child with mental illness. It speaks of the excitement of planning and preparing for a baby; comparing it to preparing for an exciting trip to Italy. You gather information on fabulous sites to visit, plan your itinerary and learn a little Italian in anticipation of the big event. When the day comes for your arrival you are shocked when instead of going to Italy, you are welcomed to Holland.

You exclaim you didn't want to go to Holland; you want to go to Italy as planned! But in Holland you have landed, and it is there you must stay. So, you learn Dutch, purchase new guidebooks, and find your way in your new home. Over time you settle into your life in Holland and find there are good opportunities, unique people and a special way of life there. But you often wonder what your life would have been like if you landed in Italy as you planned.

I shared this essay numerous times in the classes I taught and with parents of children with mental illness. For many, tears would come as they connected with the reality of thinking you were going to be a parent to the "normal" child you expected and prepared for in Italy. Instead, an unexpected detour to Holland with a child with mental illness was the experience they received.

This is not to say Dale and I don't love our children with mental illness, but it's just not what we expected and prepared for. Our Holland kids, Sarah and Taylor, have been a rich blessing in our lives. Alex, our Italy child, was the final piece of our puzzle to make us complete.

All our kids were distinctly different in temperament, personality, coping skills and interests. But as is the case in most homes, kids will be kids. They were still just kids wanting the same experiences and things as other peers their age.

Whereas the impact of bipolar disorder on Sarah and Taylor was apparent in many facets of their daily lives, for Alex, it wasn't a daily concern. It was something intimately related to his home and family life, but he had the separateness we didn't often experience. Bipolar disorder wasn't on the top five ways he would describe himself to others. It certainly mattered, but Alex's perspective would always be inherently dissimilar from his siblings.

Alex grew up having a shoe firmly planted in two worlds; the "normal" and the bipolar disorder world. But for Alex, that was all he ever knew, which allowed him to move between the two. In school, his was an education devoid of special school services or 504 plans and he excelled in traditional and nontraditional learning. Alex showed interest in mainstream activities; orchestra, media, creative writing. Academic and social situations generally came easy for him. He made and kept a diverse group of friends.

It was through these very strengths and opportunities that Alex would be reminded how his brother and sister struggled, because learning and social skills were so challenging for them.

For me, Alex gave me the opportunity to be a "normal" parent. With Alex I learned to have confidence in my mainstream parenting. I was a gentler mom with him. Sometimes I wanted to put that simple, predictable, and genuine child in my pocket to remind me that I was a good mother. Alex wasn't a mystery of tangled emotions that I had to preemptively figure out. He liked to sit by me and have me read him a book, or for us to watch a video together. He wanted to be with me and it wasn't more complicated than that.

Alex always showed strong character as a loyal and dependable child and is the same as a young adult. Simply said, I could count on him. Growing up he was dependable in finishing a task at home and in being where he said he would be. At church he was given a steady amount of responsibility and service opportunities because he would follow through. He grew into a good leader.

Alex has an added measure of compassion and empathy that blesses those who are his friends and who work with him. He is patient and calm in times of stress and he has the gift to see the good in people and situations. He manages people well and people are drawn to him.

He brought satisfaction to uneventful moments in our home. As Alex grew, he helped us remember what "normal" looked like, and enthusiastically invited all of us to join him there. Alex tutored his siblings to play gently, take turns, listen intently, and not to be easily offended. He reminded all of us to chill out.

For Alex, life as a child in the Greenwell home was a balancing act. Dale and I didn't necessarily tell Alex that some of the house rules didn't apply equally to him, but nevertheless, he learned he often had his own set of rules. Alex took on extra responsibilities to help lessen the load for me and Dale. He was usually unaware he was doing it. We took for granted that Alex would figure out his role in our family as he went along. We expected him to join our rollercoaster, keep his arms and legs inside the ride, and participate in our journey.

For our family it was more complicated because all the kids were siblings of a child with mental illness; Taylor and Sarah to each other, and Alex to both of his siblings. The sibling who was not in crisis had to step up and help in situations which could be confusing, sometimes dangerous, and almost always unpleasant. But for Alex, I had the most sympathy. Regardless of whether the crisis was with Sarah or Taylor, Alex always had to take on the role of being the "okay" kid. I don't remember Alex having a crisis as he grew up. I am not minimizing his experiences as a typical child growing up. I know he must have struggled with issues and situations that were hard for him. I'm sure he did, but we weren't used to looking at Alex in that crisis mode.

Alex was a peacemaker. He was always flexible and willing to accept unexpected changes to our schedules or our plans. If Taylor or Sarah had a therapy appointment, Alex had to come along too. With the time demands of mental health treatment I had to figure out the most efficient way of making it work. I tried to arrange for childcare or play dates for Alex at least once each week. I called my neighbor Janet who had a daughter Alex's age. Janet was so accommodating and welcomed Alex into their home. I was grateful to have a safe place for Alex where he could be a carefree kid. She never pushed to know the details of what was going on with therapy. She was respectful of our privacy and assured me Alex would always be welcome. I knew Alex enjoyed the respite as much as I did-probably more.

He was generally cheerful and playful, and we all enjoyed him. He had a tender heart and could be easily saddened when either of his siblings were in distress. His efforts to make them feel better included drawing a picture, giving a hug, or his biggest overture of all—sharing one of his beloved stuffed animals. At the end of each day, Alex would pop his head into our bedroom to say I love you.

Alex had to develop a sixth sense when there was conflict, especially if Taylor became aggressive. He had to know when to stay out of the line of fire. When he was a toddler, I worried he would accidentally get in the way of one of Taylor's meltdowns. But he never did. At a very young age he had to manage and keep himself busy as I dealt with the crisis. From the beginning he seemed to know these things naturally, although he didn't understand why.

Alex was sympathetic of his sibling's bipolar disorder. He tried to understand what was happening from their point of view. Whenever we had a major incident, Dale and I would try to take Alex aside and talk about what had happened. Sometimes he didn't want to talk about it; he wanted to move on and not always dwell on mental illness. As he got older, he became more expressive about his angst and frustration. We talked about Sarah and Taylor having a sickness in their head that sometimes made it difficult for them to control their actions. We talked about being angry at their illness and behavior but trying not to be angry with them. These mini-conversations occurred over time as Alex grew up. I am sure Alex was sometimes sick of bipolar disorder always taking center stage in our home. Opportunities *not* to talk about mental illness were a welcome change for Alex. Dale and I tried to follow his lead as to what he wanted to talk about, his level of understanding, and how much he wanted to know.

One of my favorite activities with Alex from the time he was a preschooler and even as a young adult was to go grocery shopping with him. He was my helper, running to pull items off the shelf and put them in our cart. I called him my buddy and we would wander the store, taking our time. He would look for "coupon machines" to spit out coupons to use for our list. He would ask for things, like treats, for me to buy. He could be persistent, so I told him I could only buy the extra special things if they were on sale. He'd scan the isles looking for sales and when he found a good one, he would negotiate like a car salesman to have me put it in our cart. As Alex got older, we developed a shopping vibe where he would ask for something, and I would pretend I already intended to buy the item. We both knew I would usually let him get his way, but it was easy because he didn't make a fuss or throw a tantrum or behave unreasonably. We shared a running commentary about people we saw and things we overheard, chuckling under our breath. I felt like the good mom and he was the good kid.

Alex's anger was usually short-lived, but he certainly had an opinion of what the ultimate consequences for the kids should be. He was fair, and he expected us to treat him fairly. He grew to accept the inevitability of new episodes with Sarah and Taylor over time. He would be on guard when situations started brewing and tried to avoid them, but it was kind of like watching a bad car accident; you want to see it and you don't want to see it at the same time.

As Sarah and Taylor got older, they became more verbally threatening and aggressive with each other and with Alex. Usually I was at home, and most incidents were averted, but I couldn't protect Alex all the time. Sometimes Sarah and Taylor would take offense when they thought Alex received preferential treatment. Normal sibling rivalry was certainly in play, but I tended to err of the side of keeping Alex away from Sarah's and Taylor's negative behaviors from the time he was little until he started junior high school. By then Alex seemed to be able to hold his own and didn't want me to fight his battles.

Throughout his life, Alex has been expected to overlook his siblings' shortcomings as they relate to their illness. As Alex became a teenager, he began to speak up for himself, especially with Taylor. One day when I was away, they got into an argument, and Alex tried to get away from Taylor by locking himself in the bathroom. Taylor tried to knock the door down and kept yelling at Alex. Alex, who had intimate experience with Taylor's temper, was frightened. When Taylor got into the bathroom Alex tried to push Taylor out of the way, but Taylor would not back down. Alex cowered in the bathtub, yelling at Taylor to go away. Eventually Alex had to force his way through to the other bathroom pass-through door, putting a hole in the door in the process. Alex didn't know what to do and later said he'd been "traumatized" by the incident. But at least he had a sense of being able to fight back. As he got older, he didn't want to talk to Dale or me about his feelings when something happened. He would say everything would be fine and asked us to accept that at face value. I could often see he was angry or shaken up, but he seemed more concerned with being left alone for a time.

Alex also had a perfect view of his siblings' successes. He had sympathy for them when they struggled, but he had pride in them when he saw them overcome hard things. As Taylor started to learn to walk away from confrontation instead of engaging in a meltdown, Alex joined us in celebrating Taylor's progress. When Sarah willingly joined us in a family activity and seemed to enjoy herself, Alex let her know how much he liked having her around. The ultimate success for Alex was if he could get the family to gather together for a board game and have that one hour be fun and lighthearted. As a sibling he could pick out the little successes to celebrate that someone on the outside might not notice.

When Alex was sixteen, we were talking about a job opportunity at the mental health center where I worked. I was telling him it was an ideal situation because I could put in a good word for him, the pay was decent, and he already had experience working with children with mental illness. He thought it was a terrible idea. After some coaxing he told me he didn't want to work with children with mental illness. He said he grew up with it all around him and didn't want to deal with it for a job.

In a moment that almost broke my heart, Alex said one of his greatest fears was having a child with bipolar disorder. I didn't know how to process that information. For a long time, his comment sat in the back of my mind fermenting until I could consider it objectively. The message for me was an acknowledgment of how intrusive and sometimes devastating bipolar disorder can be. I suppose, given a choice when Dale and I started our family, I would have fervently wished not to have a child with bipolar disorder. I had to accept Alex's fear as valid. However, I also understood Alex was not rejecting us as a family. His intimate understanding of the strains of bipolar disorder on a family would help him cope with whatever his future would be.

Alex always knew we had high expectations for all the kids, disorders or not. They were to get good grades, attend their church activities, complete daily chores, and be responsible for their behavior. Alex generally did those things as he flew under the parental radar. We got used to Alex not making a fuss. However, as Alex got older, he began to make it clear he felt we were not the boss of him. Dale and I established clear and precise consequences for the kids early on to manage their behavior. As Alex became a preteen, he told us the "bipolar consequences" would not work for him. He proclaimed himself an independent thinker and felt he could govern himself without all the structure. Heavy and long conversations followed as he moved through junior high and high school. In trying to understand Alex's viewpoint I wondered if his firm resolve and "I am in charge of me" attitude partly came from his role as the "normal" and therefore "different" kid in our family. He was often required to take care of himself and learn to adapt to unexpected circumstances. He knew how to think on his feet and to rely on himself in the moment. He was no less stubborn than his siblings.

The saying "hindsight is 20/20" certainly is true in considering how seemingly small decisions impacted how Alex was raised in a family of people with bipolar disorder. I perceived parenting Alex to be so simple and straight forward as he grew up because he didn't confound me with baffling behavior. He is the youngest. He didn't hit or kick me and he didn't hurt my feelings or make me cry. He liked to be with me, even for boring stuff, and he liked his siblings even when I was frustrated with them. What could be easier than that?

But now I see that with his go-along personality and attitude, desire to please, and intuitive care giving, I relied on Alex to be an emotional support for me far more than I should have. I didn't necessarily see him as a confidante. He was more a welcome distraction from the pressure of other responsibilities. As a preteen and even as a young adult, I took for granted the fact that Alex understood what my stress was like because he knew what our environment and the players were like. So, my hindsight has me regretful that I unnecessarily shared some of my parental burden with a kid who just needed to be a kid. Even through his "normal" he still lived through a filter.

As the "Other One" in our family, Alex wasn't the one who got left out or forgotten. He certainly had to think on his feet and probably make sense of things that were pretty hard.

In the end, parenting Alex, and parenting Sarah and Taylor were very different. Just like Italy and Holland are very different places. Different is real, and different is okay. But our destination has always been the same with all the kids. Our goal was to raise strong, independent, dynamic, compassionate, creative and loving members of a family. We had to come at it from a variety of avenues, but it only made us better parents. Besides, who wants to live predictable? Not me.

BLESS AND RELEASE

I was emotionally drained almost every day, but even with my overwhelming reality, I never wanted to walk away. These were my children, and I loved them. I was the best person to be their mother, and I would somehow overcome the barriers. They were never a burden to me, and I would do anything for them. I cherished the weeks and even months of what we considered "normal" when we were all in sync and bipolar disorder wasn't the center of our lives.

Sometimes reality wasn't only seeing the difficulties we faced in caring for the kids, but the reality of the daily burdens Dale had to carry alone. Working a job and helping manage the kids was a full-time commitment but having a spouse with a mental illness became an extraordinary responsibility. Dale was my cheerleader, my voice of reason, my partner to do hard things and to remind me to laugh. Every day we worked together to make it through and many times all we had to do was look each other in the eye and we knew in that moment we "got it". I was often well for more than a year at a time, but when I got sick, the depression might last for months and months. When at my worst, Dale had to work, shop for groceries, cook dinner, make sure everyone was safe, including me, and get us to bed each night. How could I not feel like a burden?

One day we were driving home from a psychiatrist appointment where I'd received yet another medication change. I felt black inside, disgusted with my own company, even. I asked Dale why he stayed with me when I was in such a horrible condition.

He seemed surprised at the question and said, "I would stay with you no matter what."

"But why?" I asked. "How could you possibly want to be with me?"

He countered by asking me a question. "Karen, what would you do if I got in a car accident and became paralyzed? Would you leave me?"

I was shocked at the idea of leaving him. I would stand by him for whatever our future would hold. We had made that commitment to each other years before.

He said, "It's the same for me. It's just your disability is hidden and mine wouldn't be. It is a privilege to care for you and the kids when I am needed, and I know it's only for a little while and then you'll be better."

"But how," I wondered, "do you have the ability to carry on knowing our bipolar disorder will never go away and that there are three of us with it?"

"It is faith," he said. "I have faith God will provide me with all I need to care for us emotionally, mentally, physically, and financially. I know this because what we've needed at any time of crisis in the past has always been there for us. I am especially buoyed up during your episodes because I know there is little I can do to make it go away, and it is hard to see you suffering. I try to do all I can to comfort, support, and carry on until you can again stand by me. I know it will always get better."

When I was healthy, I could see Dale's commitment to each one of us and the faith that sustained him. But I realized Dale's faith looked different from mine. He would *know* things would work out all right; I didn't always know they would. Sometimes I just had to trust in Dale's faith.

My own faith played a large part in dealing with the extreme crises in our lives. There were many situations where I became overwhelmed and incapable of handling a situation. I'd have no resources on which to call, and then suddenly, through a quick prayer and a deep breath, I would find myself blessed with abilities I did not know I had. All was well. This became especially true when Sarah and Taylor were suicidal or thinking of harming themselves. It was my faith—which for me I would *feel* things would work out all right—during the times Sarah cut herself that enabled me to handle things in a gentle, logical way when I knew I was anything but. It would all come together, and I'd know what to do.

After most crises, I would usually go to my room and cry a little bit, then utter a prayer of gratitude that I'd been able to handle the crisis. These events strengthened my faith and the hope I could do whatever I might be called upon to do.

Dale once said he married me because he loved me; he didn't marry bipolar disorder. That was just something we had to work around. In the end I had to keep on believing there had to be more to this life than living in constant crisis and that our family deserved to have everything we needed, including good mental health. We were more than bipolar disorder.

The conviction and faith of knowing we would be better lead to unexpected realizations. I believe a "spark" exists with bipolar disorder. It is an unforeseen gift. It must be deeply embedded in our personality because all three of us have it, but in different ways. Manic cycling enhances this spark. When we interact with others it bubbles up from the place which brings a glint in our eye. We become charming and charismatic. Whether in front of a group or only with friends, we all have this extra lift, and people are drawn to us. Each has this ability to be "on" when we need to be, which proves helpful in performing or presenting. We express ourselves with passion and enthusiasm. It brings us a confidence and feeling of peace when we need it. And when we are in a manic phase—watch out.

It can be seen in Sarah as she lifts and tilts her head while singing at her recitals. She is extraordinarily composed and confident; her beautiful voice a pleasure to listen to. She seems to be at ease as she directs people, old or young, in any activity of which she is in charge. Sarah expresses her ideas intelligently and thoughtfully. She also possesses the gift of creativity. Through her artwork, her depth of emotion is apparent.

Taylor not only has the perks of bipolar disorder but the added benefits of ADHD. These conditions create a powerful ability to hyper-focus and attend to important subjects. Taylor has a presence when he speaks, as he debates, and with others. He exudes confidence and a well-rounded knowledge about the world. For Taylor, one of the benefits of bipolar disorder and ADHD is found in the intensity with which he works. Always a leader, he can quickly assess the big picture and figure out ways to have others share his vision. He does an amazing job at anything he puts his mind to.

As I teach and give presentations, I am confident in my ability to express myself and am comfortable in both large and small groups. My smile comes naturally as I interact with people. I believe there is nothing so thrilling as watching people have an "aha" moment from something I just taught. It is a delight to teach and share information. My gifts include the compassion for others who struggle. I want to reach out to them to give hope. The outlet for my creativity is scrapbooking the story and adventures of our lives to enjoy when times can be a little challenging.

In the community education class I teach to the parents and caregivers of children with mental illness, I conduct an exercise in which participants are asked to list eight to ten words which describe their child. There is no indication given as to whether these should be positive or negative words. They are given the outline of a child and asked to draw lines to separate the handout into puzzle pieces. Finally, they transfer the words they wrote to a puzzle piece on the handout. In the end, they have the outline of a child separated into puzzle pieces with descriptive words about their child. I ask them to raise their hand if they included their child's diagnosis as one of the puzzle pieces. There is always a long pause as they look over their papers. Inevitably, a parent gasps or shakes their head when they realize they hadn't listed the diagnosis at all. The realization that for all the attention and focus given to their child's diagnosis, in the end, the diagnosis is not the way they would describe their child. I've never taught a class when this exercise didn't have some impact on how the participants viewed their child.

We spend so much time focused on the negative symptoms and on the chaos their illness brings that we forget to look at all of them.

Then we talk about how a child is so much more than their illness. The diagnosis doesn't define the child; it only describes a part of them. Sometimes we lose the forest through the trees, and then we and our children miss out on the good of who they are.

So, who are we? Essentially, we are like everyone else. Someone with asthma should be aware of their limitations and often must take lifelong medications. Someone with diabetes must keep track of their body's functioning and adjust their activities and food intake to ward off any complications. Different illnesses but similar realities. For people who have chronic illnesses, life means managing our diagnosis and living despite our struggles. We don't stop living because we get sick. We wait it out, doing what needs to be done therapeutically, and pick up where we left off. We are much more like others than we are different. We only must lift our heads to see that there is a lot of life to be lived. We learn to let go.

When I first heard the term "bless and release," it struck me as profound. I repeated it over and over in my head because I wanted to remember it. I understood it on a visceral level and decided to make it my new motto.

The dictionary defines *bless* as "to ask God to care for and protect someone or something" and *release* as "to set someone or something free." To give something to God's care was to set it free. That was what I wanted to do with my life.

There was a lot of bless and release in my life. Sometimes it was an easy task, but often I got caught up in the minutiae of life and forgot I really could let things go. I needed to remember the relief that came when I allowed myself to be free.

When the concept of bless and release first came into my life, the stresses on our family were intense. Both Sarah and Taylor were struggling in school and at home, Dale was away much of the time, and I felt guilty for not having enough time to devote to Alex. Then I remembered "bless and release."

Could I really let go? Could I count on others to pick up the slack? Could I walk away from things that *seemed* important to focus on things that were really vital? Could I handle the anxiety of not doing everything for everyone? Could I see myself outside the mental health world and in a world of normalcy and good health? Could I give up living in a state of crisis for living in a state of calm? Could I trust myself not to grab it all back? Slowly I realized that, yes. I could.

I would stretch out my arm, bend my wrist downward, and, with a quick flick toward the sky, let go. The more attitude I gave the wrist flick, the farther the burden flew. Sometimes I had a lot of attitude and loved to feel the weight of my burden leave me. But to bless and release was much more than just a physical motion. It took faith to let go. A lot of faith. I had to believe there existed a higher reason for all the happenings in my life. I believed in my family and our worth, regardless of the struggles we had. I had faith we were inherently stronger than our weakest moments, and I believed it would all work out, even if I didn't know what that looked like.

It has been years since I learned about bless and release, and I've used it often. Sometimes I joke about letting everything go all together, but that would be running away, and I know better. Some burdens we must carry. I've taught each of the kids to bless and release. They seemed to instinctively know what it meant. I hope they use it sometimes. I've learned that letting go doesn't make me weaker or less competent but stronger. I've learned there is wisdom in putting down burdens that, for the moment, are too heavy to carry.

I knew this to be true and wanted to share this new perspective with others in a positive way. I found I could do my part to lift another's burden. Blessing and releasing in my life became doing and sharing. As Sarah and Taylor grew, I found myself drawn to people I met through a support group, a mental health lecture, or school advocacy. It was liberating to have people who, like me, understood the daily reality of mental illness. We compared notes on what parenting techniques had worked or what services their child had in school.

I was hired to write a newsletter for Allies with Families. It was a start, and only a few hours a month, but I saw myself as an adult again, capable of earning money, and not permanently tied to some of the chaos at home. I wanted the newsletter to be useful, and contain information I wanted to know, or information I wished I had known when the kids were younger.

About this same time, I began teaching National Alliance for Mental Illness (NAMI) classes to families of children with mental illness. I loved the interaction and was drawn to share my experiences. I learned so much from the other parents and family members, who taught me about the resiliency of families. I made new friends and started to develop relationships in the community. For the first time, I had people approach me looking for solutions. I participated on a lot of school issues and was validated advocating on behalf of families who believed I could help them maintain hope.

There was so much to be done. I had to monitor myself as I became actively involved in advocacy. I had to be aware of the wear and tear to my marriage and family as a result of my focus on children's mental health. Dale supported my efforts, but he also knew everything would come at a cost if I wasn't careful. We talked about the benefits of interacting with families and opening conversations about mental illness in the community. However, I could also be eaten alive by exposing myself and our family in ways that were not validating or uplifting. I had to continue to bless and release the things that did not allow us to maintain our mental and physical health. Dale and I established tangible boundaries and limits to our involvement in mental health advocacy so it didn't overwhelm us, and especially me. It was a careful balance.

Allies with Families was asked to write a child-specific education program curriculum. I took on the project. It was a great opportunity, and a lot of responsibility. It was like being asked to write an educational book for parents and caregivers of children with mental illness. It was overwhelming as I started to develop a program which would be relevant, informative, and strength-based. I researched current data about children's mental illnesses and treatments. I adopted hands-on activities designed to help people understand the impact of mental illness on their families. I included information on brothers and sisters of children with mental illness and their unique issues. I strove to include comprehensive and relevant information for families across all situations. I wanted the information to be real, not to minimize childhood mental illness, and not to place guilt on the shoulders of parents. Families would benefit from attending an insightful, honest, and wellness-based education program.

In the end I authored a six-week education program called "From Hope to Recovery." From the beginning, the program enjoyed favorable evaluations, family involvement, and community interest. I gratefully blessed and released this program out to the universe to find its way to those who would benefit from it. My heart has been greatly rewarded to see the impact the program has had on individual lives.

After "From Hope to Recovery," I became fully engulfed in mental health advocacy, working for Allies with Families part-time. I was blessed to be able to work from home, so I could be available for mommy things. As I learned the art of juggling responsibilities I thoroughly enjoyed, I built relationships in the community through a variety of presentations. Contacts I made with diverse individuals years earlier now became helpful in getting the message out to parents, physicians, mental health centers, and universities.

It was a busy time but also rewarding. I continued to work with parents of children through a local county mental health center. My mission was to address stigma and talk about what was right with families rather than what was wrong. I enjoyed the days I could be the professional, dressed in my presentation clothes, feeling like I was making an important contribution. I knew I had been fortunate to have been a stay-at-home mom and later a work-at-home mom while the kids grew up. But being able to go to presentations, conferences, school meetings or one-to-one conversations with other parents helped me realize my inner sense of confidence. My idea of what I want to be my "normal" evolved. Time in the mental health field gave me a sort of respite and tweaked my perspective to my potential as not only Taylor, Sarah, or Alex's mom but as an individual making a difference for many.

PAINFUL REMINDERS

Sarah was about sixteen when she started talking to me about the negative "Do you remember whens" in our family. The more she talked, the more I didn't want to remember any of it. I didn't want to go back there. It was as if she needed to reprocess some of our most traumatizing history. Her memories brought out the tension and panic I experienced when I was faced with a situation I didn't know how to resolve. To remember Taylor's meltdowns and how I needed to go into overdrive to protect him and the rest of us from his rage was painful. I didn't like remembering how unfair it was that these situations happened when Dale wasn't home. I could never figure out if we had the problems because he wasn't home very often, or because I seemed to be unable to keep peace in the home, or, worse yet, because I was the trigger for Taylor and Sarah. Years later I still didn't know the answer, and it bothered me. Picturing us during these times physically hurt my heart and brought back emotions I thought I wouldn't have to feel again.

Sarah asked if I remembered when we would fight about the choices she made. Of course, I remembered. Just talking about it, I immediately sensed the pressure start in my stomach, rise to my chest, then creep into my throat. As I listened to her, I wanted to run away, just like I used to want to run away from dealing with her as a teenager.

Did I want to remember these things with Sarah? Not really, because in the midst of these crises my heart physically ached as I

281

watched the pain Sarah and Taylor went through. I hated bipolar disorder and the disruption it had caused in our lives. As Sarah asked these questions, I wanted to cry. I knew I did the best I could, but sometimes, like now, I wished I could put it behind me so I wouldn't have to relive it again.

But then I realized that with each revisiting of that part of our life, I could be grateful we'd made it through all right. The important thing was for me to make sense of the experience, to understand the higher purpose. God knew I could handle it, and I believed He wanted me to know I could handle it too. It kind of balanced out. If I had to experience grief and pain, I could also enjoy the strength and confidence.

One day I visited with a mom who was completely worn down. She had little confidence that her situation would ever get better. Her daughter had recently entered day-treatment. She and her husband were required to go through seven months of intensive treatment with her. Seven months seemed like an eternity. I knew exactly how she felt. I told her about Sarah's years of lying, stealing and her disrespect. I shared about her cutting class, the continual frustration, the residential treatment, and the requirement to learn DBT skills along with her.

I shared how I resented having to spend almost one year doing treatment work when Sarah had the problems and behaviors, not me. I shared with her how I expected Sarah to change, but after a few months of intensive DBT therapy we all changed. We had more success in talking with each other and I'd come to understand that we all shared some of the responsibility for what had been wrong. I thought treatment was about fixing Sarah, but in the end, it helped our whole family learn healthy ways to cope with mental illness. I told the mother that therapy didn't make everything go away, but it did empower us to resist the belief that everything would never get better.

The mother's face slowly changed as I told my story. She leaned forward to speak with me about what to expect. No more hiding behind her crossed arms. We talked about how our actions could lead our daughters from a place of depression and negativity to coping and living like a teenager should. Certainly, this family had a long road ahead, but knowing it could get better was comforting, almost critical. She went from hopeless to hopeful.

Ironically, I left her house feeling such guilt. Sharing so many personal experiences with a stranger made me feel disloyal to Sarah. I was sick to my stomach and my chest hurt. I wanted to undo what I had done.

That night I went to my now adult Sarah, gave her a hug, and asked to talk to her.

"First of all, I want to apologize for sharing some pretty personal stuff about you with a client's mom today." I said, looking her earnestly in the eye. "I feel like I have been disloyal to you. The worst part is this mom won't ever get a chance to see how amazing you are."

I gave Sarah a blow-by-blow replay of what I'd said and explained why I shared it with the mom.

I took a deep breath and said, "I just wanted to be fully honest with you."

Sarah's face softened. She looked at me with kindness. "You don't need to apologize mom." she said. "I know the kind of work you do, and I am proud of you for helping parents and families."

Then she reminded me she had given me permission to share her personal information long before and that by doing so she could also have a part in helping others. She was very gracious.

When we had the opportunity to do the PBS show about living with mental illness, both Taylor and Sarah were positive that it was a good thing. They wanted to be honest about our family and not hide who we were. They continued to feel that way and went on to do their own mental health advocacy and community mental health education.

I know it's the right thing to do, but it's not easy. As I share our stories with other parents, professionals, and people in the community, I almost universally receive positive and heartening feedback. But how can I not see the image of my little boy on his way to the police car with his stuffed animal tucked in his arms, or the pleading look in my daughter's eyes and the lines on her arms when I share their stories? With each retelling of our past comes the heaviness.

Then I remember the successes we have had, and my heart lightens. Often as I talk with others, I tell them as a form of disclosure, that if they ever happened to meet my children, they would never know they had a mental illness. They look like any other young adult; they are exceptional individuals with wonderful talents and abilities. Their struggles may be a little more intense, but they have developed the skills to manage their illnesses and face their struggles on their own terms. In short, my kids are marvelous and a blessing to all who know them, and I am proud to be their mother. I realize that I am like any other mother who's walked a long road with her child and come out the other end enriched, because she's had the privilege to share their journey. That brings joy to my heart and perspective to my life.

UNSPEAKABLE REWARDS

Being a parent is absolutely the hardest job on earth. Caring for, mentoring, shaping, loving, and directing a child from infancy to adulthood is a high-stakes endeavor. We never know what we are going to get. We learn and develop skills and stretch our abilities beyond what we think is possible. Being a parent is, without question, the most rewarding job as well. Our children have now become adults, and we survived and survived well. If I knew then what I know now, I would be willing to do it all over. It wasn't easy, but it was worth it.

Dale was a good father. He was responsible, took his role as a provider seriously, was attentive to needs as soon as he knew of them, and was a compassionate listener. I believe I was a good mother. I was dedicated, sensitive to needs, had a good sense of humor, and deeply committed to family. Together we were good. Our ways of parenting complemented each other. Others often commented what good parents we were. We wanted to believe them.

Each of our children was a gift, but they were so unique it seemed impossible to compare our experience parenting them. With one we learned patience and to stick to our guns. With another we learned to have clear boundaries and communication. With one we learned to outlast the drama and keep a smile on our face. But with each of them we learned to love, and love deeply, regardless of the circumstances.

AFTERWARD

HEROES

We haven't lived happily ever after—yet. But we do continue to live the best we can. We understand we are only as strong as our next challenge. Life always gives us room to grow and lessons to learn.

While writing this book, a devastating depression took me out of commission for almost eight full months. I couldn't work, I couldn't drive, I couldn't follow a conversation, I had to quit my job, and I couldn't access that place of peace and resilience I had come to take for granted. But all along the path to wellness I had a firm knowledge that I would get better. Living through bipolar disorder and depression before has given me a unique perspective on how much the human soul can endure, especially when surrounded by caring individuals who are invested in one's well-being. In the past, getting better has depended largely upon me telling myself I can hold on one more day. But this time was different. Overwhelmingly different.

My children are now young adults, and it had been almost eight years since I'd had such a severe depression. Dale and I had always been honest with them when I got sick. We'd decided long ago that the depressions were a part of what it meant to be me, but it helped them to know we had a plan in place and were going to carry on best as we could until the depression passed.

During this depression I needed to go to the grocery store to get some food for Dale while he drove a horse carriage during the

Christmas season. I knew he would probably have done it himself, but for some reason it became something I had to do to show support. Since I couldn't drive, Sarah took me. As we got to the store, and it seemed as if Sarah could sense my vulnerability at being in such a big place, away from the safety of home. I vaguely had an idea of what I wanted and started to wander through the aisles. I saw granola bars, which I thought were a good idea, but I couldn't figure out a way to verbalize my choice. I couldn't remember what they were called, and I couldn't explain the fear I had in my heart and my head at that moment as I knew I was going crazy.

She gently put her arm around me and said, "Yes, Dad will like a granola bar. That's a good choice. Is there something else you want to get?"

I saw bananas and slowly shuffled over to them. Sarah patiently waited for me to select the right one, which took so much time because the sheer number of bananas overwhelmed me. Seeing the tears rolling down my cheeks, Sarah again put her arm around me and quietly asked if I needed anything else from the store. Then my sweet daughter ever so gently led me through the store as my battered, depressed brain tried to make sense of what I was doing. She didn't rush, she didn't get impatient with me, she didn't second-guess what I wanted. She protected me both physically and emotionally from the environment around me. When we got to the car and she saw how exhausted I was, she praised my courage. She said Dale would be proud of me, and that we were going home now so I could rest. She was extraordinarily kind and loving, and in that moment, she was my hero.

A few months later I was sitting on the couch in our living room with Alex and my mom before one of Alex's orchestra concerts. While I knew this outing would be difficult for me, I figured I could sit quietly and enjoy the music for an hour. My mom, while compassionate, still didn't understand that depression was more than just being sad or thinking negative thoughts. She suggested that what I needed was to do something to get my mind off it, to get busy, to serve. I was struggling with merely getting through the day. I could not find the words to help her understand how the monster in my head had literally squished all good thoughts out of my life. I didn't have it in me to explain again how it felt to have bipolar depression. As tears rolled down my cheeks, I looked at Alex, and quietly whispered, "Tell her; just tell her." And then I started to sob.

Alex took a deep breath and tried in a simple and kind way to explain to his grandmother that this depression was more than just pulling myself up by the bootstraps. He talked about how unbelievably tired I was and how hard it had been for me to even get up and get dressed. How I had been resting all day, so I might attend his concert. Feeling overwhelmed, I blocked out their conversation and allowed myself to go deeper and deeper into my sorrow.

Suddenly Taylor emerged from his room and said in a forceful voice, "What is going on here?" Alex began to explain to Taylor he was trying to help grandma understand about my depression when Taylor cut him off and looked at me and said, "You need to rest."

He said, "You know this is too much for you right now. You need to go to bed and take a nap."

He came to my side, helped me down the hall, and waited by my bedside until I pulled the blanket up around my shoulders.

He then gently said, "Get some sleep and you will feel better."

I heard him go to the living room. Together he and Alex tried to explain to my mother about what was happening to me and what everyone could do to help me get better. Alex took a more emotional approach, and Taylor explained the more practical realities of what happens in depression. In that moment, they were my heroes.

During the months of my acute depression, each of my children stepped up to help. Alex took it upon himself to get me out of the house every day, if for nothing more than a drive to the gas station to get a drink. Taylor checked in and let me pop my head into his room as I shared an "aha" moment of bipolar and the way it impacted us. Sarah called me and visited me to help ward off the loneliness.

They say you get what you give out, but I've gotten so much more. There was no greater joy for me when my children turned around and, in my time of need, took care of me. I pointedly tried to tell them how grateful I was, but once Taylor said something that forever changed my heart.

In his matter-of-fact way, he said, "Mom, this is what you taught us to do. This is how you took care of us, and now we are just taking care of you."

All I could do was weep with gratitude for the kind of amazing people my children had become. When I shared this experience with Dale, he echoed Taylor's sentiment. He said they were only manifesting the service they had seen for so many years and now things had come full circle.

My children are young adults, and the reality of who they are often astounds me. As parents it is our responsibility and privilege to help mold our children. Dale and I realize that molding and influencing our children doesn't mean we can decide what their life path will be. That is up to them.

Sarah was destined to become who she is today. Our fiery red-head had more sass and spunk than we imagined or were prepared for. Sarah, who spoke full sentences at eighteen months old always wanted to know "why." Sarah liked to be out in front of people; always brave, bold, and engaging. She wanted to show she could belong, and tried hard to make a place for herself. But in her enthusiasm, she was overwhelming. Sarah would put herself out there to try once again to figure out the mystery of fitting in. Sarah would get stuck and ineffectively spin her wheels until she reached out for help. She could trust deeply and demand loyalty, all the while holding herself to the same high standard.

Memories of who Sarah was helps to fit the puzzle pieces of who Sarah is today. As Sarah left high school, she realized she had to make changes to get unstuck and to move away from tough situations in her past. Sarah moved forward to another phase of her life and made tangible, achievable goals. She knew she wanted to make a difference, because she truly cares for others. Sarah became an American Sign Language Interpreter and connected with people in the Deaf community. Sarah also worked with at-risk, inner city youth at the Boys and Girls Club as a teacher and mentor. She intimately understood the importance of their need to belong. She encouraged the kids to enjoy and celebrate differences. She taught them to take responsibility for their actions and to learn from them.

As Sarah ventured out and became independent, she still touched base back home. Sometimes she needed to "check her understanding" about something she was thinking or experiencing. After more than a decade of therapy, Sarah was genuinely learning how to accept her past and incorporate the skills and insight she had gained. She had to commit to use her skills to give her direction to build her future. Like everyone, she stumbled and had to start again, but oh my, she has come to an amazing place.

Sarah is currently seeking a Bachelor of Arts degree in theater performance and has been listed multiple times on the Dean's List for academic achievement. In her theater program she is drawn to play women who are passionate, fierce, and intelligent because that is who she is. She strongly advocates for diversity, acceptance and the value of all people.

She is happily married to a gentle soul who without question loves her. He is her rock and with him she can feel safe. Together they are a dynamic pair and are the parents of a wonderful baby boy.

Sarah and I have not only called a truce, but we have grown an honest and lovely relationship. She is the person I call when I need to look at the humor of bipolar disorder and I know she "gets it." Sometimes we both have a moment that gives us pause to remember what we have been through, and that together we can bless and release.

If Dale and I were to believe everything the "professionals" told us about Taylor's future, we would have wanted to throw in the towel. To be sure, we didn't know what the future would hold for Taylor, but we knew we just had to focus on the present. We believed if we did everything we could, it would all work out. And it has all worked out.

Taylor was scary, out of control, unpredictable, and aggressive. For a long time, he could single-handedly determine what kind of day we all would have; good or bad. His very presence was that powerful. He was loud and physical, talking non-stop and demanding your full attention. He wanted you to be interested only in what he was interested in. He played hard and was intense in his body and mind. Basically, he was a lot, almost all the time.

What one would see only as aggressive tendencies in the younger Taylor, have today become valued traits of assertiveness which have propelled him forward. In looking back, we can see the very gradual, very steady progress and growth that has brought stability to Taylor's life.

Taylor never enjoyed therapy, in fact he generally disliked it. But he went, and he must have learned something, because the skills Taylor was taught directly relate to his successes today. Taylor admits he doesn't naturally show a lot of empathy, but he has learned to consider the perspective of others to help him interpret situations and people. He can talk about emotional things and ideas. He can often intellectualize about people, feelings, and situations, thereby helping him make sense of his adult world. Taylor has been successful in building and nurturing different kinds of relationships in his life. He

294

has never been one to have many relationships at one time, but genuinely and honestly cares for, and is willing to sacrifice for those he loves.

Taylor is precise and goal oriented. Taylor's progress in his university education is thoroughly considered and planned. His Bachelor of Science degree has led him directly to his master's degree and then to his chosen profession. Taylor is a planner and has chosen a career in City Planning and Management because putting together pieces of the plan is logical and dynamic for him. He excels in what he strives to do because he does the work beforehand to prepare and plot his decisions.

He is an influencer. When Taylor was younger, he influenced by attempting to make others do what he wanted them to do. He was pushy and one sighted. Taylor continues to be an influencer, but it is because of his thoughtfulness of concepts and situations that he is effective in bringing ideas and people together. He uses his amazing verbal and language skills to share solutions and to introduce alternative ideas. Taylor will still work to convince us to agree with his point of view. Sometimes he can be frustrated if we don't see things his way. But things don't seem to be such a big deal anymore. I really enjoy Taylor; it is a pleasure to be his mom.

As Alex enters the world of young adult, his path is wide open, and he is deciding what he wants. Alex views his future with a mixture of what should be, what might be, and wouldn't it be cool if this could be? He doesn't need to be in too much of a hurry to decide. As the youngest, the distance from our story has not been very long. He has a lot of time to discover and see what comes his way.

He wants to explore the world, perhaps traveling as a journalist and reporting on different cultures and people. Or he speaks of getting a degree in education and to work with young children.

Alex is much more social and gregarious in situations outside our home. He enjoys being with his friends and spending time in groups. Like Sarah, he is drawn to diversity and can easily integrate with different types of people and cultures. His decision to go to a university away from home has encouraged him to develop positive traits he desires. Always cheerful as a child, Alex continues to be engaging and fun with all ages of people. He loves working at an elementary school, teaching reading and mentoring young children. He enjoys the individuality of the kids and looks forward to being with them.

For right now we seem to be happy. Having vision for the future, taking care of the present, and learn from the past. Kind of our family motto that keeps us all moving along.

Dale and I often speak of the reality that within the next five years we will likely not be geographically near each other for our next bipolar episodes. It was a perfect storm for me to have my family physically present during the difficulties of my last big depression. But time and distance will not keep us from supporting, caring, and nurturing each other in times of distress. It may look different, but we will be there, come what may.

They are my heroes: Dale, Sarah, Taylor, and Alex. We have been through a lot and it warms my heart and softens the sting of depression to know that we are resilient and strong, even when faced with unimaginable trials. The greatest reward is knowing that in the end we will conquer and live to face another day.

TAKING ONE FOR THE TEAM

It's been a long journey. From the devastating depths of suicidal depression to the phoenix of hope rising to see a new day, we have survived. Luckily, along the way we found ways to find joy and humor in life. We were blessed, very blessed. Although not unscathed, we have found within ourselves the ability to separate ourselves from the mental illness we carried.

From my breakdown in Alaska to our lives even now, we recognized that early intervention; consistent, quality treatment; structure; and coping skills developed over time held the key to our wellness. But there has been more.

I envision a photograph with dozens of people lined up on bleachers all looking at the camera, some smiling, some not. They look like a pleasant bunch, a little eclectic maybe, but all willing to gather and represent themselves. As a family we view the photograph with mixed emotions. This is our team-our treatment team we have amassed over almost thirty years of mental health care. It is because of some of them we are alive.

The psychiatrists are easiest to process. Happily, they haven't been many. They came with expertise. We selected most of them because of recommendations we received. For some, their job seemed to be just that—a job. Due to the shortage of child psychiatrists, the doctors we had were in high demand. We considered ourselves lucky to see them because they excelled at what they did, but there never seemed to be enough time for us to have what seemed like a complete visit.

There was one doctor who kept our fifteen-minute appointment time to the second only to literally have an alarm go off, abruptly close the file, and then rudely stand up and point us out the door, even when we had not resolved our questions or needs. I would think, "What about the myriad of questions I need to ask?" But there were other doctors who went well over our appointment times because they seemed to be as invested as we were to help our children.

We willingly-well, mostly willingly-submitted ourselves to their chemical cocktails to have some of our most disturbing and life-altering symptoms become more manageable. It was difficult to wait out the side effects and wonder if we would ever get better. We didn't know what would happen, but we believed medication was going to be a tool for good.

Doctors Flint and O'Reilly were exceptional in helping us know what to expect, what not to expect, and in helping us hope things would change for the better. We were grateful to have a relationship with them as they truly cared about us outside of our patient number. That brought huge amounts of trust and a willingness on our part to do whatever they encouraged. They remain an intricate part of who we are.

Dr. Flint was magic, at least we believe he was. He took confused parents, newly thrown into the world of mental illness, and an unruly, seemingly out-of-control Taylor down the road to find stability. He had the ability to personalize his treatment to Taylor's unique needs and had the courage not to throw different medications at us. He was patient, thoughtful, and had a gift for healing young children. He never talked down to us and always conveyed a sense of confidence in our parenting. Dr. Flint saw the good in Taylor we were missing due to his chemical imbalance and helped us embrace the amazing kid Taylor was and had the potential to be.

Dr. O'Reilly saved my life, literally. I came to him already feeling broken, deep in a depression that had lasted close to a year. Medications, which seemed frightening to me in the mysterious ways they might affect my brain, became the lifeline I needed. He offered hope and healing to Dale and me through each conversation we had when it seemed like healing would never be found again. When I started to recover we made a plan—a tangible, doable plan to help us know what to do if the darkness ever returned. Of course, it did return, and because Dr. O'Reilly had spent time with me, he knew my specific illness profile, and was able to proactively keep the worst of the illness at bay and move strongly toward wellness.

His paramount message to me—that even with bipolar disorder I was a functioning, successful, and dynamic individual was hard to wrap my head around. But I trusted him. After sixteen-years, our doctor-patient relationship ended as Dr. O'Reilly moved on to other endeavors. It made me sad, even to the point of grief, until I recognized the gift he had given me to want to live and to live well.

Also, in our line of team members there are social workers and interns who worked with the kids as they attended day-treatment. They showed patience and a stick-to-it attitude that helped Sarah and Taylor regain ground lost when they were ill.

It was comforting to have some of the staff step in and help with the parental duties I couldn't do while they were in day-treatment—keeping them on task, doling out consequences for behavior on the level system, doing schoolwork, social skills tasks, assisting the therapist in groups, and managing a bunch of kids from the treatment center as they went on much-needed field trips to the zoo or museum.

My appreciation goes to a skills specialist who nurtured Sarah during a time of profoundly low feelings of self-worth. With this woman Sarah believed she was competent, even gifted, as an artist. She returned home from their outings with a smile on her face and a willingness to keep doing what she needed to do.

I remember the recreational therapist who recognized Taylor's energy as not just ADHD but an exuberance which came naturally to him. She made sure Taylor had his own space and encouraged his rough and tumble self, so long as he followed the rules and stayed safe. When he left her care from day-treatment, she got down on his level and looked him in the eye and told him he truly was a good kid and could do anything he wanted to do.

Therapists have unique personalities and points of view. We celebrate a mini miracle when we find that person who fits exactly what we need at a given time. Therapists by nature are elusive, listening and knowing so much about their client, and we in turn knowing so little about them. How is it we allow therapists to ask incredibly personal information of us, yet they do not volunteer their own? I wonder why we do that. Usually it works well, but sometimes it does not, and when that happens it leaves the client feeling exposed and vulnerable.

Taylor saw Kate Fallon for years, starting when he was six years old. He was awfully closed about any feelings he had, with the exceptions of anger and excitement. But underneath all those intense emotions existed another range of emotions which included sadness, resentment, fear, confusion, frustration, jealousy, rage, and anxiety. So many things overwhelmed him, but he didn't have the verbal or cognitive skills to know how to deal with them. To keep both Taylor and the rest of the family safe we were extremely invested in helping him learn to identify and talk about his feelings, and Kate lead the fight.

Kate didn't only focus on Taylor's therapy but helped educate me in the ways of managing Taylor's explosive behavior and the other difficulties we had with him at home. Her confidence in my parenting ability came at a time when I didn't know if I would ever parent effectively. I especially liked Kate because she validated my experience as Taylor's mom. I just needed to be heard. I could be honest about the challenges we had because she judged our family for who we were and what we were trying to do.

Taylor didn't like going to therapy with Kate because she would make him talk about his emotions and they would go over situations that were uncomfortable or made him feel vulnerable. He would often come out of a session seemingly lighter and behaving better, and we would have a few good days together at home. But sometimes he seemed like a dark cloud, and we knew to lie low and be quiet while he settled down from his session.

It was heartening when I saw Kate frustrated with Taylor on occasion; at least I wasn't the only one he could get to. Kate became part of our celebrations when we saw Taylor mature and manage himself better. She always expressed interest in his latest soccer game and shared in the excitement when he bought his horse. Taylor rode in a city parade with Mary. Kate took the time to come stand on the street corner with our family and wave at Taylor as he rode by. It touched my heart that she was invested in my son, even when he rarely reciprocated her kindness. But she had to have known she made a difference.

From almost twelve-years-old through seventeen-years-old, Sarah struggled to know what to do with herself and her mental health. We needed a "super-duper" therapist for Sarah; one who was tenacious, focused and would put up with her drama. We found the perfect fit in Samuel Frasier. Samuel was formidable, well educated, well-spoken, and very direct. He exuded confidence in his skills and was well thought of by his peers. I liked how he stuck with Sarah in all her stages of falling apart, and with confidence seemed to say, "Yes, I can help her; she will be in good hands. I will take care of her, and we will make great progress."

From the beginning Samuel recognized Sarah's strengths and her courageous efforts to take care of herself. He had worked with youth who'd struggled with issues such as Sarah's and from the beginning seemed to have a plan of attack. That vote of confidence and the skills we all learned brought hope, and over time a way for us to rebuild a connection with Sarah.

He taught us DBT therapy skills and made us learn acronyms to help us know how to more effectively communicate with Sarah specifically and as a family in general. He gave Sarah a great gift—the gift of self-validation. When she learned to define who she was, who she wanted to be, and who she could become, she was happier and able to face hard things.

I had always considered being in therapy with Samuel hard. He could be a task master and expected a lot out of us as parents, making it clear to us the time to make a difference for Sarah was now. We trusted him partly because we saw him work as hard as he asked Sarah and us to work. He showed up at our home one Saturday to help rake leaves and gave us object lessons and skills instruction as we worked side by side. He made himself available by phone when the crisis with Sarah felt way bigger than me and I needed direction. Samuel not only helped us in creating behavior systems to reward and consequence Sarah but taught us effective methods to use for all the kids.

When Taylor grew out of his connection with Kate, maturing into a preteen young man who needed to connect with a male therapist, we hesitantly had Taylor start therapy with Samuel. We were apprehensive about the kids going to the same therapist. But we knew we could trust him to keep Taylor's and Sarah's treatments separate and to honor the confidentiality vital to the process of therapy.

Taylor's experience with Samuel was different than Sarah's ; not better or worse, just different. Taylor and Samuel connected on a cerebral level much of the time. Speaking Taylor's language, Samuel slowly introduced a new world of possibilities to Taylor's strict black-and-white, all-or-nothing mind. Taylor expressed his anger and frustration in a more mature way with Samuel and often left the office feeling liberated. Samuel called Taylor out on his stuff, but Taylor seemed to hold his own.

Like Kate, Samuel stood by us during the suicide attempts and scary moments that accompanied bipolar disorder. They provided structure and a sounding board for us as we tried to figure out what we needed to do to help the kids. But it became more than that. It went beyond the obligatory concern of a professional and was life-changing.

Also scattered throughout the group picture are the exceptional teachers, coaches, and church leaders who saw beyond the mental illness and viewed us as whole, healthy individuals. It is great to have moments where nobody talks or worries about bipolar disorder, because it doesn't matter. As these occasions happen more often, I experience a sense of belonging. We are more like them than different from them.

That's our team. But the picture would not be complete without the five people who stand at the front of the group: Dale, Karen, Taylor, Sarah, and Alex. We want to be better in spite of bipolar disorder and all the hardships we've encountered as a family. We inherently know we matter more than the illness. Rather than believing people with mental illness are damaged or limited or incapable of success, we know we are amazing, and we believe in our absolute worth as individuals and as a family.

Karen Greenwell is a mother and certified mental health professional. She earned a BA in Psychology and authored a 6-week children and family mental health education program: From Hope to Recovery. As an advocate, educator and trainer, Karen has presented throughout the United States. Her goal with *Bless and Release A Mothers Journey Through Mental Illness* is to provide validation to families who struggle with mental illness while offering practical advice in how to best manage it.

Karen enjoys reading and eating warm brownies right out of the pan with her kids.

Dale—"Count me therefore a partner."

Sarah, Taylor, and Alex—"The harder the conflict, the more glorious the triumph." Thomas Paine

Thank you for reading <u>Bless and Release: A Mother's Journey Through Mental Illness</u>

If you have enjoyed this book please leave a review at:

https://www.amazon.com/Bless-Release-Mothers-Journey-Through

Your positive review will make a difference in getting the conversation started about mental illness, how it impacts families, and how we can build support and services in our communities.

Thank you.

46356394R00172

Made in the USA
Middletown, DE
27 May 2019